CW01498255

NEW DIRECTIONS IN LATINO A
Also Edited by Licia Fiol-Matta & José Quiroga

Forthcoming Titles

NEW CONCEPTS IN LATINO AMERICAN CULTURES
A Series Edited by Licia Fiol-Matta & José Quiroga

Forthcoming Titles

The Portable Island

Cubans at Home in the World

Edited by

Ruth Behar
and
Lucía M. Suárez

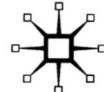

First published in 2008 by
PALGRAVE MACMILLAN®
in the United States—a division of St. Martin's Press LLC,
175 Fifth Avenue, New York, NY 10010.

Where this book is distributed in the UK, Europe and the rest of the
world, this is by Palgrave Macmillan, a division of Macmillan Publishers
Limited, registered in England, company number 785998, of Houndmills,
Basingstoke, Hampshire RG21 6XS.

Palgrave Macmillan is the global academic imprint of the above companies
and has companies and representatives throughout the world.

Palgrave® and Macmillan® are registered trademarks in the United States,
the United Kingdom, Europe and other countries.

ISBN-13: 978–0–230–60477–3

Library of Congress Cataloging-in-Publication Data

The portable island : Cubans at home in the world / edited by Ruth
Behar and Lucía M. Suárez.
    p. cm.—(New directions in Latino American culture)
Includes bibliographical references and index.
ISBN 0–230–60076–X
    1. Cubans—Foreign countries. 2. Exiles—Cuba. I. Behar, Ruth,
1956– II. Suárez, Lucía M.

F1760.5.P67 2008
304.8089'687291—dc22   2008005341

A catalogue record of the book is available from the British Library.

Design by Newgen Imaging Systems (P) Ltd., Chennai, India.

First edition: November 2008

10 9 8 7 6 5 4 3 2 1

Printed in the United States of America.

Transferred to Digital Printing in 2010

For our parents, queridos Mami y Papi:
Alberto y Rebeca Behar
Roberto e Hilda Suárez

Isla, tierra frágil, Patria mía
cuánto te he faltado estando aquí.

Island, fragile land, my Country,
how faithless I've been to you, being here.
—Laura Ruiz

CONTENTS

ILLUSTRATIONS

Preface and Acknowledgments

The Portable Island began with Lucía and me sitting and talking in my living room in Ann Arbor, Michigan where a framed watercolor painting titled *Muchacha que llora pececitos* (Young woman weeping little fish) by Rolando Estévez hangs. On the surface this artwork doesn't appear to be "especially Cuban," even though Estévez is a Cuban artist who lives in Matanzas, Cuba, and has never lived anywhere else. His watercolor has a Chagallesque, dreamy, floating feeling. There aren't any Cuban flags or palm trees to signal that the *llorona*, the weeping woman, is a *cubana*. But if you look closely, you see that the pattern on the woman's dress consists of dozens of little boats and little fish, and that a couple of those little fish are the tears that flow from her eyes. That is when you understand that the work is undeniably Cuban, that Estévez made it in the aftermath of the biblical-style exodus from the island that took place in 1994, when thousands of *balseros* flung themselves into the deep dark sea on flimsy rafts, like so many Noah's arks, in search of a better life in the United States.

So there we were, the two editors of this book, in the presence of that Cuban weeping woman, and we were talking about Cuba, of course. What else? Cuba had been our bond, the glue of our sisterhood, for the past fifteen years. We'd met when I went to North Carolina to give a lecture about "bridges to Cuba" at Duke University, where Lucía was then a graduate student. Sometimes when you give a lecture, there is one person in the room who needs to hear what you're saying so badly that you can feel their hunger for your words. The day I gave my talk at Duke, I was speaking to a roomful of people, but the person who was listening most attentively was Lucía.

Like me, Lucía had recently traveled to Cuba. I was returning to the country left behind in childhood, while Lucía was reclaiming the country her parents had left just before she was born. I wanted bridges with the island and was determined to keep returning to Cuba to understand the sensibilities of those who had stayed, those who kept waving goodbye to the ones who were leaving. Lucía, on the other hand, who had gone to Cuba to interview Cuban women writers, had discovered that many of those writers had subsequently left the island. She was concerned that her interviews, all about writing *in* Cuba, had quickly become obsolete, when Cuban writers were writing *outside* of the island.

At our first meeting we connected instantly as we exchanged opinions, which clashed sometimes, about the volatile relationship between the island

and its diaspora. But we discovered a shared passion to understand what home might have meant to us if we'd grown up in Cuba rather than the United States. And so we continued to stay in touch. We were thrilled when, after finishing her dissertation, Lucía took a job at the University of Michigan. From being in a teacher-student relationship, we went on to become colleagues. Over the next seven years, we'd have numerous conversations about Cuba, watching with fascination and trepidation as our island awakened the curiosity of the rest of the world and a veritable deluge of books, films, photographs, and dispatches from Cuba began appearing almost daily as we entered the twenty-first century.

But there was something different, something haunting, about our conversation when the idea for this book occurred to us. It was summer in Ann Arbor, the season that seems miraculously lush after the terrible winter when clouds from the north make everything gray. The leaves were gorgeously green, the days long, sunny, and languid, and the fireflies lit up the slow falling of the night. We were talking about Cuba and feeling sad because Lucía was about to leave Ann Arbor and take a job at Amherst College in Massachusetts. It was July, 2006 and her departure would take place in August.

As the need for us to say goodbye to one another loomed on the horizon, we thought about the wrenching separations that Cubans had been experiencing for close to fifty years. All our conversations about Cuba now truly hit close to home. We would not be living within walking distance of each other anymore. We would not be able to swing by unannounced at each other's house and stay for dinner. We would not meet for a lunch of bi bim bop anymore at our favorite Asian restaurant. We would not be able to simply grab books from each other's bookshelves and "promise" to return them soon. All of a sudden it dawned on us that our conversations would now be held from a distance. Maybe, no longer colleagues and neighbors, we would talk less often, or not at all.

We'd probably never again live in the same city. But we wanted to keep talking to one another about Cuba, despite the geographic distance that would soon separate us. And so, with the weeping woman looking over us and giving us her blessing, we decided we'd edit a book together to keep our conversations from ending. This book would be *our* portable island.

Here, we each claim Cuba, each in her own way. For me, Cuba is the homeland that I have sought to recover through anthropological, literary, filmic, and spiritual journeys, and repeated visits to the island. For Lucía, Cuba is the place she has come to know through intense reading of Cuban and Caribbean literature, limited visits to the island, and journeys to other countries that seem to connect her further to Cuba. Working on this book, we have learned that even though we have different ways of experiencing Cuba and belong to slightly different generations, neither of us can totally let the island go. We have come to accept that while we continue to seek a connection to Cuba, our longing to make it ours is inseparable from our understanding that we won't ever recover the island of our past.

Writing about our imaginary islands and inviting other Cubans—who find themselves at home in all the different worlds they inhabit—to also write about their imaginary islands is a remedy for staying connected with one another as well as with our floating community. Whether islanders with feet still firmly planted on island soil, or exiles, immigrants, or perennial wanderers seeking home somewhere else, we are all Cubans and all in this together. One thing we know for sure: nothing is more crucial for Cubans than to avoid the curse of loneliness.

*   *   *

It is a delight to be able to give our thanks to all the contributors to this book, who believed in our vision and generously gave us the gift of their beautiful work.

For our vision to become a reality we needed a publisher to back us and we are most grateful that we found such support at Palgrave Macmillan. Gabriella Pearce signed up the project and we thank her for opening the door to us. Luba Ostashevsky became our editor as the book took shape and she worked enthusiastically with us, making sure every detail was handled with the utmost care. Thank you, Luba. We offer our thanks as well to Luba's assistants Joanna Mericle and Colleen Lowrie, for their expert handling of all the logistical matters.

We were fortunate to have the opportunity to present an early version of this book at the Latin American Studies Association meeting in Montréal, Canada in September, 2007. With a few of our contributors, Pedro Pérez-Sarduy, Eliana Rivero, Jorge Duany, and Nara Araújo, we presented a panel entitled "Post-Bridges," and received very helpful commentaries from our audience that included other contributors to the book as well as many from our diverse intellectual communities in Latin American studies.

We wish to give special thanks to the Faculty Research Award Program at Amherst College. The award, supported by the H. Axel Schupf '57 Fund for Intellectual Life, covered the costs of translation. More than half of our contributors wrote their essays and poems in Spanish and we are indebted to David Frye for his lyrical and thoughtful translations into English. David was also our in-house editor and we thank him sincerely for carrying out numerous essential tasks, including copyediting and formatting our text to prepare it expertly for publication.

Ruth is grateful to the University of Michigan for support during a sabbatical leave in 2006–2007 that gave her time to devote part of her energy to this book. The Latin American and Caribbean Studies Program at the University of Michigan generously provided a subvention to aid with the presentation of the artwork. Ruth also wishes to thank her husband, David Frye, for his patience, kindness, understanding, and love. She thanks her son Gabriel, who accepted her need to return to Cuba with the utmost grace while he was growing up. And she thanks her parents for having fallen in love in Cuba so she could be born there.

Lucía is grateful to her friend and colleague Jossianna Arroyo, who read an early version of her essay and provided much needed conversation and support during their summer together in Brazil. Thanks also go to her friends and colleagues Karen and Benigno Sánchez-Eppler. They read the very first draft of her essay to their children on a car trip to Princeton. The family comments were quite thought-provoking. Lucía remains indebted to her husband Blake Williams for his unfailing love and support. Even though his own ancestors hail from Sweden and Wales, and his childhood was rooted in the rainy Northwest, he makes an amazing *lechón asado* and regularly brings the heartwarming scents of Cuban foods to their home in the Northeast. She thanks her daughter Arianna for her joy, her energy, and her curiosity about her Abuelitos' Cuba, and her mother's work on Cuba. Lucía also thanks her parents for giving her an intimate memory and an infinite love for their lost island-home in the Caribbean.

RUTH BEHAR—Ann Arbor, Michigan
LUCÍA M. SUÁREZ—Amherst, Massachusetts
October, 2007

José A. Figueroa, *Exilio* (photograph)

Introduction in Two Voices

After the Bridges

Ruth Behar

Such a small island, such a great role in history.

—Alma Guillermoprieto*

Cubans today can be found all over the map, living in places as far afield as Argentina, Amherst, and Australia, and Matanzas, Michigan, and Moscow. We're no longer torn simply between the island in the sea and the mirror island Cuban exiles built in Miami. We have become one of the most intensely diasporic people within our contemporary globalized world. Since the Revolution of 1959, a remarkable 12–15 percent of the Cuban nation has resettled outside of Cuba.

As I write these words, on the verge of the fiftieth anniversary of the Revolution, I am struck by how portable our homeland has become, how Cuba itself has become a portable island. Wherever we Cubans go, we take the island with us, lugging it along in our memories and dreams. Even when we're convinced we've left the island behind, no matter where we land, ready to start anew, there always seem to be people eager to remind us of our island past. The sounds of the Buena Vista Social Club reverberate throughout the malls of Iowa and the chic parties of Paris. The island haunts all of us Cubans; it won't let us go, no matter what distance we travel to get away.

Displacement has an emotional impact not only on those who leave, but also on those who stay. Back on the island, it is the responsibility of those who stay to wave goodbye and shed tears for the departed. They must also charitably welcome back those who later feel the compulsion to return to the living source to *recargar las pilas*, to recharge their batteries, as Cubans like to say. Movements back and forth, from the island to the diaspora, or from the diaspora to the island, between cities, between continents, and across oceans and rivers have made travelers of us all, even Cubans who only dream of going places.

I became obsessed sixteen years ago with the need to understand the Cuban search for home, whether on the island, outside the island, or between the island and the diaspora. On a second return trip to Cuba in 1991, I was plagued with panic attacks and inexplicable fears, but I made a vow to myself that I would continue to return. I would treat the island not as the forbidden country it had been turned into by the United States embargo, but as a normal country where I had friends and loved ones who awaited me.

Out of that commitment to form a connection with Cuba, the land I left as a child, came my anthology *Bridges to Cuba/Puentes a Cuba* (University of Michigan Press, 1995). *Bridges to Cuba* sought to initiate an artistic and literary dialogue between Cubans on the island and Cubans in the United States. Ties between Cubans were broken in the 1960s and 1970s as the island split into "revolutionaries" and *gusanos,* the so-called worms of the Revolution, which was the term Fidel Castro used to describe those who left and largely resettled in Miami. The severed nation started to heal in 1978 and 1979 during the era of the family reunification program that brought 125,000 Cuban immigrants back to Cuba for brief visits with relatives. It was also the era of the Antonio Maceo brigades, which allowed idealistic Cuban-Americans to return to Cuba and do volunteer labor to prove they weren't "worms" like their parents. But the movements of Cuban-Americans on the island were closely surveiled; they weren't allowed to stay with their families and were forced to stay in hotels. Then, by a strange coincidence, the same number of Cubans who returned as visitors was matched by the exodus of 125,000 Cubans from the port of Mariel in 1980, which the island viewed as a purging of the "scum" of its revolution. Again the gap widened, making the ninety miles of the ocean border between Cuba and the Florida coast the longest ninety miles in the world.

By the early 1990s, at the moment I went seeking bridges, island Cubans and diaspora Cubans were in need of ways to reconnect and reconcile in the midst of the social and economic crisis brought about in Cuba by the collapse of communism in the Soviet Union. Cuba suddenly felt stranded—more an island than ever. The Soviet subsidies that used to prop up the economy vanished. The depletion was so extreme it evoked a feeling of wartime and came to be known as "the special period in a time of peace." The Cuban government scrambled for alternative methods to survive in the global market. Increased investment in tourism was one solution. A more positive attitude toward Cubans in the "exterior" was the other. Cubans abroad were urged to return again and fewer restrictions were placed on their movements. Their remittances were welcomed with open arms. After the U.S. dollar was declared a legal currency in 1993, Western Union set up shop in Cuba. The *gusanos* became *mariposas* (butterflies) who flew back bringing gifts for their families; those who were once viewed as *traidores* (traitors) became *traedólares* (dollar carriers).

Cubans had been torn apart by politics for three decades, but the hope of *Bridges to Cuba* was that they could be reunited through poetics, the poetics of bridges, of claiming a common language of history, culture, and memory. Yes, this idea was romantic and sentimental and more than a little bit naive. I discovered how quickly some of my fellow Cubans let me know I was an idiot savant, not just a *comebola* (a fool), but the worst sin of all, a *comemierda* (a shit-eater).

Yet, in spite of the critics, my call in 1992 for contributions for a double issue of the modest literary journal, *Michigan Quarterly Review*, on the theme of *Bridges to Cuba* was met with enthusiasm, even desperate gratitude, by a vast network of Cuban writers, scholars, and artists. They learned of the project by word of mouth at a time before anybody had e-mail, and among Cubans, word of mouth can be much faster than e-mail. As the island opened up, numerous Cuban-Americans of undecided political sympathies went back in search of their lost homes and were eager to tell the stories of their return journeys. These children of exiles contacted me from such diverse places as Boston, Las Cruces, Colorado Springs, Chicago, New York, Durham, Tampa, and Los Angeles. Many were university professors. No one knew one another. It became my role to connect the dots on the map and bring us all together.

Along with the stories I collected from Cuban-Americans, I sought out the stories of my counterparts in Cuba. I wanted to know how Cuban intellectuals, writers, and artists of my generation, who had grown up on the island, thought about the idea of the bridge. On brief, intense, lightning-bolt trips to Cuba, I would meet with people from the crack of dawn until late into the evening, hardly sleeping. I knocked on doors at three in the morning and was received with utmost nonchalance, as if that was the most natural time to visit. I found it shocking that a number of writers willingly gave me the only copy they had of a manuscript, so anxious were they to get their work translated into English and circulated to a reading audience in the United States. In that era, as unbelievable as it seems today, no Cuban writing from the island was being published in the United States.

Bridges to Cuba was a project poised on a threshold. It was conceived before the adrenaline rush of people-to-people travel from the United States to Cuba ushered in a new era in the late 1990s. As the past century came to a close, Americans flocked to the island in the role of grassroots diplomats, making up for the long hiatus brought about by the lack of official ties between the two nations. Curious and well-intentioned Americans proceeded to reconquer the island with their gazes and their desires and their guilty admiration for Cuba's survival in the midst of their own government's hostility. American journalists began to cover Cuba again. A full-scale Cuba boom erupted, leading to an explosion of writing, art exhibitions, photographic images, and musical compilations reviving everything Cuban under the sun for American and global consumption.

But before mojitos and salsa dancing became fashionable once again, a sizable number of Cuban thinkers and artists agreed that what we needed as a people were bridges, not walls. *Bridges to Cuba* sought to close the gap between Cubans "here" and "there." This was a goal that made sense at a moment when Cubans were living, geographically and psychically, in fixed locations on the map.

Now, fifteen years later, circumstances have changed dramatically. The severe impact of the Cuban special period led to the sudden wave of world-wide tourism streaming into the island. Expanded communication with travelers from capitalist nations in Latin America and Europe, especially Spain, Italy, France, and Mexico, made it possible for Cubans to create a wider network of ties. Many Cubans who had been reluctant to leave and get embroiled in the politics of the island/exile split were able to relocate to "third countries." Tempted by economic, cultural, educational, and artistic possibilities available to them elsewhere, they uprooted themselves and in this way participated in redrawing the boundaries of the island.

Cubans find themselves now in a "post-bridges" moment. The bridges to Cuba extend from places much further than the ninety miles that separate the island from the United States. What name to give to our present situation? Many of us are wondering, after bridges, what's next?

This book is an effort to address this question. Initially, we thought of gathering again all the people who participated in *Bridges to Cuba* to produce a sequel that would be called "After the Bridges" or "Post-Bridges." But what we wanted, we realized, was a new vision of the Cuban search for home that was more international in its sweep. While inviting some of the original participants in *Bridges to Cuba*, we also wanted to reach out to a wider range of Cubans in the United States, Europe, Latin American, and Cuba who had not been part of that project. The hyphenated identity of Cuban-American was no longer inclusive of the varied displacements Cubans had undergone. We now had to think of the possibility of Cuban-Mexican, Cuban-Russian, Cuban-German, Cuban-Spanish, Cuba-Rican, Afrocuban-British, and other identities far too multilayered to name with a simple hyphen. Our aim, we decided, would be to gather together a broad collection of personal reflections on the expanding array of cultural fusions that have come to define twenty-first century Cubanness.

Cubans were everywhere, weren't they? On our computers we opened a file and called it "Global Cubans." Then we asked ourselves: Are we right? Are Cubans as global as we imagine? We decided to find out by contacting writers and scholars dispersed throughout the world and asking them to contribute personal essays about how they experience home, homeland, travel, and the gifts and losses of diaspora. We also invited several Cuban artists who address these experiences in their work, both to add a visual dimension to our reflections and to be able to confront feelings we have found impossible to describe only in words.

We discovered that Cubans do inhabit places all over the globe. Many have spent time living in Africa and Asia. Cubans obsessively travel, more than other immigrants, which is surely due to the fact that returning to the island is fraught by Kafkaesque regulations and emotional burdens. But the majority of Cubans who are professional writers, intellectuals, or artists occupy a distinct regional nexus—the United States, Europe, and Latin America, and of course Cuba itself. We may know many languages, but we prefer to express ourselves mainly in Spanish and English.

The important thing is that we *feel* ourselves to be almost unbearably globalized. There is no place we can go in the world where our Cubanness passes unnoticed. Invisibility isn't an option. All eyes, it seems, are always on Cuba. Everyone everywhere has an opinion about Cuba that they are eager to share with us. This Cuba that everyone claims to know is not so much a place as a set of iconic references: Fidel, Che, red-kerchiefed Young Pioneers, the Pompeii ruins of Havana, cigars, rum, sensual women, cranky but glorious old Chevys that still run fine, and the Buena Vista Social Club.

Simply to be Cuban is a global condition. Our island is small, but ever since José Martí envisioned our independence in the nineteenth century, we have thought of ourselves as a chosen people with a unique purpose in the world. The Cuban Revolution, for better or for worse, took that megalomaniac fantasy, what scholars politely call exceptionalism, a step further, and since 1959, we have become accustomed to being players on the world stage. We Cubans dared to imagine a great role for ourselves in history, and the rest of the world has not let us forget it.

There is a huge literature obsessed with Cubanness as an essential state of being. But we have not had enough conversations about the increasingly fragmented lives Cubans lead. Few know about the Cuban experiences that have emerged from the recent quiet journeys in and out of the island. The Cuban government now allows for a low-intensity exile by offering a category of residence permits known as the "PRE" (*permiso de residencia en el exterior*—"permission to reside abroad"), which allows Cubans to live elsewhere for eleven months as long as they spend one month each year back on the island. While in transit, Cubans stay in touch, creating social networks unreachable by governments and their lowly tools of surveillance. In the past ten years, Cubans have also resettled permanently in a wider range of cities in Europe and Latin America. Even in the United States, while Miami remains the classical Cuban hub, it is no longer the primary destination for the newest wave of Cuban immigrant writers and intellectuals. Miami, too, is no longer exclusively Cuban, but pan-Latino, and increasingly a global city. In Cuba, the weight of all these far-flung diasporas has made those who've stayed feel as if they too have become unhinged.

One day the title for this book came to me: "The Portable Island: Cubans at Home in the World." To be Cuban is to understand that the island travels with you. But how do Cubans travel with their island? What fragments of memory, language, and history do Cubans take with them? What does it feel like to wait on the island for those who return, suitcase in hand? Our book, written in first-person, offers a chorus of responses. Scholars, critics, writers, and poets, all were asked to speak directly about their experiences. We chose to privilege the personal voice to gain an emotional as well as an intellectual understanding of our situation. There are plenty of pundits ready to shout their position on Cuba. But we have too few whispered stories by Cubans that address the joys and sorrows, and the fraught ambivalence, of searching for home in these tumultuous times.

Ultimately, the contributors took the risk of entering the realm of the personal in their own way. Some speak about their lives in poetry, or as members of a generation, or as researchers who see themselves as part of a larger community. Some speak from inside the island, some from outside. Some who were inside a year ago are now outside. Some who are outside return again and again to the island, temporarily, or even permanently. To give some structure to the discussion, we divided the book into sections that address departures, returns, the things we carry in our suitcases, and the impossible desire to go beyond geography and stop being so unceasingly Cuban. But the various contributions also transcend these categories and can and should be read in other ways too.

As we explore what it means to be Cubans located or dislocated in Matanzas, Michigan, Miami, New York, Barcelona, Moscow, Paris, Puerto Rico, Amherst, Havana, Los Angeles, Chile, and Mexico City, among many other places, inevitably we must ask ourselves what our crisscrossing journeys have taught us about who we are, where we want to be, and how we envision our present and our future. Are we Cuban by default, or because we actively seek to craft a Cuban identity that can still make sense in an age when the soul is global? Do we decide to be Cuban or do others decide for us in our supremely consumerist era?

The new century is unfolding at a quickening pace and the long-awaited last chapter of the Cuban Revolution seems finally to be arriving. Watching and waiting, we Cubans have ended up becoming a tribe of nomads. Wherever we go, with humor and pathos, we build up anew our imagined island, troubled by our possible irrelevance but never losing altogether our sense of our own importance as we keep trying to be the free people we were meant to be.

Is it a comfort that our island is portable? Or does it make us inconsolable? Either way, our island is portable not only for those who no longer reside there full time, but even for those who live in Cuba, for they are the witnesses to the endless departures and returns, and they know what fits and doesn't fit in a suitcase. And who knows? Any day those inside may themselves be packing a suitcase to go somewhere else. For that is the thing about us Cubans—we revere our island, but the sea is always fogging our eyes with visions of other places.

We each carry a different piece of Cuba in our suitcase. Piece by piece, we will put the island together again and try to make it whole.

Or maybe we are learning to live with the realization that the island can never again be made whole. Maybe we now understand that it was never whole to begin with. Maybe the island is as whole as it can ever be in each suitcase we carry from one destination to another.

NOTE

* The quote from Alma Guillermoprieto appears in her essay "Fidel in the Evening" in *Looking for History: Dispatches from Latin America* (New York: Vintage Books, 2002), p. 127.

Our Memories, Ourselves

Lucía M. Suárez

> *Life is always, necessarily, a tale: we tell it to ourselves as subjects, through recollection; we hear it told or we read it when the life is not ours.... Autobiography does not rely on events but on an articulation of those events stored in memory and reproduced through rememoration and verbalization.... Language is the only way afforded me in order to "see" my existence.*
>
> —Silvia Molloy[1]

Unable to hold onto a mythic Cuba, we turn to noting the ways in which Cuba and Cubans have evolved over the past half-century, and how our needs for exile, migrations, and diaspora—as well as the very meanings of these terms—have evolved with us. In the twenty-first century, travel defines us: traveling beyond the confines of the island; staying, returning, caught in between; here (Cuba) and there (no longer only the United States). For example, I have lived in Cairo, Paris, Belo Horizonte, Bahia, New York City, Durham, and Ann Arbor. Most recently, I have made yet another move to Amherst, where the late Antonio Benítez Rojo taught and wrote about Cuba, multiplying thus his never-ending connections to his "repeating island." As our memories and pathos *transculturate* with new homelands, we explore our new sites of residency with enthusiasm and harbor our Cuban anchor in the private and creative spaces of the imagination. Thus we entertain a panoply of identifications rooted in Cuba. Eliana Rivero, for instance, calls herself "Cuban-plus" (Cuban plus American). We could argue that we have all become Cuban-plus (Cuban plus Spaniard, Cuban-Puerto Rican, Cuban-French, and so on). Though some of us writing in this collection have never left Cuba, the inevitable economic changes, continued departures, emotional returns, and new-formed relationships with international tourists force us all to think about the daunting condition of Cuban absence and presence.

When Cuban artists, intellectuals, and writers gather at conferences, we revel in the stories we share of our travels far and wide. Where do Cubans go? We are found in the United States, and beyond, in countries such as Australia, Mexico, Puerto Rico, Spain, Germany, Italy, and France. The growing diversity of Cuban experiences has led us to ponder the new relationships we have established with different cultures and geographies. Displacement, resettlement, and even staying in a Cuba that has changed dramatically have had a profound effect on our sense of Cubanness. Many of us speak third and fourth languages that are neither English nor Spanish. It is safe to say that the continuing departures from Cuba have taken on a life of their own. The Cuban diaspora is multiple and incessantly multiplying. Consequently, the imagined and real, ever-changing Cuba has become a portable emblem.

* * *

The logistics of Cuban exile, migration, and disapora are manifold. Over the years, migrations to the United States, for example, have been studied extensively by a number of sociologists.[2] Cuban-American sociologist Silvia Pedraza opens a 1996 article on Cuban migrations to the United States by citing an insight of C. Wright Mills to the effect that "the sociological imagination lies at the intersection of personal troubles and historical issues."[3] Pedraza tells us the story of how Cuban migrations have shaped the American landscape and argues that these migrations also mirror the developments of the Cuban Revolution. In this account, she distinguishes four waves of Cuban migration. The first wave left between 1959 and 1964; its members, drawn largely from Cuba's elite, tended to be the most anti-Castro, and even three decades later were still waiting for Castro's immediate departure or overthrow and refusing to accept the changes that eventually restructured Cuba's economy and ideology. Pedraza terms them "those who wait." The second wave, consisting of Cuba's petite bourgeoisie, came during the chaotic year of 1965 when "hundreds of boats left from Miami for the Cuban port of Camarioca" (266). This was the migration of "those who escaped" from newly imposed food rationing and stringent government and social control, while seeking economic opportunities they did not feel were available to them in revolutionary Cuba. Third came the mass exodus from the port of Mariel in 1980 by the so-called Marielitos, whom the Cuban government branded as *escoria*(scum), the antisocial elements of society. To that government, they "represented a large public slap in the face: no longer the immigrants of the transition from capitalism to communism" (269). The Mariel migration caused changes in U.S. immigration policies with Cuba, and, to a certain extent, blemished the image of conservative, white, professional Cubans. They comprised, according to Pedraza, "those who search" for better opportunities. The fourth group delineated by Pedraza fared the worst; they are the *balseros*(the rafters), "those who despair."

In contrast, exile to another host island, the U.S. commonwealth Puerto Rico was quite different. According to a 1997 study on Cubans in Puerto Rico by sociologists José A. Cobas and Jorge Duany, "Cubans who migrated to Puerto Rico were more representative of the propertied classes. . . . Cubans specialized in trade and akin activities and dominated some business lines."[4] During the 1960s, Cubans were warmly welcomed in the neighboring island, but their relationship to the people in their new home was wrought with tensions as Puerto Ricans began to define Cubans as snobbish, white, and rich; "economic competition and political differences between segments of the Cuban and Puerto Rican communities generated antagonism toward the exiles" (49). Partly as a result of these tensions, between 1970 and 1980 about 3,000 Cuban exiles left Puerto Rico for Miami (45).

In a recent book, Pedraza updates her research, suggesting that her new study captures "the processes of political disaffection of participants of this major drama."[5] She concludes that the different waves of "Cuban exodus that is now nearly half a century old and has brought more than a million Cuban immigrants to American soil, an exodus that harbors distinct waves of immigrants, [are] alike only in their final rejection of Cuba" (2). Her book offers us a convincing account of the revolutionary stages that led to departure from Cuba to the United States, and her narrative underscores a strong sentiment of "disaffection" with the revolutionary dream.

Paralleling Pedraza's four-stage categorization of migration to the United States, Mette Louise Berg has traced three "clusters of diasporic generations" to Spain, which she calls "the Exiles," "the Children of the Revolution," and the "Migrants."[6] These generations reflect distinct phases of the Revolution, and therefore of the evolving conditions that have led to migration, as well as assimilation. Berg argues that the three generations have little in common with each other; each group has a dramatically different experience and memory of the Cuba they left behind. Many of the exiles that arrived in Franco's Fascist nation in the 1960s and early 1970s supposed that Spain would be a mere way station to the United States. Others stayed, as according to Berg, many were "first- and second-generation descendents of Spanish immigrants" (19). Most Cuban exiles of the period found jobs easily because they had solid management skills and spoke English. Four decades later, their children "define themselves as Spanish and think of the link to Cuba as something pertaining to their parents" (20). Berg's second diasporic generation, the Children of the Revolution, consists of those who arrived after the death of Franco and Spain's successful transition to democracy. Berg notes that many in this group were artists and writers, often migrating alone, who had benefited from the education and opportunities created by the Revolution in Cuba (21). Finally, the migrants are those who left Cuba for economic reasons during its financial crisis after 1990. Many migrated through Russia and have joined in the ranks of other undocumented immigrants. Berg emphasizes that they tend to "not nationalize their memories" (24); instead, they remember their Cuba in terms of friends and family. In her presentation, the three waves of migration do not create a single Cuban diasporic community; instead, each claims and remembers a different Cuba, from a different personal and economic vantage point, in a host nation that has also witnessed major political and economic transitions over the course of the past fifty years.

Tracing a similar pattern to that of Pedraza and Berg, Holly Ackerman categorizes Cuban waves to Venezuela in terms of the "Foundational Groups" and the "Third and Fourth Waves."[7] Again, the patterns of integration, memory, and community are directly related to the historical point of departure from Cuba, the group's race and educational skill set, and their political or economic need for exile or migration. Migrations to Venezuela have been much smaller in number than to Miami, Puerto Rico, or Spain, and according to Ackerman they represent a success story of integration and democratic participation. The first arrivals between 1959 and 1967 did not necessarily leave Cuba for political reasons, but rather because they could no longer live the lives they wanted in Cuba. They chose to move to Venezuela "because of a common language, a familiar culture, and the probability that they could find immediate work" (92). A number of them already had business experience or family ties in Venezuela. Compared with the first wave of Miami Cubans, they were relatively open to conversations with the Castro system. In 1980, when the third wave, composed of political prisoners, arrived, the established Venezuelan community "reached across this divide" and helped integrate the new arrivals (99). The "Fourth Wave" includes the most recent series of migrations to Venezuela. In light of the change in the country's politics with the elections of Hugo Chávez to the presidency of Venezuela in 1999, and his close ties to Fidel Castro, this group is mostly composed of Cuban advisors and contract workers. As a result, some of the earlier exiles have departed from Venezuela; it may no longer be considered the ideal place for them. In conclusion, Ackerman suggests, "As scholars and policy makers analyze the situation, diversity of exile communities could be a vital part of diplomacy and peaceful resolution" (102). This open closure makes me especially hopeful. In the process of building bridges and creating new nodes of knowledge about Cuban lives in the world, we would greatly benefit from thinking positively and acting constructively.

What has become clear over the past seventeen years is that Cubans are not bound to political binary oppositions that respond to struggles played out between Cuba and the United States or that are built upon nostalgic memories of an idyllic pre-Castro past. Cubans live in many countries, have different and changing political views, and write literature that reflects these forceful international cultural experiences. Our lives unfold in places as distant as Russia, Angola, and Cuba; our memories are written in French, Spanish, and English, and have been translated into over fifteen languages. Not only do we cultivate homes throughout the world, we have begun to be historically present in national histories, other than those of Cuba and the United States.

This has led to new models of dual, and sometimes multiple, identifications. In his chapter, Jorge Duany, a Cuban-born immigrant in Puerto Rico, reveals that when he was young he would say he "was born in Cuba, but grew up in Puerto Rico." In recent years, he has come to say "I live in Puerto Rico, but my parents came from Cuba." This shift succinctly reflects the way identifications get reshaped with lived experience in a host country turned home country.

While we have sociological, critical, and historical studies clarifying the numerous exoduses from Cuba to a variety of host countries, no book exposes the very deep, heartfelt and personal mutations that the demographics of Cuban diaspora, return, and remaining on the island has implied. Within a Latino/a context, Suzanne Oboler observes that

> [...] migration is evidence of "history on the move." From the perspective of the social actors caught up in this flow, while at the same time being the bearers of the historical transformations underway, which migration makes manifest, the process acquires its own human and personal dramaturgy.[8]

With *The Portable Island*, we are presenting "history on the move" from the intimate meditations of Cubans whose experiences have led to reconsiderations of "identity on the move," anchored by a floating island, always there and ever changing. To unveil the inner thoughts that often hide behind the sociological texts, we asked our authors to contribute writings of autobiographical nature.

Some of our contributors confessed that this was the most difficult writing exercise they had been invited to complete. At least two of our authors, perhaps because there is still an inner censor, or because the reality of relatives on the island is still precarious, wrote with caution. We were respectful not to ask for deeper revelations at this point in their lives. Autobiography takes time; specifically, coming to terms with the sometimes contradictory realities that make up our lives is a long process. How we remember ourselves is one thing; how we write ourselves for an international audience demands daring. Yet many of us feel that, at this point in the telling of our lives, departing from, returning to, or having stayed in Cuba, we have the advantage of history to give clarity to our drama of identity. This forces us to grasp the present while reflecting on the past, contextualized from its future. Central to our stories, our memories, ourselves is how emotions shape our writing.

In her groundbreaking study, *Cuban-American Literature of Exile*, Isabel Álvarez Borland highlights which emotions have come to play a pivotal role in Cuban-American autobiographical writings. She distinguishes affect by generation:

> If anger, despair, and sadness were the traits expressed by the first exiles, vacillation and ambivalence will be the prevailing emotions for the Cuban Americans who came from Cuba as adolescents. The history challenged by the exiles has to be confronted by the second generation in order to put it aside and to go on, even if this process is painful and at times fruitless.[9]

The anger that beleaguered the first generation in exile was not always shared by their children, who had not lost a home, and whose curiosity for Cuba led to conflicting relationships, caught between trying to honor the parents and needing to explore, and perhaps even find a connection to the island. Ruth Behar has written extensively on this ambivalence. In *The Vulnerable Observer* she examines how this conflict led her to question her own authority. "Every ethnography I knew depended on some form of ethnographic authority.

But as an ethnographer for whom the professional ritual of displacement continually evoked the grief of diaspora, I distrusted my own authority."[10] Across the generations, it seems that anger gave way to grief.

Ruth Behar did not become handicapped by the burden of grief. She reconsidered her questions and concluded forcefully:

> From the global arena to the intimate stirrings of the human heart, the disintegration of the old world order has provoked, as the writer Margaret Randall suggests, "a general reevaluation of stories...." New stories are rushing to be told in languages we've never used before, stories that tell truths we once hid, truths we didn't care to acknowledge, truths that shamed us.
>
> As with the island of Cuba, everything has already happened and everything has yet to happen. And that is absolutely terrifying, but maybe, finally, it will prove absolutely liberating. (33)

How do we—how can we—liberate ourselves from the weight of anger, despair, ambivalence, and grief? A decade after Álvarez Borland's study, and twelve years after Behar grappled publicly with grief, new emotions have come to the fore. In *Cuban Palimpsests*, José Quiroga exposes how authors like Abilio Estévez have confessed to "disillusion" and that the "anger felt by [Reinaldo] Arenas has now turned into melancholia."[11] Quiroga signals disenchantment as a pervasive emotion felt by many Cuban writers. Pedraza suggests that disaffection plagues today's Cubans.

With this collection, we emphatically recognize the numerous emotions that haunt us, and the many ways in which we "continue to wear our hearts on our sleeves" (Behar, 32). We also highlight another emotional dimension of Cuban lives: acceptance. Pedro Pérez Sarduy, who lives in London, proclaims in his chapter that, "as a 100 percent Cuban, and also as a person of African descent, I find it a great relief not to have to struggle with the ghost of identity." Pérez Sarduy accepts his writing life, its international musings, its reality in London, and its rooting in Cuba. But this acceptance has come as a result of changes. He observes how twenty-five years ago "few had a clear idea of where Cuba was located. There were none of today's clubs and restaurants with allegorical names from the largest island in the Caribbean." In the time span of a quarter of a century, London has become multicultural, welcoming or at least recognizing, the diverse Caribbean presence in the city. More interestingly, Pérez Sarduy underscores how "African descent Cubans are an integral part of the island...[which] goes to show how things have changed in Cuba." Acceptance is personal, national, and global. Acceptance also comes through "letting go." For example, María de los Ángeles Torres concludes that "Cuba...is no longer home, it is a point of reference." She accepts that her life is in Chicago.

Acceptance is the first step to the necessary reconciliation that awaits the Cuban nation. Nara Araújo's literary journey to a present in which she has returned to Cuba after living many years in Mexico, not as an exile, reveals a sentiment shared by many Cubans of different generations, gender, and political persuasions. She writes that she does not want to "judge my fellows, but instead understand and forgive." This sentiment opens the door to hope. Verónica Pérez Konina, who lives in Moscow, writes, "I hope, when that day [of change] comes, that all Cubans—in Cuba, abroad, and we 'half' Cubans—will join together and do everything possible to create a happy future."

The migratory meditations in *The Portable Island* cover five decades of history and are written by different generations from many sites of experience. Our Cuban Condition is highly philosophical, intersecting and *transculturating* with numerous home spaces. This collection is by no means exhaustive; yet we believe that it offers a broad representation of the trials and tribulations of Cuban exile, migration, and diaspora.

The artwork, essays, interview, poetry, and theater piece included in the following pages have a contemplative quality that steers away from harsh definitions or bold political positions. Our texts bring to light the emotional impact displacement, travel, and new homes have had on our intimate lives, our dreams, and our expectations. *The Portable Island* pays special attention to the varied relationships that we have to Cuba. These deeply intimate stories reveal what we remember, what myths and realities of and about Cuba we are struggling with, and how we construct our present life narratives. Many of us continue to dream of new models of revolutionary and humanistic living. We recognize that change is a formative part of the Cuban national, political, and economic landscape. Thus, with this book, we hope to encourage new conversations and more nuanced configurations of Cubans "at home in the world."

Notes

1. Silvia Molloy, *At Face Value: Autobiographical Writing in Spanish America* (Cambridge: Cambridge University Press, 1991).
2. Renowned researchers on the topic include, and are not limited to, Nelson Amaro, Alejandro Portes, Rubén Rumbaut, and Silvia Pedraza.
3. Wright C. Mills, *The Sociological Imagination* (New York: Grove Press, 1961), cited in Silvia Pedraza, "Cuba's Refugees: Manifold Migrations," in Silvia Pedraza and Rubén G. Rumbaut, eds., *Origins and Destinies: Immigration, Race, and Ethnicity in America* (Belmont, CA: Wadsworth Press, 1996), p. 263.
4. José A. Cobas and Jorge Duany, *Cubans in Puerto Rico: Ethnic Economy and Cultural Identity* (Gainesville, FL: University Press of Florida, 1997), p. 49.
5. Silvia Pedraza, *Political Disaffection in Cuba's Revolution and Exodus* (Cambridge: Cambridge University Press, 2007), p. 2.
6. Mette Louise Berg, "Memory, Politics, and Diaspora: Cubans in Spain," in Andrea O'Reilly Herrera, ed., *Cuba: Idea of a Nation Displaced* (Albany, NY: State University of New York Press, 2007), p. 17. The critical and sociological essays in this book trace the historical and sociological dimensions of Cuban migrations to Spain, France, Puerto Rico, the United States, and Venezuela, studying the nature of diverse Cuban migratory experiences.
7. Holly Ackerman, "Different Diasporas: Cubans in Venezuela, 1959–1998," in Andrea O'Reilly Herrera, ed., *Cuba: Idea of a Nation Displaced* (Albany, NY: State University of New York Press, 2007), pp. 90–106.

8. Suzanne Oboler, "History on the Move...Revisiting *The Suffering of the Immigrants* from the Latino/a Perspective," *Qualitative Sociology*, v. 29, n. 1 (Spring 2006), p. 125. See also, Jorge Duany, *The Puerto Rican Nation on the Move: Identities on the Island and in the United States* (Chapel Hill, NC: University of North Carolina Press, 2002).

9. Isabel Álvarez Borland, *Cuban-American Literature of Exile: From Person to Persona* (Charlottesville, VA: University of Virginia Press, 1998), p. 49.

10. Ruth Behar, *The Vulnerable Observer* (Boston, MA: Beacon Press, 1996), p. 21.

11. José Quiroga, *Cuban Palimpsests* (Minneapolis, MN: University of Minnesota Press, 2005), pp. 142, 143.

PART I

En La Maleta: With a Suitcase in Our Hands

Perhaps the only true home is the one that we lose.

—Richard Blanco

Sandra Ramos, *Y cuando todos se han ido, llega la soledad* (And when everyone has left, solitude arrives) (calcograph)

CHAPTER 1

Wherever That May Be

Richard Blanco

The sole cause of a man's unhappiness is that he does not know how to stay quietly in his room.

—Pascal, *Pensées*[1]

I could be on my way anywhere—Paris or Chattanooga, San Francisco or San Antonio—the engines drone carrying me above a white sea of clouds, or an ocean glinting like sequin, or the ridges and lines of open land like the palm of my hand stretching 33,000 feet below me. Inevitably, I turn to the route maps on the back pages of the airline magazine, trace the red arc of our flight with my finger trying to guess where I am by comparing what I see over the wing's edge against the world unfolded on my lap: *Are those these mountains? Is this that river? Is that city this city or this one?* Inevitably, my eyes begin moving from arc to arc like massive bridges leaping across rivers and countries, oceans and continents, taking me on a virtual tour of all the places I've lived, the places I've traveled to, the places my wanderlust has imagined in search of paradise. Inevitably, I get lost in the crisscross of arcs and questions about the meaning of home that have echoed in my mind since childhood.

*   *   *

From Madrid, where I was born, a long elegant arc crosses the Atlantic to Miami, where I grew up in a house with a terracotta roof framed between two mango trees and two myths. The first myth was the Cuban homeland, *la patria,* always on the nostalgic tongues of my parents and grandparents: *En Cuba el café era más sabroso* (In Cuba the coffee was much tastier). *En Cuba los mangos eran más grande* (In Cuba the mangoes were much bigger). *En Cuba no llovía tanto* (In Cuba it didn't rain as much). *En Cuba el mar era más tranquilo* (In Cuba the sea was calmer). According to them, I came from a marvelous Eden (though I'd never been there) and one day soon, after the Revolution was over, we'd all go back to live out the rest of our lives there. But Cuba was a paradise I could hardly imagine from photos of Old Havana printed on the tacky place mats of La Carreta restaurant, soggy images of *La Catedral* and El Morro Fort waterlogged under our drinking glasses; a utopia I was supposed to see in the black-and-white faces of cousins I met in photos, always grimy and disheveled, wearing sandals, tank tops, and papery housecoats; a dreamland I couldn't draw with the black ink of letters my mother would read aloud from aunts announcing the birth of a grandchild or death of a relative I never met, or asking us to send them bubble gum, a few yards of taffeta for a wedding dress, or a used pair of old sneakers. Unlike those who left Cuba with real memories, I had none. How could I yearn returning to a home I had never been?

The other myth was the *Yunited Estates* of America as I saw it on 1950s and 1960s reruns of *I Love Lucy, Leave It to Beaver, The Brady Bunch,* and the like. I thought this was the *real* America, not Miami. In Miami, all the checkout girls, teachers, waitresses, and neighbors spoke Spanish and came from towns in Cuba my parents were sure to have visited; in Miami there were Cuban supermarkets (no one went to Winn Dixie) and *cafeterías* serving homemade *pastelito* pastries and shots of espresso all day long, decades before Starbucks; in Miami almost every house had a framed map of Cuba, a glass of water atop the refrigerator to ward off evil spirits, velvet furniture in the living room upholstered in clear vinyl never to be sat on; in Miami Brian Kunkle was the boy beat up at recess because he had red hair, freckles, and ate peanut butter-n-jelly sandwiches. No, the *real* America was somewhere on Channel 6 where every house was fully furnished with Dacron sectionals and coffee tables with candy dishes; where everyone wore hats and used coasters; where everyone ate after-dinner mints and said weird things like *gee, swell,* and *gosh* in perfect, elegant English. But how could home be a television show?

Overshadowed by these two myths, I believed home was elsewhere, a place to be recovered, or arrived at, someplace I had never been to, a hope, be it (as it was) the illusionary Cuba of the 1950s or the America of the 1950s I knew on TV. Eventually the two myths would connect with a hyphen, making me a Cuban-American with two languages, two cultures, and two countries. But how could I have two homes?

*   *   *

Instead of praising Cuba, my mother complains all the way from the airport in Rancho Boyeros to my aunt's house in the Almendares section of Havana: *Can you believe all this dust? I don't remember the city being so filthy. Look at that, all the buildings are falling apart. How dare they rename the streets?* We were in Cuba, but not really, not the Cuba my mother remembers, not the *paradise* she left behind. Cuba had changed without her permission, though nothing had changed for me; I had no actual memories to hold up against the present, no before and after scenes flashing in my mind. The street names were the same and the city was just as beautiful as it ever was. The cracked and moldy tiles of my grandmother's house had never looked lovelier; the seashore at Varadero was exactly the same blue as the last time my grandfather saw it; the road where my mother and father met hadn't changed; the sugarcane fields fluttered the same, the fried pork and black beans tasted the same, and the palm trees and mountains stood the same. I had lost nothing because I remembered nothing. And although I reveled in the Cuba coming to life before me like a pop-up book of family stories and anecdotes transformed into three dimensions, I still felt an empty craving for my mother's Cuba, strangely envious of her memories. I too wanted to feel robbed of a past, of a country, of a home that could never be recovered. But there are no flights to my mother's Cuba on the map, no red arcs mooring it to any other city or country. My mother's Cuba floats isolated in the Caribbean Sea, with no way of reaching it except through my imagination, no way of claiming it as a home I found, or a home I lost.

* * *

From Miami you have to fly through Atlanta or Philadelphia to get to Hartford. But I rented a U-Haul, packed everything I owned in 1999, and drove north on I-95 from my seaside apartment in Miami Beach to Hartford, America, the right side of the hyphen, or bust. Alas, I *the poet* would arrive in New England to teach creative writing and become the Cuban Robert Frost; alas, I would see snow, take sleigh rides, drink hot cocoa by a fireplace quoting Whitman; I would meet the Cleavers and the Bradys and visit Samantha Stephens' house in Westport; alas, I would be an American, I would be home. Not quite. Connecticut was and wasn't the America I had expected or hoped. There were fireplaces and snow, and people like the ones I saw on television, but I soon realized I could never really be one of those characters, a real part of the quintessential *show*, a real American the way I had envisioned I could (or should) be. What's more, I ended up living in a Puerto Rican and Italian neighborhood south of downtown with people who seemed just as lost as me, even though we were in "America." Perhaps even more lost because of what seemed like a looming pressure to assimilate—but into what? I refused the pressure (and the temptation), but began to see myself as some kind of pathetic Ricky Ricardo character banging on congas nobody could (or wanted to) hear.

My dream of being an American seemed to have completely vanished after living two years in Hartford. I needed a new home to dream about, to reach for, and began traveling extensively in search of that paradise, that one place meant for me, that city I belong to heart, soul, and mind. I drove through the Brazilian countryside following the ghost of Elizabeth Bishop's poems through waterfalls and villages; I woke up in Paris speaking French to a man I'd never see again, and laid naked on the beaches of Barcelona. I drank cheap red wine with Romans on the Spanish Steps, and skimmed through Dante while sipping espresso at cafés throughout Florence. But it was in Venice where the complete sense of the Cuban diaspora crystallized for me in the red, white, and blue image of a Cuban flag fluttering from a third-story window, its single white star appearing so lonely and yet so proudly hung for all to see above the Grand Canal. *Que coño hace un cubano en Venecia* (What the hell is a Cuban doing in Venice)? I thought. It dawned on me that I had more than just two countries or cultures to choose from. I could be a Cuban-Venetian or a French-Cuban. *Home* could be Venice or Rome, Austria or Mexico, or Guatemala.

*   *   *

From Hartford you must stop in Miami or Houston before getting to Guatemala where I lived for five months. I had moved there with my partner who had temporarily relocated to work with a Guatemalan doctor testing a new treatment for cancer. We were living in Antigua, the former colonial capital, a charming and picturesque city dotted with ruins of cathedrals and convents as well as teeming with cafés, restaurants, and shops. An ideal "home" for a poet, I thought. And if it was good enough for Gore Vidal who lived there several years, then it should be good enough for me. I'd wake up everyday to the sight of three volcanoes framed in my bedroom window, then take a slow walk along the cobblestone streets to Café L'Opera owned by an Italian expatriate. I'd have a mugful of espresso while scribbling down images and thoughts in my journal for two hours, then stroll through the central plaza and end up at the farmers market buying fresh vegetables and fruit. A beautiful life, in a beautiful city, in a wondrous land, but it wasn't mine. It would never be mine no matter how many times I climbed Pacaya and stared into the volcano's mouth, or I stood atop the Mayan temples of Tikal at sunset listening to monkeys screeching through the jungle, or bathed in the lagoons of Chamuc Shampey, or read the ancient *Popol Vuh* stories of creation where we are made out of corn not clay. I would always feel like a tourist, and outsider here. This could never be home, I thought, and began looking back to America with a new perspective: *Perhaps I should give America another try; perhaps I was just living in the "wrong" part of the country. Maybe if I moved to another city I would feel at home in my own country.*

*   *   *

My finger arcs across the map from Guatemala, to Hartford, to Washington, DC where I never thought I would live. I relocated in 2002 following my partner's career once again, though I was glad to abandon Hartford and my academic pursuits. In retrospect, I realize that I held a perverse, foolish hope that somehow living in our capital city would instill in me a love for America that I had never known and reveal my true place in this country. And it almost did. Many times driving home after midnight past the Washington Monument glowing under a full moon, I remember thinking, *This could be home after all; maybe this has been home all along?* But in the end, I just couldn't commit emotionally to America. I was actually afraid of finding home, preferring to keep dreaming of it instead because that was the mode I was used to. Having no sense of what home really meant, I began looking back toward Miami with a nostalgic eye. I began to long for the palms, the call of sea gulls on the beach and Caribbean Spanish drifting through the streets, the aroma of Cuban coffee from sidewalk *cafetería* windows at every corner, and the taste of my mother's *vaca frita*. It seemed more and more that Miami was my *natural* home, the only place that could ever accommodate the likes of me, for better or for worse. But I was bound to Washington and could not return to Miami, not yet.

*   *   *

I count thirty-two red arcs converging on Miami like petals at the center of a flower. Thirty-two routes leaving or returning as I did in 2004 to resume my former career as a civil engineer and urban designer. I began working at the same consultant firm where I was employed before I left, and purchased a home in the same neighborhood where I was living previously, expecting to live in exactly the same city I had left behind six years before. But, like my mother's Cuba, Miami changed without my permission. My neighborhood has been dubbed *Little Buenos Aires* by the Argentines who have immigrated into the area, I can't get a decent *pastelito* pastry for miles, the attendants at supposedly Cuban *cafeterías* refer to Cuban coffee as espresso and serve it without sugar, and everywhere there is a cacophony of different Spanish accents from Colombian to Chilean bouncing against each other. Perhaps Miami has become more diverse (or at least more pan-Latino) and that's indeed a good thing, but I still can't help feeling as though *my city* has been hijacked in some sense. Cuban no longer seems to be the dominant culture and, for better or for worse, I feel on the cultural margins of the very city where I grew up. Although the street names haven't changed, the streets themselves are now shadowed by Trump Towers and condos with pretentious names like *Oceania* and *Aqualina* turning a once low-key tropical paradise into a developer's *Chiquita Banana* version of New York City, referring to parts of Miami as the *Upper East Side* or the *Upper West Side*. Please. Unlike my parents who cannot return to live in Cuba, I've been able to return to live in Miami, but it is not *my* Miami. I am reminded of that every time I go visit a favorite restaurant or store only to realize it has become yet another *chic* nightclub or fancy European furniture store, or demolished altogether to make way for a fabulous new condo tower. Every morning, as I cross Biscayne Bay on the way to my office, I scan the countless construction cranes across the sky raising a new city that seems to be appearing right before my very eyes; a new skyline that has betrayed me and seems indifferent to my memories and my history as if I had never lived here. In this way, I have come to a much closer understanding of my parents' own displacement in time and their overwhelming nostalgia for a Cuba that doesn't exist anymore. *My*

Miami is a *place of mind* that I can't really return to either. Perhaps the only true home is the one that we lose.

*   *   *

I could be on my way back from anywhere—Venice or Venice, California; London or New London, Connecticut. Inevitably, the captain announces our final descent, I fold up the map of the world, put my tray table up, and stare through the shoe-box window at the gathering of lights and buildings, the crosshatch of streets and highways slowly coming into focus as a city. Inevitably, I remember Elizabeth Bishop's lines from "Questions of Travel":[2]

> Should we have stayed at home,
> wherever that may be?

and I tell myself that home is merely a fiction we construct, colored with our desire for permanence, our fear of change and resentment against fate. *I am a citizen of the world, I don't have to belong anywhere, this is my legacy as a child of exile,* I tell myself as we land and I am returned to a place that doesn't feel like home, still hoping it would.

NOTES

1. Blaise Pascal, *Pensées*, trans. Alban Krailsheimer (Harmondsworth, UK: Penguin Books, 1966), p. 37.
2. Elizabeth Bishop, "Questions of Travel," in *The Complete Poems: 1927–1979* (New York: Farrar, 1965), p. 94.

CHAPTER 2

I Will Die in Paris in the
Sudden Rain...

Verónica Pérez Konina

(Translated by David Frye)

I've always wondered how national character influences personal character, and what this thing they call "nationality" consists of. If I don't like dancing salsa, can I be considered Cuban? Can I be Russian when I detest vodka? And why can't I simply be an earthling, without belonging to any given country?

Two countries and two cultures have determined my character and my life. And these countries are completely unlike each other: opposite poles that I've had to link together in my inner world. One is cold and enormous, the world's largest country and its coldest one to boot. The other is small, a tropical island, "the land of eternal summer." The first is Russia, where I was born in 1968; the second is Cuba, where I lived for twenty years, until I emigrated in 1989. There are no people on earth less like each other in behavior and attitudes than the inhabitants of these two countries. Cubans are cheerful, open, lively; they love to dance and have fun. Russians are very reserved, find it impossible to speak to someone they don't already know, are rather unpredictable in their actions, undergo sudden mood shifts, passing from bottomless grief to joy without any apparent reason, and are prone to depression. They say that climate determines character, which is why the people of the south are more communicative and cheery than those of the north. For me, having both cultures in my veins, it has been truly problematic to combine the Russians' reserved character with the Cubans' joviality. That's why I'm joyful but so timid. When I used to live in Cuba I loved to dance but was embarrassed to do it in public. I empathize with the people around me, but find it hard to talk with a stranger, and for many years I had no friends.

Having lived the first part of my life in Cuba, up to the age of twenty-one, I hardly knew the real Russia, yet I considered myself Russian (not in appearance, as I am very tan, but in character). Nothing could have been further from the truth: the Russian character is just as Dostoyevsky describes it, like Raskolnikov and Sonya Marmeladova at the same time. For me, coming to Russia meant discovering that I really was Cuban.

The few times I came here on vacation in childhood, I was so small and came for so short a time that I couldn't get to know people or see the country. These were one or two month vacations when we stayed at my grandmother's house; I would see my aunts and uncles and cousins, visit Red Square, maybe see a little theater, and that was it. There was no opportunity for me to make friends or play with other children. My image of Russia was idealized and very literary, for I learned about it through nineteenth-century and early twentieth-century literature. Dealing with real life in this, my second country, was all the greater a shock.

My first unpleasant experience here in Russia came at the age of fourteen, when I decided to spend a year in this country and get to know it at last. Doing this wouldn't affect my studies, because I was already studying at a Russian school in Cuba, and I could live with my mother's unmarried sister and with my grandfather. My mother was always against this plan, not only because she didn't want to let go of me, but also because adolescence is a difficult enough phase and not the most appropriate moment to be living without your parents in an unknown country, but my father insisted. He thought that a year in Russia would be enough for me to decide in which country I'd rather go to college. My father was a psychologist, and I suspect that having a psychologist at home complicates things, because you can never be a good psychologist for your own family. Since my father's plan was to rid me of the desire to live in Russia in the future, I can state that he nearly accomplished it, as life was very hard for me that year.

To begin with, my mother wasn't from Moscow but from the outskirts, and provincial cities were quite neglected in the Soviet Union (as they still are today), with poorly stocked stores and buildings in disrepair. Moscow was the country's façade, the image for the tourists, and the provincial cities were all neglected. I saw a Russian television interview with a foreigner who visited a provincial city on a trip to Russia after World War II. Viewing the sad state that the city was in, he thought it must have been occupied by the Germans and that they had caused the disaster. When he mentioned this to a city resident, he quickly discovered his mistake: the Germans had never entered that city, which had been in this condition since the 1917 Revolution. My family lived in a similar place, and it also looked like it had undergone a Nazi occupation.

Some of the kids in the school where I studied were alcoholics (at fourteen years old!), and two girls were prostitutes. When I got sick and was admitted to the city children's hospital, I discovered the place was like a branch of the prison: children were admitted without parents, were not allowed to walk outside—and were forced to clean the floors! All this seemed completely inconceivable to me. In Cuba, the level of medical care was much higher, and besides, children were never admitted alone. I couldn't believe that the patients—the children—would be forced to clean the building, that there weren't any employees in charge of the cleaning, and I refused to do it. Then they forbid me to see my aunt (who would come to the hospital every day to bring me something to eat, because the food was also atrocious) or receive any outside food. The nurses were also our jailers; they took away everything my aunt brought me and called me "Jew" and "Armenian" to my face (since I am dark, they didn't think I looked Russian enough, so that's how they tried to insult me).

That was a very difficult year. It was also the year Brezhnev died, 1982. Even at the age of fourteen, I could see how cruel that system was. For me, too, the Soviet Union had become the "evil empire." After these experiences, I stopped believing in socialism and all the other ideas they tried to squeeze into our heads at the Russian school and later at the University of Havana. I discovered that socialism was a prison system: the school was one prison, the hospital was another, the army was a prison with an administration that was sometimes worse than an actual prison; the degree of freedom depended on which place you found yourself in, but the only freedom that was permitted in a socialist country was inner freedom. From the age of fourteen, I've been a dissident.

Things have changed quite a bit here in Russia now. It was precisely the possibility of change and of saying what I thought that led me to return to this country, in spite of the bad impression it had made on me as a child. In addition, life under so many years of socialist government has made the people here come up with protective mechanisms against any rules the state imposes, which has allowed life to become freer in Russia than in any other country. Every law can be evaded, any rule can be ignored. This is a totally individualistic society, every person is responsible for himself, but no one interferes in your life. It's a harsh, complicated life, but a life that makes you grow and mature.

My life can be divided into two parts, each corresponding to a country. I spent my early years and adolescence in Cuba, and for me Cuba is the magical land of childhood, the place we'd all like to return to some day. Never-Never Land, the country of Peter Pan. Russia is maturity for me, and it's always a test, the inexplicable world of Gogol's *Dead Souls*; it is the endless steppe, the snow piling up to the second-story windows, the 30-below-zero freezes; every year, when winter comes to an end, you think: I've survived another year! And you feel a touch of pride for such an achievement.

My first years of life in Cuba were very happy ones. I'm one of those people who love nature deeply and can stare in amazement at a landscape or a flower, and the neighborhood I lived in was an enormous garden. The neighborhood was Cubanacán, one of the residential suburbs of Havana where the rich people lived before 1959, which is now home to professors, scientists, and the "new" elite—bureaucrats and diplomats. The Victoria de Girón Medical Institute, where my father worked, is located in the neighborhood, and that is why we were given a house in such a privileged area. It was a large house, painted pink, that we shared with another family of professors from the Girón Institute. In front of the house grew a huge *flamboyán* tree whose branches covered the entire right side of the roof. Its red flowers were like tongues of fire every time it bloomed. I was quite intrigued by the fact that each flower had, in addition to its red petals, one multicolored petal with a white base fringed in all the colors of the rainbow. For me, it was a magic petal, a petal you could throw to the wind while making a wish, like in a Russian tale I once read—"The Flower of Seven Petals." Even though the *flamboyán* only had one magic petal in each flower, there were enough flowers in my tree at the time to take care of all my wishes.

There was another flowering tree at the end of the garden. Its flowers were large, white, and sweetly scented. We called them daisies, but I think they must have had another name, though I'm not sure. It was around that tree that we played house, and I was like Pedro Luis Ferrer's character in his song *Romance de la niña mala* (Ballad of the Bad Girl):[1] the girl who climbed trees, got onto rooftops, threw rocks, and fought with the other children.

Those trees were home to my favorite animals (after the dogs and cats that always lived in my house back then), the lizards. I devoted all my free time to hunting them, and came to be very skilled at it. Not a day went by that I didn't catch one. I liked the green ones that could change color quickly; the gray ones didn't change colors, so I didn't like them as much. I'd catch them and bring them home. I always wanted one to live with me, in my room. Since they, for their part, hunted mosquitoes, it seemed to me that a lizard could be well fed if it lived in my room, while at the same time there'd be fewer insects inside (there was quite a large number of them then, but later there were fewer and fewer because of the campaign against dengue fever, a disease transmitted by mosquito bite; along with the mosquitoes, the butterflies and dragonflies also disappeared).

Our garden was also visited from time to time by *zunzuns,* tiny and beautiful little birds, otherwise known as hummingbirds. The *zunzun* is the world's smallest bird. It lives from the nectar of flowers, like a butterfly. When it flies, it flaps its wings so rapidly that they cannot be seen; all you see is a tiny, bright green body hanging in midair, and a long beak, which it inserts for a moment into a flower. Then the bird disappears, as if by magic.

The world of my early childhood was all but uninhabited by people. Adults existed in a parallel dimension, and other children, it seems, didn't play much of a role in this multicolor garden. Nor do I remember playing with dolls, which never interested me. Playing games with other children was something I discovered years later, when I started going to school and my vision of the world had changed. Everything around me continued to be harmonious and clean, but I was different. I felt out of nature. Once, at dusk, watching the white clouds float overhead, I thought I'd like to be like them, white, clean, but I felt deep down that it was impossible. But why can't I be clean, like one of those white clouds, if I haven't done anything wrong? I thought, deep inside myself. I found no answer. It was a sense of shock that I still remember today, like discovering a truth that you can't explain but that you feel will turn out to be very important. Years later, when I studied a bit of the Bible, about original sin, that explained to me why I felt dirty and couldn't be white as a cloud, but the memory of that afternoon remained etched in my mind as the discovery of an inner world that did not depend on the nature around me.

The neighborhood children treated me as if I were different from them, probably because I was serious, and was also the only girl who had studied outside of Cuba, who had traveled on a plane, who had seen the world. Just to bother me, they kept asking, "But have you seen snow?" And I certainly had seen it, as a four-year-old girl, when I lived in Russia for an entire year. This made them envious, because in Cuba everybody dreams of seeing and playing in the snow. They think that snow is a miracle. Here in Russia, however, after spending nearly six months surrounded by snow, what you really want is a bit of sun and warmth.

Personally, I have always liked the sea more than the snow, the warm sea that also formed part of my childhood world. The first few months in Moscow I found it hard to conceive that the city had no sea. Whenever I drove somewhere in a car, I'd realize that I had been staring out the window, looking for the sea; it always seemed that the sea should be somewhere nearby, that it would only take driving up that street for the horizon to open up to a view of waves and for the smell of salt spray to overcome me, but it was all in vain. It was odd not to have the sea to gaze at. A city without the sea is, for me, a closed city, like a maze without an exit.

My earliest years in Cuba had been spent in Mayanima, a neighborhood along the coast of Havana, and the sensation of enormous open space, the freedom that a view of the ocean gives you, is the image of happiness for me even today. The sea is happiness, and whenever I get a chance to spend some time on the beach I jump at it. Many times I've been to the Black Sea, the Baltic, the Red Sea (from Egypt), and the Mediterranean (from Spain).

I lived on the beach at Mayanima for nearly a year, and I remember there were hundreds of crabs that would come out every afternoon to crawl around and look for food, so that the sand seemed to skitter with them. It was the crabs' beach. Then it wasn't anymore. I think all the crabs were eaten in the 1970s. One of the crabs was a smoker—it would steal my father's cigarette butts and carry them off to its cave. And there was a drunken butterfly that perched on his beer cup to sip the dregs. It was a huge black nocturnal butterfly, one of the kind that measures more than four inches across, and it seemed completely natural to me to think that it had finished off a full cup. (Of course, it was my father who had drunk the cup, but he liked to joke, and I believed him.)

It was around then that adults started asking their foolish questions. I've always found it hard to answer such questions. There are people who ask them because they don't know how to talk to a child. The most foolish question was about my nationality. Are you Russian or Cuban? As if it were up to me. As if it made a difference. Whether I said I was Russian or Cuban, nothing inside me changed. People usually ask these things as if the answer were obvious. It's like when they ask a child whom he likes better, his mother or his father. It's a little game for adults, watching the children suffer, because when a child is forced to choose between two figures as important as their parents, he really feels under pressure. It's the same thing, being asked to choose which nation you belong to, when your parents come from different countries. I couldn't decide which one to go for, especially since I was dealing with two cultures as unique as Russia and Cuba. Which do I prefer: nineteenth-century Russian literature, or the carnival celebrations in the little towns of Oriente province, where everyone runs out into the street to dance? Well, I'll keep them both, because I like both. Choosing between Russia and Cuba would be like choosing between my father and my mother, my Cuban father and my Russian mother. Choosing one would betray the other, which is why I prefer to say that I'm both at once. I'm half Russian and half Cuban, like those mythical animals that were both man and animal; I'm *polovina*, as the descendents of Russians and Cubans were called in Cuba; I'm *mitad*, half person and half animal.[2] Of course, I'd like to be half of a more or less likeable animal, a dog or a horse, for example, or a lion or lioness, and not a serpent. In Mayanima we "borrowed" the house of one of my father's colleagues to live in until I was four; my memories of the butterfly and the crab are from my earliest childhood. At first, my mother didn't work. I remember her washing clothes by hand in a wash tub, while I could squat down inside a water bucket, where my whole body fit, so small was I back then. When we strolled around our neighborhood near the sea, people stared at us with curiosity and made comments out loud. My mother still spoke no Spanish, so they could say whatever they wanted. But I did understand. The children who lived there almost always shouted "The Russian girl!" and "There goes the little Russian!" at me, though physically I don't look Russian at all. It really bothered me when they called me that, so I came up with this retort: "I'm no little Russian girl. My name is Verónica Pérez Cubana!" My name is actually Verónica Pérez Konina, but at the age of four, my second surname[3] "Konina" sounded almost the same as "Cubana" to my ears. The joke is that Konina is my Russian surname, my mother's name.

When I lived in Cuba, I never enjoyed feeling like a Russian among the Cubans—unlike my mother, who never attempted to stop being "foreign." I've always been attracted to the "common folk," the man in the street, in spite of belonging to a family of university professors. Perhaps because the housing they gave us was located in an old "bourgeois" residential neighborhood where only professors lived, I wanted to get away from the "petit bourgeois" oasis of Cubanacán and find out how "normal" people lived, and was very curious to know what life was like for people who didn't have professors for parents. I've always been an outsider: in Russia, because I came from Cuba, and in Cuba, because my mother was Russian and my father was from Oriente province, which made him an internal emigrant even within Cuba; I've always had my own view of things.

You might say I've always felt a bit foreign, "too Russian to be Cuban and too Cuban to be Russian," to paraphrase a North American poet of Cuban origin, Lourdes Casal. I read her poem "For Anna Veltfort" one summer afternoon in Alamar, the most Russian-seeming neighborhood that exists in Havana. It is a neighborhood of concrete buildings that look like match-boxes, all alike, where the writers with the most brownie points at the Union of Cuban Writers were given apartments. I went there with another writer, who didn't have enough points and didn't have a house either (because houses were handed out by the state), to visit a friend of his. It was the writer who lived in Alamar who gave me Lourdes Casal's book, because he thought I had a lot in common with her. Both writers, discovering that I was bilingual and spoke Russian as well as I did Spanish, started speaking in French and reading French poems on purpose, so that I couldn't understand them. I sat down to read Lourdes Casal. She had won the Premio David, the same prize I would win the following year. I liked her book a lot, and it amazed me that they had given her such a prize.[4]

I was too Russian to be Cuban, too intellectual to be like the young people my age, but I've always tried to cross those borders, to be like everyone. My motto has been, as Celia Cruz sang, *Ay, no hay que llorar, que la vida es un carnaval, y las penas se van cantando* (Ay, you shouldn't cry, because life's a carnival, so sing away your sorrows)...

Russia, the country of my adulthood, has forced me to look at life more deeply. It takes a lot more resources to survive here than in Cuba. The houses keep the heat running for almost half the year (from mid-October to late April or early May), and fortunately it is central heating. You have to buy winter boots, boots for fall, overcoats, sweaters. If you have children, and I have two, you have to buy them new clothes and shoes every year. Russia's nature, the fir and birch forests, the lakes, are the only things I like about the landscape.

The most difficult thing for me, as an emigrant in Russia, isn't the language, given that Russian is like my second language and sometimes even like my first, but the impossibility of understanding the people. If you haven't lived in this country, haven't watched the same movies they've all watched, haven't listened to the same songs, haven't gone to the same daycare center and the same school, then you have little in common with the people here, and you can't understand them. In Cuba I could read people by their faces, there was no need for words to tell what kind of people they were, what social strata they belonged to, even which neighborhood of Havana. The way they dressed, combed their hair, the gestures they made—it all formed part of an easily decipherable code. Not in Russia. Lots of times I don't know what to expect from the people around me, I can't tell just by looking whether it's worth it or not to talk to a person. That's why emigrants are almost always solitary people, as is true in my case. Family and work are my only consolations.

Even though Russia is a developed country, in regard to human relations it is still in the medieval era. Muscovites can pass as civilized, they have been "brushed" by world culture, but the people of the outskirts—the ones in my student dorm, for example—really were rather uncivilized. When I arrived in 1989 as a Cuban student at the Gorky Literary Institute, I suffered my second shock. Not to dwell on hygiene—after all, every country has its own norms, and we Cubans are meticulous about cleanliness—but those collective toilets in the hallways looked like something out of a horror film. This was in the dorm of the literary institute, and when you say literary, you mean culture.... The toilets were cleaned from time to time by a brigade of alcoholic ex-convicts with little experience in that type of work, and I don't think they ever cleaned the kitchen, which was crawling with cockroaches and always covered in filth.

But it was precisely Russia's alcoholic culture, or lack of culture, that caused me the biggest shock. In Cuba people drink very little—there's no comparison—and they are incapable of downing some cologne or a bottle of medicine that contains alcohol just to get drunk.... In Cuba you drink to go dancing, to have fun; drinking is a means, not an end. In Russia you drink to forget the world. Russian writers, moreover, think your talent can be measured by your capacity for drinking vodka. They are aggressive, ill-mannered, often ignorant. Of course, I can't speak about all writers, just the ones that graduated from my institute. In writers' workshops, they'd insult you in the meanest ways, and everybody thought it was the most natural thing in the world. My workshop tutor, Andrei Bitov, would always say, "Verónica is a Westerner." I never understood what he meant by this. Now I realize that I was the only one who didn't understand that Russians can insult each other and just keep going, as cool as cucumbers. People are less hypocritical in Russia than in Cuba, they prefer to tell you the truth to your face, but it's almost always a truth that you'd rather not hear. They go out of their way to tell you unpleasant things, they'll never tell you anything good. The workshop was pure suffering for me. Moreover, I had to translate everything I presented there into Russian, or write it directly in Russian, and writing in that language didn't feel right to me. I tried to write a few stories in Russian, but they didn't turn out all that well.

That's how my literary career got interrupted for nearly fifteen years, until the moment came when I could once again speak in Spanish, think in Spanish, and write in Spanish; that is, when I began to work as a Spanish instructor in the Instituto Cervantes, and went back to writing in Spanish.

Sometimes the students at Cervantes ask me questions about Cuba, but I always evade them. There's nothing in my everyday life that can remind me of my country, which is how I have planned it, because I like to avoid those memories. Speaking about Cuba makes me suffer. My dreams are the only things I can't control; I see my country in my sleep, then wake up feeling sad. Fortunately this doesn't happen very often. I talk to my students about Cuba when I don't have any other choice. There are a lot of people among the older generation of Russians who still sympathize with Fidel and the Revolution, and if they discover that I'm Cuban, they express their sympathy for Cuba and its political course. One of these older students told me one day that she had seen Fidel from a distance during his last trip to Russia, and she admitted her admiration for him. Then she went on to compare the situation in Russia, where in her opinion everything was terrible, with that in Cuba, where everything was great.

"The Chinese have a saying, the worst thing that can happen to a person is to live in a country during a time of change," she told me. "Russia's been in a period of change for a long time, and it seems like the changes are never going to end. That's why we're so bad off. The Cubans are lucky, because they've been able to avoid changes." At that, I couldn't hold back any longer, and I told her, "We Cubans are only hoping to get to see changes like these ourselves, and to experience them in the flesh. At any rate, I hope I can see such changes with my own eyes. Maybe my father didn't get to see them, but at least I'll see them for him." I hope, when that day comes, that all Cubans—in Cuba, abroad, and we "half" Cubans—will join together and do everything possible to create a happy future.

My father, who unfortunately didn't live to see the longed-for changes on the island, came from Oriente province, from a small town named Palmarito de Cauto, near Santiago. He left town at the age of fourteen to join the militia, finished school later in Havana, and in 1962 was one of the first Cuban students to come to Moscow and study at the university. His dream had always been to study philosophy, but that field was reserved for Russians, so he turned to Russian psychology. When he finished his degree and returned to Cuba married to a Russian woman—my mother—it was clear that there would be nothing for him to do in his home town, which didn't even have a hospital, much less a psychiatric clinic. That's why he had to look for work in the capital. So both of my parents came to Havana as outsiders. My mother had the status of foreigner, for which everybody envied her, because she had a better chance of "obtaining" food in a country where getting enough to eat was and remains a constant problem. My father, one of many "Orientals" who had moved to the capital, owed his education to the Revolution that sent him to study for free in another country. On his return he was given a place to live in Havana and achieved his goal of becoming a professional. None of this could have happened without the Revolution; his father was a simple cane worker, and the highest he might have dreamed for his son would have been a technician's post in the sugar mill. The fact that people like my father were later forced to leave their country is proof that something has gone wrong. It is hard to emigrate when you're fifty years old, and have the better part of your life behind you! My father never foresaw the changes that have taken place in the world: perestroika, the fall of the Berlin Wall, and especially the fact that he himself was forced to come to Russia and live here for the rest of his life. Nor did I think, in 1991, the last time I traveled to Cuba, that I was about to leave my country forever. I think that lots of people had the same experience; they thought they would be going away for a short time, until the end of the "Special Period," which was actually a period of special hunger, one that continues today. My mother left Russia in 1967 thinking that she had left the country forever. I came to Russia in

1989 as a Cuban student, married a Russian, and then my parents came too, my mother in 1991 and my father in 1993. Thus my family's peregrinations came to an end, returning full cycle to the same point where they started, in Moscow. In the early 1990s, people were leaving Cuba in any way and direction they could; that was the time of the so-called *balsero* crisis, when people were risking the ocean on rafts and inner tubes to reach the United States. According to one statistic, half of these *balseros* were lost, and forever will remain, in the waters of the Gulf. My father didn't have to undertake such a dangerous crossing, but his departure from Cuba put an end to our life there, for when he left his job at his institute, he also lost the house where we used to live and where I had been so happy during my childhood years.

I think Cuba can be seen as a country whose population has been dispersed around the world; there are the same number of people living on the island as abroad now. Of course, Cuban culture has become popular in many countries as a result. Even in Russia, young people are learning to dance salsa, and many of them move on from discovering Cuban music and dance to studying the Spanish language.

Every country makes some important contribution to world culture. Cuba's contribution is precisely its sense of joyousness, its people's capacity for rejoicing under any circumstances. In Russia, people don't have this ability to feel joy; they are more embittered, more bitter. They don't know how to rejoice in the simple things, they need too many things in order to be happy, but even when they have them they still can't enjoy them. The young people are a little different, more receptive, more cheerful. I think the Russians are going through what the Jews of the Old Testament experienced when they left Egypt: they had to wander in the desert for more than forty years to stop being slaves, and a new generation had to grow up outside of captivity. Younger Russians are different, but the ones who grew up under the socialist system are beyond cure.

I can say that, living in Cuba, I always missed Russia, because I thought my character was like the Russians', and now in Russia I live missing Cuba, but the Cuba I remember no longer exists. Then too, I've lived almost as many years in Russia as I did in Cuba; my children were born here, and they are completely Russian. They study Spanish as a foreign language and have never been to Cuba.

Once I saw an interview on Russian television with Andy García, a North American actor of Cuban origin, who said that for him, his father had been like a little piece of the home country that he had gotten out of Cuba. I don't remember his exact words, but that idea was burned into my mind as if I had said it myself. I was also lucky enough to get my father out of Cuba. He lived for more than ten years in Moscow, and when he died in 2004, I felt as if I had lost the little bit of the home country that he represented for me. His death was sudden, no one anticipated it, and at the time it grieved me so deeply to think that he would remain forever in this cold and inhospitable ground that I would have paid anything to transport his body back to the land where he was born. He always wanted to return to Cuba, if only for a visit, and never wanted to be buried in Russia, to stay here always.

We buried him on a rainy day in March. The sky was gray, and snowflakes were falling hard as sleet. The open grave was full of dirty, frozen water. The gravediggers had tried to disguise the puddle at the bottom of the grave with pine branches, the only branches that are green in that season, but I found it so painful to see that black pit in the earth, I felt like screaming. That's why I couldn't watch when they lowered the coffin and began piling the earth on top. I only looked when the damp earth had already been heaped high. It was the kind of dampness, so typical of Moscow, that chills you to your bones. We were all freezing, and it anguished me to think that his bones would remain forever in so cold a place. Or does that not matter any more after you are dead? "I'll die in Paris in the sudden rain, on a day that I already can recall...."[5] Vallejo was my father's favorite poet, and he always liked to recite that poem from memory. But it wasn't in Paris, it was in Russia, in freezing rain with sleet.

In May, when everything dried out and the trees were dressed in green, I went with my mother and children to visit his grave for the first time since the funeral. Up until then, there had been so much mud that it would have been impossible to reach it. To tell the truth, we didn't really know what to do there. Cleaning the little pile of earth, throwing out the remains of bouquets and wreaths, and sitting on a bench there—that was all we were able to do in his memory. We had no experience of visiting anyone in the cemetery. We had brought along some candles, which we stuck into the ground and lit. The wind tried blowing them out, and we found it very heartening when a lizard crawled out to sun itself for a long time on the grave without taking note of our presence. We saw that as a good sign, a message from the beyond, but we thought it even more heartening when we discovered, not far away, a tombstone with a name in Spanish! The name was written in Cyrillic letters, of course, but there could be no doubt about it, a certain Antonio Ruíz was buried near my father. The man had died some twenty years earlier, and, judging from the dates carved on the tombstone, he may have been one of those Spanish "war children" who had been evacuated to Russia in the late 1930s and who had never been able to return to their country afterward. And if he wasn't a war child, who cares, he was someone of Hispanic origin, and my father wouldn't be so all alone any more; someone who spoke his language and shared his culture was buried by him. Making this discovery was a great joy for my mother and for me.

As María Zambrano said, "My country is my language." She always felt connected to her country through language, and for me as well, my country has become the oases of Spanish that exist in Russia, and there my father will have his bit of home country, his Spanish-speaking territory. As the Instituto Cervantes in Moscow is for me—my second home, a bit of an intellectual country, allowing me to survive.

TRANSLATOR'S NOTES

1. The best-known song in Ferrer's 1977 album *Mariposa*, based on a poem by Raúl Ferrer, it narrates a father's defense of his rebellious young daughter against the criticisms of his neighbors.

2. *Polovina, mitad:* Russian and Spanish, respectively, for "half."
3. In Spanish-speaking countries, people customarily have two surnames, the first from the father and the second from the mother.
4. The Premio David is awarded annually by the Union of Cuban Writers and Artists (UNEAC) to a promising young writer. Verónica Pérez Konina won it in 1988, at the age of twenty, for her book of short stories *Adolesciendo.* Lourdes Casal won not the Premio David but a related special prize from the Casa de las Américas in 1981.
5. From Peruvian poet César Vallejo's poem "Piedra negra sobre piedra blanca," published posthumously in his collection *Poemas humanos* (Paris: Presses Modernes, 1939).

CHAPTER 3

Exile and Bougainvillea

José Kozer

(Translated by Mark Weiss)

For a Jew like me, who's lived for over forty years outside his native land, being what's called an exile is neither novel nor surprising or discouraging. It's never seemed to me a major issue, it's neither odious nor a source of despair; nor, for that matter, pleasant or agreeable. It's perhaps a burden, given the historical situation, a burden that inclines us to self-justification, to explanations as intimate as they are public, although when we remember the uselessness of passing our lives giving explanations and cease to offer them, to ourselves and others, exile becomes, if not comfortable, at least bearable: neither devastating nor wonderful. For me, at least, it has lost much of its force and become merely a state of being, or better, a situation: if one wishes to grant it relevance as a theme one can treat it as a destiny, like any other: a fountain, a spring rich in healing waters, a vein to exploit with subtle dedication when one's art requires it, a vein of such inexhaustible depth and size that one can extract from it the full, endless range of the most dissimilar experiences, the most complex and variable referentiality. The exile can define himself as one who doesn't have just the one tree, the one flower; it is given to him, rather, to know, to examine, to fall in love with, to use the multiplicity of flowers and trees, gathered in his incessant wandering to all points of the compass, such that the man born in the tropics ends up, one could say, singing of the snows of the north, and he sings of the flat-roofed masonry houses of his native place but equally of the peak-roofed northern houses, their copings and lofty mansards.

I turn to the figure of the French explorer and traveler Louis Antoine de Bougainville (1729–1811); though not one of my heroes, given his racism, awkward Eurocentrism, and reactionary politics, as Gobineau and de Maistre attest, he will serve to show us an important aspect of exile. This navigator, who circled the globe and established an unsuccessful French colony in the Malvinas, and in whose honor was named that beautiful shrub, no less a global traveler than he, the bougainvillea, *bugambilia* in Mexico (in Cuba *buganvilia* or *buganvil*, a word that also carries an indecent connotation in the language of the street), brought from Tahiti a "savage" to demonstrate in the flesh the Rousseauian concept of the "natural man." In Paris our good savage discovers opera. And Bougainville is surprised to learn that, after the Tahitian has been in Paris for a while, said opera is the only artifact of civilization that interests or attracts him at all; he's only drawn to the most extreme artificiality that the world of opera represents in the arts. The natural, we assume, means nothing to him, but it's the unrealistic, grotesque, and exceedingly mannered stage business of opera that mesmerizes this man of nature, giving life and sense to the disarray in which he finds himself.

I recount this anecdote because (although I have no taste for analogies, which always seem to me a dangerous intrusion in the act of interpretation, and which, because of their very logic, may not be accurate) my own experience as an exile has certain points of contact with that of Bougainville's Tahitian. When I arrived from Cuba, in 1960, as a twenty-year-old, and settled immediately in New York, where I remained for thirty-seven years, I was changed at many levels. The most fundamental was my relationship with my language (and my Havana dialect): my sense of language changed completely, becoming Alexandrian and diasporic; it became in a sense Byzantine and artificial: a living opera. In place of the fetters of my native, monolingual Cuban, a linguistic proliferation unfolded, and continues to unfold, within me; the mixing of English and Spanish expanded the ways I perceived and received the grace of my language. As I said in a poem called "Babel," "my native, maternal / language / is intricate."

By "intricate" I refer in part to that artificiality that in a sense is characteristic of art. Given the lived experience of exile, the language that I speak and write is, in some ways, an artifice, when compared with the usual way of learning, growing, and living within a native, singular language, from which one never absents oneself nor imagines being uprooted involuntarily. Thus, for example, I rarely use the Cuban word *cotorrita* for that little insect that I love so much, preferring the Mexican word *catarina*, which I find more useful poetically. I haven't the least qualms about using—interiorizing— Mexicanisms, Peruvianisms, Hispanicisms. At home, for another example, there is the curious phenomenon that my wife, of pure transplanted Spanish stock, has come to say *botar*, a Latin American term for "throw out," while I, a Cuban hybrid, in general, and casually, say *tirar*, in the Spanish manner. Thus, she *bota algo a la basura* (throws something into the garbage) and I *lo tiro* (throw it out).

Exile, finally, turns things upside down, pushes them sideways, incorporating baggage from everywhere and anywhere: everything is reversed, becoming a *mejunje*, a stew (*menjurje*, in Cuban) of tones, words, turns of phrase, provenances, from the full range of Spanish. It seems to me that an ever-approaching future will bring us naturally to an evermore hybridized Spanish; not like the hybridism of the past, which involved the adoption of gallicisms or anglicisms, but the incorporation of the most diverse, richest forms of speech from the diverse nations in which Spanish is spoken. Soon, I think, we will hear, without really noticing, a Mexican saying *camaján* (con man) or *tremendo sal p'afuera* (knock-down-drag-out fight), we'll hear an Argentine redecorating his native speech with Cuban overtones. If this in fact comes to pass, this linguistic rapprochement would be healthy for our family of countries and for its citizens. For a while we would decry it as artificial and a threat to our national values, we would refuse, violently at times, to participate in the kaleidoscope, the stew, of this new, complex Spanish; after a few decades, however, it would become natural to us, and the linguistic transfer would bring us closer.

The artificiality forced on us by the diaspora would become natural. And for this garrulous and tropical Cuban the experience of the cold and silence of the forest would become natural as well: exile has taught me to love, with my entire being, the juniper (which gives its flavor to gin) and the amazing dogwood, without losing my connection to the *uva caleta* and the *hicaco*.

I present these trees as poles of reference, but I wish to make clear that both poles are now alive, appropriated, naturalized, within me. Without the experience of exile I doubt that I would have been able to come to feel such a deep affinity for the Mexican *ocote* (ocote pine) or the Spanish *encina* (holm oak), no different from my feeling for my maternal *laurel de Indias* (golden ficus). I don't think that the harshness and the luminosity that I experience every day upon discovering the presence of a word that I haven't heard or used for decades (having lived in a context where English takes precedence, and is sometimes the only language) would have been possible without the difficult, fruitful experience of exile.

Here, for example, are two terms from Cuban popular speech: *chévere* (great, generous) and *paluchero* (bullshit artist). I heard the first constantly in my country, the second I only learned in exile. *Chévere* and its cousins *asere, ecobio, mi sosio, monina, nagüe*, or *yérnica* (all of which mean "chum," "buddy," "pal") are words that I never used in my Cuban adolescence: they belonged to a different social class, they were not merely of the street but pretentious in the context of my Havana dialect. They belonged to the slum dwellers, the brothels, the mentality of bullies, and juvenile delinquents. If I were to have said, for instance, in the Havana of 1957, that someone seemed *chévere* to me, I would have sounded hollow, phony, as pretentious as if I had thrown a Latin word into a Spanish conversation.

Nonetheless, time and distance, and certainly an element of nostalgia, has led the word *chévere* to be incorporated into my vocabulary. Why? In part, I think, because class barriers have lost for me much of their importance; but also because the experience of exile revitalizes words foreign to one's native dialect, facilitating their incorporation. This process seems odd at first—we feel, as a Cuban would say, like *postalitas* (phonies). But the word becomes naturalized, assimilated, and recorded by the blood and the heart in the most natural way, through use. There appears to be something akin to a law of linguistics to which every exile becomes a signatory: that the artificial will become natural; and the foreignness of otherness itself, to call it such, will disappear.

Words are also lost, a plethora of words that, no longer used in daily life, remain buried within us. These words, once natural, may suddenly surface, but with an artificial timbre, a foreign echo and sonority, almost as if they weren't in the dictionary, or better, as if they had been but were no longer. The word that once was natural returns as something artificial. Astonished, delighted, we use it again, we rediscover it, and we begin, almost like a child with a new toy or a box of chocolates, to use it at every opportunity, until, through a process of reabsorption and forgetting, it regains its original nature, its initial naturalness. Except that now, and it's what I want to emphasize, it's been enriched by layers and layers of personal experience that give it an uncommon luster and density.

To summarize: there are two processes related to the exile's loss of language, its distancing and recovery. On the one hand, there is the process that leads from the artificial to the natural, as in the example of *chévere,* above; on the other, there is the process that goes from the natural to its loss, and to its recovery as something foreign and artificial that now, enriched, becomes naturalized once more.

What we call a *paluchero* in Cuban is what peninsular Spanish calls a *baladrón, echador,* or *alardoso* (braggart, boaster, show-off), with his endless chatter. As I've said, it was after several years in exile that I first learned this word; I can remember from whom I heard it and where, and almost the day and hour. I was astonished: I finally had an exact equivalent for an English word, which enriched my conversation, but which I'd never been able to reproduce in my native dialect. I refer to "bullshitter" and the expression "bullshit artist," meaning someone who habitually asserts untruths. Suddenly, and with intense relief, I could vary my discourse and use comfortably, in each of the two languages that, though they remained distinct, had become, finally, equally natural to me, a word that was no longer missing in either. I had the original word and its translation, as well as its retranslation into the original. Oh happy land, lost paradise recovered!

Franz Werfel wrote in "The True Story of the Recovered Cross": "Mistrust is one of the most poisonous plants of political exile. Each immigrant distrusts the others and, if he could, would suspect even himself, his spirit already shattered by belonging nowhere."[1] In his turn Czeslaw Milosz in *The Captive Mind* calls attention to "the abyss that exile was for me," which he terms "the worst misfortune that could have befallen me, because it meant sterility and inaction."[2]

I cite two writers for whom I have the deepest respect. I well understand their grief and that feeling of menace that can manifest as suspicion or impotence when one becomes stateless. I think, nonetheless, that each of them presents a vision of the exile that precedes the current enormous displacement of people, cultures, modes of perception, and interests, whether over- or underestimated, that, how deeply one can't know, is once more changing the Western world. Where Werfel saw suspicion and Milosz sterility I find opportunity for growth; in place of profound grief or a tragic fate I prefer to emphasize the benefits, and no small number, of the exile's condition. In the face of the difficulty implicit in that condition, I see, through personal experience, the occasion to amplify, deepen, free one's being, forging, for example, a more ecumenical and polyphonic language that without pretence or affectation can express a new order in which exile, though far from a utopia, is also neither the worst of misfortunes nor a source of paranoia. I think it's time to turn one's back on the sometimes opportunistic exaggeration of the situation of the exile. Let the exile instead use his experience as a weapon in his social and spiritual quest.

It should go without saying that to turn one's back on the romantic vision of displacement doesn't imply surrendering the struggle to diminish the occurrence of exile and emigration born of social injustice, although a degree of this injustice will probably always be with us.

NOTES

1. Franz Werfel, "La historia verídica de la cruz restaurada," in *El secreto de un hombre* (Barcelona: Libros DB, 1983), p. 63, translation of *Die wahre Geschichte vom wiederhergestellten Kreuz* (Los Angeles: Privatdruck der Pazifischen Presse, 1942).
2. Czeslaw Milosz, *The Captive Mind* (New York: Vintage International, 1981), p. xi.

CHAPTER 4

The Land Is in Me

Damaris Calderón

(Translated by David Frye)

You are Born to Yourself

I've lived outside of Cuba for a dozen years, but I don't think I've ever left it. No matter where I go, for good or for ill, the land is in me. I have images of myself as a woman traveling on a train that never stops, looking out through a small window. Sometimes I get off, sometimes I keep going. At first it was sad, now it's unmarked, it's neither festive nor tragic, it just is. When I go to Cuba I think I won't be able to say farewell to Cuban soil, won't be able to come back and leave my folks, my family, behind. When the plane leaves the ground it's a painful process, like I'm sloughing off layers of myself, a sensation of rending and of relief, I leave myself back there, some part of myself stays on the ground, another part flies up, leaves, doesn't belong, in the end it's like the anesthetized lethargy that follows an amputation, just so, I'm always (or almost always) moving between two ways of being torn in half, when I arrive in Chile I head toward the Andes in search of the Malecón. I don't believe in Ithacas: I know that no land can contain me, I know there is no calm.

There's a beautiful book by Claudio Guillén, *El sol de los desterrados*, in which he speaks of the endlessness of exile and the endlessness of (existential) literary responses to that phenomenon.[1] He speaks of expatriation as a solar metaphor, seeing it as an experience that opens you up to what's universal (contemplating the sky, the stars, the other, from space), and he mentions the Cynics and the Stoics as figuring among the expatriates (or the self-expatriated), and of exile as loss, as an imbalance of self and of the civic subject, and from this point of view Ovid appears, with his *Tristia* and his *Ex Ponto*, as the paradigm of grief, of love for the land from which he's been dispossessed and to which he returns through evocation and writing. Now, I don't believe that both postures (metaphors) are necessarily contradictory, but rather are complementary. I believe that, whether or not you sought it out, whether or not the process was entirely conscious, exile, diaspora, departure opens you up, forces you to grow as a human being, to confront another culture, other norms, other aspects of yourself that were unknown and perhaps nonexistent or deeply buried, and that your departure revealed. You are born again, to yourself.

CHILE: BOOKS. LAND'S END.

By living in Chile, a country that I, like the majority of Cubans who emigrate, did not choose, I kept my language, Spanish, though naturally with a different accent. The cultural norms, however, were quite different. I arrived in Santiago, invited here by a journal that some Chilean friends published, when I was twenty-seven years old and had a few literary connections in my country, and here I "started from zero" by working in a publishing house as a secretary, as a proofreader, later as an editor. I've held a motley mix of jobs. In recent years I've devoted myself to teaching, learned to lose myself in the crowd, and be anonymous. I arrived in 1995 and worked in the publishing house but handled the most diverse jobs, answering the phone, keeping the petty cash, proofreading, and correcting manuscripts, before becoming an editor, and before *El Mercurio* awarded me their Prize for Poetry in 1999, in a competition judged by Gonzalo Rojas, which is what "introduced me" to Chile. Accomplishing all "these little things" (and continuing to do them, too, from other spaces) has required humility, an attention to others, and also a sureness and confidence in myself that I can't get from any literary prize or other validation. Also, by reading the manuscripts sent to the publishing house (whether they were ever published or not) I began to build up, at my work desk, an idea of the country, this other country. And I then lost the fundamentalisms, the nationalism, and so many other isms that we look to for self-affirmation and that are so limiting. The security of being in my land, the affection of my friends, stayed behind, I started over in a vacuum, all was leveled. The cultural aridity of postdictatorship Chile, its great differences from Cuba's idiosyncrasy (if there is such a thing), forced me to grow. I didn't suffer my loneliness in another language, but I suffered it in my own language, and I don't know which is harder. Departure, exodus, diaspora, whatever term you prefer, literally means leaving the road you're on. However, I believe that this "departure" is, should be, an opening of the self toward the Other, toward Otherness, not merely a loss. For the ancients, going down into Hell was a source of knowledge, a revelation, which they illustrated through paradigmatic descents, and in the same way one does not return from exile with empty hands.

Before I arrived in this country, the images I had of it were basically literary. Before I set foot on Chilean soil, I knew the country through the names of its great poets (Gabriela Mistral, Neruda, Violeta Parra), alluded to in some of the songs of Silvio Rodríguez and Pablo Milanés, and it was a very distant, remote place. It was *Finis Terrae* (Land's End), where the world ends, where the devil gave three shouts, or none at all, in a word, a narrow fringe of land at the end of the map in an atlas, if you look at it from the north. And then I found myself in the end of the world and saw that it could also be the beginning. I owe thanks to Chile for giving me the opportunity to know the extraordinary cultures of the Andes, largely devastated for the most part by the Spanish Empire, and then again by the neoliberal barbarism that levels everything that's autochthonous, everything that's local, in the name of progress. Here I met the mountains and learned what it is to be (to have to be) a mountain. I came to understand, in my own flesh, Gabriela Mistral's "La extranjera" (The Foreigner), came to understand her *Tala* and *Desolación*, and the desert ceased to be a metaphor. I endeavored to learn from all these things. Existence overflowed the banks of literature. Chile was taking hold of me, and I was taking hold of Chile, of its people's speech (which began to be, in a way, my own), their words, their symbols. This gave rise to a book, *Parloteo de Sombra*, which is a textual crossroads, a hybrid cartography of no-man's-land, where the streets of Cuba, of Santiago de Chile, of the Great Andean North all flow together. For many years I sketched in Cuba, but in Chile I began to paint, to do performance pieces, to explore other routes, other ways of life that also became fleshed out in my artistic creativity. As for the rest, here as in Cuba I work in a small apartment that I treat as my nun's cell, and every day, every painting, sketch, or poem, every act I do, I carry it out like a small prayer. The poet José Kozer says that islands always return to islands, and in my case, to paraphrase what Emily Dickinson said about her Amherst: if I live, I will go to Cuba—if I die, I certainly will.

NOTE

1. Claudio Guillén, *El sol de los desterrados: Literatura y exilio* (Barcelona: Quaderns Crema, 1995).

CHAPTER 5

Notes on the Movement of
Trains in Germany

Carlos Aguilera Chang

(Translated by David Frye)

Germany, for me, took the form of a tube. A long, dark tube, through which its trains traveled. This, together with the names of a few actors I had picked up from the silent films of the 1920s, was all I knew about the Reich and its various provinces. That, and a bit about its literature.

Actually, I gathered this image of Germany as a tunnel where anyone could get lost from a short story by Uwe Johnson that I read as a teenager. In it, the main character tells of a train trip between the two halves, possibly already separated by the wall, and speaks of how life outside the train cars had the ghostly intensity of a hollow landscape.

Ever since then I longed to see Berlin, which for me loomed as large as all of Europe, and to make a trip like Johnson's, somewhere, anywhere. I imagined that a "difficult" writer needed an experience like that to discover himself. And, as you know, a difficult writer is one who gets to the bottom of things, one who shows us, sometimes in shocking ways, things that others don't even dare to think, who is rough. Over the years, my views have changed. I've ceased to believe that any event can signify *the* Truth, understood as the definitive reason, and instead have started paying attention to the pointless movement inherent in all efforts, the idiotic and absurd side of them that Robert Walser might have written about.

What worried me most about my arrival in Germany was the stereotypes. Not because I believed in them very much; like any "good son," I knew that a good portion of them means nothing, that they are sterile repetitions of some sort of error. But this still left some percentage in which the worst could prove to be true. And when it came to the Germans, aside from their being punctual, cold, methodical, and philosophical, I had heard the worst—and the worst is what is outside of our poor little human control. The worst is the worst, a friend had told me in Havana, three small tears in the corners of his eyes.

Reinforcing this idea was the arson attack that burned down that hostel for Turks in Hoyerswerda, a kind of giant cauldron that had suddenly exploded, and the ever-alarming news of some Nazi parade here or there. It was *the* worst, no doubt about it, and this was the penny-opera denouement that my family and I had to confront. Filled with these fears, we arrived in Düsseldorf.

Apart from the unintelligible signs in the airport itself—anywhere else in the world, the signs are in several languages; but in Düsseldorf, only in German—our first impression of Germany was that it was the perfect space: a place where everything had been calculated (ordered) so as to leave no options for the outlaw. As a result, I was even afraid of tossing a cigarette butt into the street during our first few weeks there. I thought there would be some sort of mechanical arm lurking around to grab me by the shoulder for the slightest infraction and hold me for punishment.

The sight one morning of a young woman flicking her cigarette away, then crossing the street without waiting for a green light, was liberating for me. After that, Germany began to seem like a model train set one could live in. This vision of Germany was passed down by the Cubans who had traveled to the GDR (East Germany) years earlier. They always went on about German neatness, how it was a society where everything had been measured to the last millimeter, with no possibility for surprises. I still remember the anecdote about a person who had tossed a scrap of paper onto the street and had been stopped eight or nine blocks later, fined, and forced to go back and pick it up.

I imagined—although the person who told me this story had never mentioned such a thing—that the policeman had dragged the Cuban back by his ear, making him walk there on his knees, "so that he'd learn once and for all how Germans were different." In an extremely ordered society, I later explained to my wife, all kinds of violence were legitimate.

And then there was the weather. Anyone who has read the plays of Virgilio Piñera, the most scatological Cuban playwright of the twentieth century, will have noticed that, no matter what the temperature is outside (and, truth be told, it's always stifling in Cuba), his characters are always hot, as if they were suffering from hot flashes, menopause, as if all of reality were being concentrated by traveling across a hot iron.

Germany, according to the Cubans who had lived in the GDR, with its various winter seasons (the German spring and fall are just two more kinds of winter to Cubans) and with its pastel architecture, was just the opposite of Cuba: a kind of paradise of meat markets and consumer goods, but an unlivable one, especially in the months of scant light and abundant snow. A place where it could snow ceaselessly for years on end.

I should point out right away that it only snowed twice in Bonn during the twelve months I lived there (with only brief interruptions), and those snowfalls occurred far enough apart that the experience did not become catastrophic, as a friend from Berlin corroborated when I revealed my fears to him and he burst out laughing.

Also, the Germans didn't strike me, despite their penchant for keeping a certain distance when they first meet you, as being all that cold and withdrawn. Some were quite talkative, telling me even more than I felt like hearing, and they would laugh without stridency, as if all the traumas that my fear placed on them didn't bother them at all.

I don't mean to say that my "German life" was always pleasant. There were days when I'd go to the supermarket and it seemed to me like everyone had a killer's face. I was sure they hated me simply for looking like a Turk even though I wasn't one (or for being Chinese-Cuban, even though I don't look like one), and I tried to show my "superiority" through my indifference. But those were only brief moments—wartime moments, as it were; and it was always interesting to see how, after downing a few glasses of beer, some Germans would go from shyly reserved to clumsily gregarious without a transition. The same person who had been begging your pardon for brushing against you half an hour ago was now burping in your face, singing an unintelligible song at full blast, and starting to stare at you in a funny way. It was a struggle between a caricature and its opposite; or rather, between two stereotypes.

In *Eichmann in Jerusalem*, Hannah Arendt shows how modern totalitarian systems have turned man into a filing cabinet of stereotypes. Emptiness as law. This truth, which I learned in Cuba, has been more valuable to me than anything I've read before or heard since. Stereotypes weren't just those ideas I had unwittingly brought with me and hung up in front of the other. They were also there in the German effort to hide a certain uncouthness, and in the way their efforts proved ineffective. The moment when the living person tripped over his own shadow. As was obvious on our first trip to Berlin.

Among the many things we encountered was a work of art by Anselm Kiefer that still strikes me as one of the most powerful reflections on individuals, states of mind, and history that have ever been constructed. In the center of a half-empty hall that had once been a train station, the artist had deployed an entire archive of documents, all made of lead and steel and hidden mirrors. Walking around the sculpture, we saw how our faces were falling as we looked at these shelves of corroded files and books, and how the question of German destiny—the question that had, in one way or another, turned Europe upside down for so many years—had resulted in a double crime: that of these file cabinets, scorched by reason (and perhaps also by the reflections of our little eyes in the mirrors), and that of these file cabinets, built in the name of reason itself. A binary movement that above all signified one thing: the relation between intolerance and subterfuge is much more complex than we imagine; unfortunately, it always leads to identity stereotypes.

The same friend in Berlin who used to laugh at my comparisons between German cold and Cuban cold and at my "fine ethnic distinctions about temperature" told me, after having a cup of coffee in his apartment and sharing a *schokoladentorte*, about the woman who used to run the basement clinic in his building. For years she had been butchering a number of children in the Prenzlauer Berg neighborhood, and had even performed transplants on animals of different sizes. She had been discovered by the little bald man in the apartment across the hall, or by his son, and her trial had been followed with great suspense by the whole country. When she was arrested, she still had two medium-sized rats stored in a large freezer, among other things.

The most incredible part of the story, according to D., was that this woman was quite beloved in the area, and had lived on Chodowieckistrasse since long before the fall of the Wall, when Germany was still divided in two. She was always very pleasant, something that made her stand out among everyone else. I mention this fact because it could well become a whole chapter in my still unwritten book about "ills" (or something of the sort, since the book is always waiting to be written) and the way we all live between the images we wish to project and the images we try to hide: a hall of mirrors, repeating each other endlessly.

In fact, this friend from Berlin was an odd fellow himself. He would swing from garrulous to silent with hardly a beat in between, and he had such a fascination with spiders that I didn't get any sleep the five days we stayed at his place. He kept them piled up in a series of glass cages against the wall, and his main source of entertainment was to sprinkle a white powder on their backs and watch them start fighting. For him, this game summed up humanity, the struggle between the species.

The confrontations that he provoked with his philosophy seemed to me almost as shocking as the operations that the woman in the clinic performed on little children. After I left Berlin they made me avoid any further contact with him. I even erased him from my list of friends. One little detail—I feel tremendous revulsion toward spiders. I still remember how I had to run out of the Cine Ideal, the movie theater near the Arco de Belén in Havana's Jewish neighborhood, in the middle of the Fritz Lang film "The Spiders," precisely because its theme was a Chinese criminal gang that used arachnids for doing their dirty work. The silent images of those bugs crawling up and down the screen in close-up, and of the Chinese gangsters swatting flies to feed them, were too much for me. I couldn't sleep for five days.

When I returned to Bonn, I tried to forget this discordant note and concentrate on what I had observed. For someone who had come, as I had, from a country with a high ideological kitsch quotient, all the postcards they sell in Unter den Linden are more than interesting. There you can find reproductions of the famous image of Brezhnev kissing Honneker that raised so many interpretations and jokes, images of fragments of the Wall, views of Checkpoint Charlie, a banner at the Leipzig demonstrations. Even the little pins for sticking in your lapel drew my attention. I'm sure that these "pendants" would be useful—more so than other things—for putting together a long-winded lecture on aesthetics under socialism.

A research project that, if anyone were to carry it out, would also have to include the political murals that have been painted over the course of more than forty years of the Cuban Revolution, and the various ways they have to depict the "triumph of the stereotype," a poor epic poem. A particularly deranged mural used to grace the side of a bank in Old Havana. It showed a deformed Che Guevara, recognizable only by his attire, the star on his beret; he had some indescribable thing between his neck and his face, as if a number of illnesses had transformed him into somebody else, a cross between Kim Il-Sung and the Phantom of the Opera. Every time I saw that mural, I understood why the Cuban government needed to keep repressing people over and over again. A state that makes its own heroes look as ridiculous as that is a state that lives divorced from all reality, a state that must become a monster to survive.

This is a transformation that some Germans already knew in the flesh, especially the Ossies,[1] one that led to conversations on train trips, for example, about all the absurdity whirling around this system (socialism) and its despotic organization. Beyond a doubt, our lives had been caught in the same trap: we had watched the very same TV programs, and no matter how long we talked, it was amazing how this ideological horror had brought us fears that were different yet exactly the same, though we lived thousands of miles apart, a kind of idiocy that could only be covered up with a clumsy chat about the clouds or a long, thin, hysterical laugh.

Those who were born in West Germany, having grown up beside a different wall, seemed to me not really to understand what we were talking about, though they did their best. I often heard them arguing about what they saw as the incapacity of people who had spent their lives under the orthopedics of Stalinism: what paralysis! I'd listen to them and look up at the ceiling. It's so hard to make someone understand, even if you've lived it yourself, how an ideology can dash any illusion, can make your little legs twitch just like a cockroach's.

In Bonn, after taking a few language courses and trying to discern the distinctions among their various lines of beer, I concentrated anew on my short stories and was able to complete them.[2] In these stories, I was constructing a fiction about totalitarianism, but from the "hollow space" of different characters; and I wasn't setting them exactly in Cuba, but rather in a kind of virtual China, a caricatured land where the characters were not so much identities as empty sacks, air. (And a China made of air, it occurred to me at some point, would be, when you come right down to it, just as "real" as an island turning to ashes in the middle of the Caribbean, a floating island, as Reinaldo Arenas suggests at the end of *The Color of Summer*.)

Before this, a photograph I had seen of a Chinese sharpshooter had impressed me. It showed piles of dead sparrows all up and down a field, and, at one edge of the field, a man aiming upward, alert. This photo called forth such a strange reaction in me that I immediately wrote a poem about the power/deadsparrow/livesparrow relationship; about how, behind any idea of the state, there is always a crime, entire fields sown with symbolic sharpshooters.

Imré Kertész, who, as he himself has written, survived several horrors (Auschwitz, the 1956 invasion of Hungary, capitalism, and so on), elaborated in his Nobel Prize lecture one of the most precise questions that a writer can ask ever himself. It goes: "Which writer today is not a writer of the Holocaust?" This question, or better, this assertion, deserves a commentary of its own.

The day I flew with my family to Germany, my luggage was inspected in the Havana airport, and some of my books were confiscated. Among them was the book of photographs that Leni Riefenstahl did of the Nuba. A book of seemingly innocent photos depicting bodies, everyday scenes of men and women, rituals. For months afterward, I wondered why they would confiscate precisely a book like that, where no laws are broken. I could have accepted (though not understood) it if they had retained books by writers prohibited in Cuba, or suspicious titles, like that one by Hannah Arendt, *On Revolution*. But the German filmmaker's book about Sudan was a bit beyond my logic. What sort of feeling did the customs police have about that massive tome? What did they see in it?

Fascism, no doubt. Bits of an aesthetic that contains the Holocaust. Fetishes. After reading Viktor Klemperer, a Jewish German who has written one of the best reflections on the use of language in the Third Reich, I understand that totalitarian states are trained to detect gazes; and what those three people saw was the shock of finding their own gaze reflected in Riefenstahl's eye, the instant when horror and sublimity became a single concept.

Those ash-whitened heads, those images of men decorating their bodies, that image of Riefenstahl coming down from the mountain while a naked Nuba gives her a hand, must have been sufficient to set off the paranoia of the customs dwarfs, so much so that they threatened to withhold my passport and ran off to find their boss. They hadn't understood—understanding can sometimes be a very difficult act; but they had *seen*. And those faces, dusted with white ash overlaid with a patina of mud, may have been sufficiently pathological to indicate that these photographs were a continuation of Fascist sentimentalism on a new stage, of that "clean-dirty" so beloved of Goebbels.

And, as Kertész writes in his Nobel lecture, the Holocaust is more than an episode in the history of Germans and Jews; it is a break that cannot be reduced to a mere context. The power of indecision, the fear of the other's questioning, the fact of being stripped of every last thing and having no right to even answer back—these things transform this "complex of problems" into an ongoing roulette game; and it takes a writer to capture this break and try to do something with it—it takes a writer to laugh. Even if it's just a long, thin, hysterical laugh, the kind the Ossies made every time someone on those train trips asked them about the grandeur of socialism.

PS. Even though I've entered and left Germany many times (I currently live half the year in Dresden), the idea of belonging to no place has loomed larger for me over the years. So, when others tell me about their pride in being French, Nigerian, or Vietnamese, I find it hard to understand exactly what they're getting at. Living in Havana for thirty-one years was more of a torture than a fiesta, something that I and others lived through as a kind of grief, misfortune. And that grief, which was partly ideological but mainly was a lived reality, has continued to grow wherever I stay long enough. In the end, it looks like Thoreau was right: man should return to the woods, because there is an animal part within him that only finds its true outlet there. And that is what I do whenever I move toward one place or another, look for the woods where my animal side can come out and at the same time make fun of itself. And it is this thin laughter, sordid and tragic by turns, that this text attempts to address. As for the rest, dear reader, as you know, we have to keep moving, even if someday there are no more trains where we can sit and slowly laugh.

NOTES

1. The German nickname for people from the former GDR, that is, East Germany.
2. Carlos A. Aguilera, *Teoría del alma china* (Mexico City: Editorial Umbral, 2006).

CHAPTER 6

Easter Sunday *and* Lake Waban: Two Poems

Nancy Morejón

(Translated by David Frye)

Easter Sunday

Easter Sunday.
She was wearing a little white dress,
looking radiant.
He was decked out in rubber boots,
simple outsider's boots,
a monumental overcoat
and a time-worn scarf.
The two of them were heading out in a little car
made in Japan, one pretty April afternoon
that happened to be Easter Sunday.
He barely remembered the date.
She pointed it out to him again
and asked him to enjoy it
like someone might watch
a clown gulfing down an imported strawberry cake.
It was a Sunday afternoon, an Easter,
in the middle of Central Park—what am I saying?—
in New York's Parque Central, on the West Side,
and the avenue was filling up with coaches pulled
by horses with all their trappings.
Men in tailcoats rode them,
their faces round
like the apples he'd seen glistening
in the fleeting markets, stocked at random
on any edge of Downtown.
                             The tailcoats
glistened in the afternoon light.

He'd have liked to help her into a coach
and take a ride with her all down Riverside Drive
and watch the Hudson River flow
while he felt his heart beat loud
like that red apple rolling down the street.
She didn't understand why
his eyes kept turning to the coaches
and the tailcoats.
                        She saw
a statue of José Martí mounted on a horse
that had reared at the very moment
it was being sculpted. And she pointed out
the statue to him. He smiled, tilted
his startled head, placed
his hands on the car window
as if he were about to get out and hand
all his nostalgia to Martí.
"We're crazy," she told him
and they embraced each other, sad in spirits;
they embraced, knowing that she and that he
were far from one another
and that they could stop being nomads without respite,
crazy in love, forgiven only
by the irresistible force of the wintery air.

LAKE WABAN

I

The tree before me here
was yesterday scarcely more than
a dark torso.
A few hours of water falling
from this sky
and already its boughs
are opening up,
like naked limbs that
point to every place,
make every sign,
like rain-drenched children
suspended in space,
like these simple leaves
that form a green crown
in the breeze.
In the center is the trunk,
congenial and yellow,
deprived of light and rays,
swaying back and forth,
always naked,
still damp,

perhaps awaiting the arrival of new waters
or that other new nakedness
that here is known as Fall.

II

Amid this peaceful greenery
throb small plants caught by surprise,
and the boughs breathe in
the water's fine spray,
sumptuously vertical,
that's been falling since the dawn.
How it draws your eyes;
how your eyes would like to cut through
the water curtain, this transparent dance
waltzing to the rhythm of violins
that Haydn has led here through the window.

Fall will fall on all this greenery,
diligent, humane, retiring, distant
in its diffuse transparency.

This green is not my green.

Here all I find is this high greenery
encircling stands of timber.

But what if Plácido came all this way,
and searched here for the clear depths
of his coffee trees?

Fall will come to clean away
the motionless traces of the rain,
and the silenced poets,
asleep in their errantry,
will once again take up
the volatile quill of these twilights
to sing
the return of Fall,
a Fall that can no longer wait for anyone—.

III

The waters remain placid
and a light from on high is upon them;
songs sung in alto at the break of day,
like the first fervor of the murmurings
and the smooth calm waves of Lake Waban.
The waters are placid

and a light surrounds them—.
dear god forgive me
what is this thing my eyes are seeing
where has this black head come from

with darkness blazing from its brows[1]

floating in the middle with that blazing darkness
where has it come from
this round velveteened black man's head
his wooly hair
trembling as he drowns
his first drowning of this Fall
in the still quiet waters of this lake

Lake Waban, your waters
have washed over the sinister dream
of this drowned man, who reappears
within your tranquil waters:
a drowned man
and a *güije* pulling his head along
and the impossible forgetting of his name
within the placid waters
that the *güije* pushes to the shore.[2]

Lake Waban,
what do I have of the exile about me,
that I should come from so far off
while I long for the violins to play
a timeless charanga in your placid waters,
while I stroll through the solitude of your garden?

Lake Waban,
your waters remain placid
and there's a light on them that Fall consumes.

Wellesley, 1995

TRANSLATOR'S NOTES

1. Blazing darkness (*rayo de tinieblas*): an oxymoronic metaphor coined by St. John of the Cross to describe the soul's dark perception of the overwhelming light of God.
2. *Güije:* In Cuban folklore, an imp or water spirit that appears in rivers or lakes.

CHAPTER 7

Avon Calling

Nely Galán

I always knew that I would be a millionaire one day. Was it a case of nature versus nurture? My story begins in Cuba, a tiny tropical isle famed not only for its tropical beauty, but also for its people's ingenuity. To this day, despite the political tug-of-war and turmoil, the creative Cuban has always devised inventive workarounds to difficult situations. For example, my Uncle Manny discovered that a pair of women's pantyhose made an excellent substitute for a broken fan belt on his beloved 1959 red Cadillac when resources proved scarce.

Unfortunately, the Revolution took its toll, and in 1966 my family fled to the shores of the United States on a Freedom Flight, destined never to return. Branded "political exiles" by Castro's regime, and stripped of all that we had worked so hard for in the homeland, my mom, my dad, my little baby brother Chino, and I (at the tender of age of three) were traumatized beyond belief.

My father, formerly a suave wheeler-dealer who was always decked out in his crisp white *guayabera* and doused in Paco Rabanne, had now been relegated to working on the Ford Motor Company assembly line in Freehold, New Jersey. He would arrive home everyday in his denim jumpsuit drenched in sweat and completely exhausted, but he still maintained a great "I-love-America" attitude regardless.

As for my beautiful mother, this latest twist of fate was difficult for her to handle. In Cuba she had already escaped the grip of poverty once. The only child of nine who managed to leave the rural trappings of Santa Clara for college, she supported herself in Havana as a highly paid Cyrano whose services were sought out by the lovelorn and tongue-tied in search of her eloquent love letters. It was there that she had a brief encounter with the middle class, when she met and married my father. In Freehold, her lofty dreams were put on hold as she sewed ten dresses a week for the choir ladies at the Presbyterian Church that had sponsored our trip out of Cuba, and acted as nanny for six American kids. She also managed to cook for us and many of our neighbors, who quickly became addicted to her delicious *ropa vieja* (shredded beef) and *frijoles negros* (black beans). My mother acted like everything was fine, but I worried about the constant sadness I heard in her household singing.

As for me, I learned English in record time from the *americanos* at the church, and was quickly thrust into the role as superdeluxe translator for the entire family, as well as for our handful of Latino neighbors.

We moved from Freehold to Teaneck, New Jersey, a few years later when my dad got a job as a salesman at Goya Foods, a Puerto Rican food company. My father loved his new country; however, his inability to make enough money concerned me. He was a dedicated parent who often came home early so that he could spend more time with us. He would say, "Carmencita, you'll never be ten again. What's the point of life if you can't spend time with your kids? Look what happened in Cuba, we all worked so hard and it was all taken away. You and your brother, Chinito—that's what matters."

My parents wanted the best for us, but realized that they could only afford to send one of us to private school at the time. Or so they thought. I was enrolled at the Academy of the Holy Angels, an all-girls Catholic school for *niñas finas* ("classy girls," as my mother would say), and I performed well academically, but was soon destined to become the only student whose parents couldn't really afford the $200 per month tuition.

When my Tía Dulce dropped by, my mom would often banish me to the second story of the Tudor-style house for which the New Jersey Cuban Exile Committee had helped us obtain a mortgage. Upstairs I would work on my homework and help my brother with his, while in between I would eavesdrop on my mother's hushed conversations with my aunt. I could overhear her bemoaning about how much she missed the old Cuba, and how worried she was about my dad's inability to pay the bills, particularly my tuition.

I began to feel panicky. Every day as I put on my plaid skirt, saddle shoes, and bobby socks, I started to make a mental note of how much everything cost, and how much of a burden I was on my parents. While the strawberry-blonde girls on the yellow school bus sang "American Pie" and rolled their skirts two inches shorter every morning, I would quietly obsess about how I could bring home money. In my head, I ran through a variety of plans and schemes, and calculated the risk and reward of each option, as any budding entrepreneur would.

Lemonade stand? No, I only made 10 dollars doing that last summer. Sell my dolls? No, since I had cut off all the dolls' hair, their desirability (and hence profitability) would be limited. Write papers for other kids at school? No, I wasn't a cheater, and surely I would be caught and expelled from school. (*¡Qué vergüenza!* The shame!)

I was plagued by a recurring nightmare where I would be called into the mean principal's office, and I would walk in on her just in time to see her hunching over the microphone to announce to the entire student body over the loud speaker, "Carmen Martínez's parents can't pay her tuition, so today will be her last day!" I would just have to die, plain and simple! Every night I prayed to God, "Please, *Diosito,* if you really exist, show me a sign!"

Then I came home from school one day, and there on the kitchen table was my answer. I asked my mom, "What is that?" She replied, *A la vieja Brooks de la esquina yo no la entendí en inglés, y me hizo comprar "Skeen So Suft" de Avon, yo no sé cuándo le voy a pagar, yo no tengo...*(I couldn't understand what old Mrs. Brooks from the corner house was saying in English, and she made me buy some Avon "Skin so Soft," I don't know when I'm going to pay her, I don't have any money...)

I didn't hear a word she said after that, the wheels in my head were turning so loudly. I thought to myself: "Avon 'Skin so Soft,' Mrs. Brooks...Of course!" I knew I could fix everything the next day. I had to. I wanted my dad to have his time with us and my mom to regain her beautiful smile and have faith that my father was still Prince Charming.

My new mission in life was to convince Mrs. Brooks of my brilliant plan. Mrs. Brooks was an enterprising Irish widow who lived in a house filled with early American knickknacks and the distinctive scent of "Skin So Soft." Her living room was blanketed with white, folded Avon bags, on each of which was stapled a lined receipt inscribed with red, fancifully handwritten names. To me, they looked, and smelled, like heaven on earth.

I told Mrs. Brooks that lots of the girls in my school were asking me if I knew of anyone who sold Avon, because the new sassy pink nail polish and lipstick were "really groovy." She let me know that we were all too young to wear lipstick. I objected: "Mrs. Brooks, don't be silly. Our moms buy them, and then we play grown-up with them." Then I explained to her that there were 120 girls in my class...120 girls with disposable income. She finally conceded and said, "Okay, you sell in your class, I'll take the orders, and you'll get some free makeup."

I thought, *¿Esta vieja se cree que yo soy boba?* Does that old woman think I'm stupid? I wasn't. I knew she was trying to cut me a bad deal, but I had come armed with the knowledge that I had her at my advantage. "Mrs. Brooks, it's got to be fifty-fifty," I replied, repeating a phrase that I had heard my neighbor, Temma Ehrenfeld's father, say to a guy on the phone one day. I didn't want to reveal my true motives, and instead told her I needed the money for Christmas and birthday presents for my friends and family. We cemented my first entrepreneurial deal then and there. I was thirteen, starting an all-cash business and already learning the ropes of negotiating and profit sharing.

In my first month, I cleared $400 cash, enough to cover two months' tuition. I loved the feeling of being a business woman! No doll or game had ever been this much fun. My locker was filled with bags of perfume, rouge, and lipstick. The fragrance emanating from my locker acted as a lure for all the school girls—the rich ones, the athletic ones, the cool ones; even Judy, whose dad had won the lottery, wanted to know me. I went from being the only Latina bused in from the "bad part of town" to being the junior beauty expert.

Then came the moment of truth. My school tuition was past due and my parents were sweating it. I knew I had to part with my precious $400.

At the end of my lunch break I marched up to the head mistress' office and knocked. Sister Jermaine invited me in and asked what was troubling me. I said, "Sister Jermaine, I'm here to see you because my parents are going through a hard time."

She responded immediately, "I had assumed as much, since they are forty-five days past due on your tuition. In fact, I was going to talk to the parent P.T.A. committee to see if any of the more privileged families wanted to donate your tuition. I called your house one day last week, but no one spoke English. I was going to have Mrs. Bustos [the Spanish teacher] send you a letter."

My face turned beet red. We didn't want to be anyone's charity case! I knew I had to take action, even at the risk of going to purgatory for being "creative" with the truth. "Actually, Sister, my rich uncle from Miami sent me the money for the tuition, and he'll be paying the bill from now on," I told her as I handed over my hard-earned cash. "But you know, my parents are very proud people, and my uncle doesn't want them to know. Do you mind sending my parents a letter telling them that I've been given some sort of scholarship?"

"Absolutely!" she declared, and proceeded to pen a hand-written letter, sealed with the school's imprint in wax.

That night my parents opened Sister Jermaine's letter, which, of course, I translated:

Dear Mr. and Mrs. Martínez,

Your daughter Carmen has been awarded the Academy of the Holy Angels full scholarship for her academic achievement. We are very proud of her and believe she has incredible potential. We commend you on her success.

Best Regards,
Sister Jermaine

"Carmencita—what does this mean?" inquired my mom. My dad, with a tear in his eye said, "That our Carmen is a genius—school is free! *¡Tú ves que cuando uno es bueno, Dios lo resuelve todo!* (You see how, when you're good, God takes care of you!)." They both squealed with delight, and already I could sense that the tide had turned. My parents thought I was the best student in the whole school, Mrs. Brooks was my new best friend, and I was reaping the benefit of a great education and on the road to becoming a millionaire entrepreneur. The popular slogan of the time was "Ding-dong! Avon calling!" To me, it was the sweet sound of opportunity knocking.

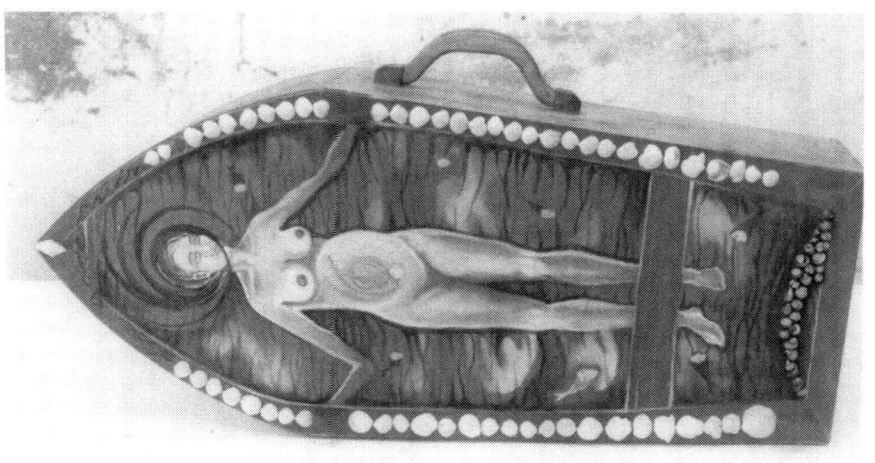

Sandra Ramos, *Bote: La vida no cabe en una maleta* (Boat: Life doesn't fit in a suitcase) (installation)

PART II

Idas: After Everyone Has Left

A suitcase proclaims the places you have left.
Or proclaims the places still to come...

— Rolando Estévez

Nereyda García Ferraz, *Couple in white* (painting)

CHAPTER 8

They Took Me to the Movies While My Mother Packed Her Bag *and Other Poems*

Rolando Estévez

(Translated by David Frye)

THEY TOOK ME TO THE MOVIES WHILE MY MOTHER PACKED HER BAG

On the unmade bed, my mother opens a suitcase.
Imitation leather, chromeplated clasps
that sea mists from one shore or the other will rust at last.
A handle, made of lead or plastic,
from which her soft fingerprints will never be removed.

The unmade bed. My mother. A suitcase.
An afternoon like any other. Like any other street named
Buenavista, or Capricho.
An afternoon, like any other place,
could be better, could be worse.

My mother opens a suitcase.
Into it she packs my sister's clothes,
the clothes of my father.
For her: only two dresses—
the latest fashion in Cuba
but long out of style in Paris or Miami.
The rest was seafoam.
Smoke from thick church candles.
Grease-laden air wafting in from the kitchen.
Scents of soap escaping from the shower.
Family silence by a weedy grave,

and the noise of a handsaw
hacking a piece of wood to bar the door and shut the house.

From the high point of the tower
where the Twelve Apostles mark the time in Prague
        I see my mother packing her bag.
From the Zócalo in Mexico
where the flag is gathered in each evening
        I see my mother packing her bag.

From the skyscrapers of New York
that sway like flustered drunks
        I see my mother packing her bag.

From the city of Berlin that, day after day,
keeps overturning the rocks of its Wall
        I see my mother
         anxiously
    packing her bag.

And a suitcase is forever unforgiving when you forget:
the thread and the needle,
the tiny little mirror,
the framed photograph of forgiveness.

A suitcase proclaims the places you have left.
Or proclaims the places still to come, with all their names:
wounded sites on the map of your right palm.
The places are called:
        Camarioca
        El Laguito
        Airlift

        Passport
        Thaw.

They're called:
        Money Order
        Refuge
        Residency
        Fire.

Sitting inside a neighborhood movie palace
as dark as the maw of a fighting dog
        I see my mother
        covered with earth
        packing her bag.

An afternoon, like any other place,
could be better, could be worse. And if someone decides,
this afternoon and your fate can move you like a pawn,

lay out your afternoon walk for you:
> Cine Abril
> Sarita Montiel
> The Last Torch Song
> Nineteen sixty-nine

And the fighting dog clamped down its jaws,
and I, my gaze fixed upon the giant screen,
see my mother sedately sitting on her suitcase.
She's not heading toward any gangway.
She's not showing anyone her travel documents.
Whirling around her body is the world—
flat and circular, standing on four elephants' backs,
> It whirls vertiginously
> > and she, seated there
> > > alone

sees each day and every night pass by in silence
> and she sees pass by:
> factories
> hospitals
> paper gardens
> concentration camps
> empty beaches
> faded towers
> unfamiliar faces
> pickup trucks
> unfinished lace.

The spinning disk won't stop. My mother seems to feel no nausea,
no attacks of laughter or of tears.
She's fallen deep into a trance
as still as death.
An endless trance of spinning disk and woman sitting on her bag.
Woman, neither sad nor happy.
Just woman, sitting on her bag.
> Woman, Daughter, Mother

who has never known I watched her
from the hard seat in my neighborhood movie palace
and that I still weep with all my tears
> that were denied to her.

THE OTHER THURSDAY

Lucrecia goes out one Thursday afternoon.
Her face as pallid as a Japanese
> a Jewish
> a Spanish
> a very Black goddess.

Wearing little makeup, the afternoon wind catches her by surprise
and sets her to swaying
like an adolescent palm tree stripped bare.

My mother runs out of the Three Round Towers
that smell of the frijoles negros
so many women like her cook at once,
infusing hallways and staircases
with the sour scent of cumin
           Of green peppers
           of a little music
           of wait for me at six
                           to watch the show
           because I'm dying
           and the tv's just the thing
           for a ritual as formal as this.

She leaves all the apartments behind
in their armor plating of cheap recycled nostalgia,
encased in windows that once upon a time
held the name Miami,
ready for a flower curtain
like an earthless hanging garden.

Lucrecia goes out one Thursday afternoon.
She's wearing a close-fitting poppy dress,
the kind women wore in the forties
to the Parque La Libertad
to be courted there by night beaus in blinding white shirts.
Fused to his summer shirt,
this beau, my father, smiles with his eyes
and digs into his pockets for his handkerchief of iron.

Lucrecia goes out one Thursday
leaning heavily on the cane of exile.
Proclaimed the queen of her own nostalgia.
Making a bouquet from the flowers of her lost land,
which she hides, suspicious, in any store,
whenever she can give the slip
to the hurried men rushing past who see her standing there
along the sidewalk curb.

Lucrecia goes out at last
and her car drives down an avenue
on the long ribbon of her birthing gown.

Lucrecia reaches the beauty salon
where the skill of another's sad hand
erects a chignon as high as the Three Towers
atop her head.
And on her everygirl's pallid face from anywhere in the world
the beautician paints the eyebrows of a María Félix reborn,
the lips of a Rosa Fornés in spring.
And wide, wide eyes
from which drip long

        Exquisite
        everlasting
fragile streams of tears in bloom.

Lucrecia goes out one Thursday afternoon
to look at herself in parking lot puddles
and discovers she has the gift of patience.
She goes out to find a piece of sky
that's just the same size, just the same time
as her hand mirror—a jewel box for storing,
among clouds and angels and airplanes,
her timid girl's face.
She,
who still
won't stand up from the bench in her park,
she,
who's holding her hand out in front of my father
and feeling
how all her blue sky ice cream is melting in her cone
and running down her hand and covering her ring
and sliding in a chilling shudder
and falling onto the white
skirts
      of her bridal
           gown.

The Chair

Here and there,
like north and south,
are two seasons.
Coming and going
with the rumbling
of snails across the curtains.

For my mother,
who doesn't live in norths or souths
but in the relative lukewarm of fallen leaves and jasmine,
snowcones upturned into a cup,
and the tapping of a fan against her breast,
here and there contaminate each other.

She's taken their seasonal attributes
and built a chair.

Not a perfect, marketable, comfortable chair.
Not Lam's chair, screaming from the *monte*
and displaying a flower vase.
Not a chair from her house, or from an old railroad platform.
Not in the middle of some constellating crowd.

Not a chair sitting all by itself,
             but rather
a chair in the sea halfway between two shores,
like a miniscule newborn isle,
a tiny land where the light of day and the light of night
fall together in the sadness of one feeble ray.

Her chair is not a compass.
Her chair is not a boat.
Her chair does not go north, does not go south.
          It does not go.

On her chair, set in the middle of the sea,
            she sits
like a primitive Venus
carved into the rock of twilight.
Her hips hang over the edges of the seat,
her salt shoulders cling to the chairback,
and, like one more cascading wave,
her enormous round breasts spill onto her thighs
           where they
suckle fish and shipwrecked sailors.

She's alone in her chair. She doesn't drift.
          Doesn't sail.
My mother, halfway between both shores.

THE TALE OF THE TONGUE

For Laura Ruiz

When my sister was born
January second, nineteen sixty-one
just after midnight, port city,
clinic clinging to the hill of Matanzas
from which we could see the sea
and hear the language of the gods,
my grandmother inspected
her fingers, tiny bunches of bananas
her sex, an unopened flower
her navel, engorged like a tiny caterpillar
her ears, two labyrinths of silverwork
her pupils, honey-colored, restless as the bees.

My father
inspected her tongue alone.
With his worker's, gambler's hands.
With his eyes, avid discoverers of secrets,
he inspected her tongue alone.

My mother,
at repose within her birthing gown,
once more made silence fall.
Hard and crisp as brown toast,
thick enough to slice.

She's got a strong tongue. Said father.

A short while later, the little girl was talking
to cats, to gladiolus
to the blackish seeds of *anón* fruits
to pumpkin seeds
to her cousins, to her jars
to all the children in her life
to her *azabache* charm
to the half-open mantle of God's great power.

A short while later the girl was talking
in proper, humble Spanish.

...Time passed by, and an airplane passed over the sea.

The girl in her little south Florida school
cursed in her sad Spanish,
cursed the girls, the teachers
and even cursed her own tongue.
Cursed and wept
with tears in her eyes and on her tongue.

But her little girl's tongue was tamed
—it was a strong tongue, as you know—
and she learned to speak in another language
            To the gladiolus
            to the cats, to the jars
            and to the new pots and pans.

The girl, now a woman, has an adult tongue.
She talks in Suntrust to the Greeks,
the Celts, the Czechs. the French,
the Muscovites, and lots of Cubans.
To the blackish seeds of *anón* fruits
and to pumpkin seeds.

She got married in Vizcaya Palace
to a German man whose tongue is hard.

When we are born, my sister and I,
in December of nineteen ninety-four
on the terrace of the Pyramid of the Sun,

Teotihuacán, Mexico City, hour not noted,
listening to the speech of the gods,
looking sadly at the scrubtrees
of a land that has brought us together again,
searching for the distant sea of Matanzas
and the sea of Miami Beach,

her tongue translates for me in bitter Spanish
the sweet
      the airy
           the strange words
that are presented to me in perfect English
by her son's tongue.

FIRE, WATER

For Ana María Coro Barreto

My father, ill, died in a Miami hospital.
My mother, the phone call, the agonizing.
A leg retracing its steps for three whole days
through every garbage dump across the city.
The elegant dumps. The plastic tubes through which
my father's leg slid
without a shoe, without a sock, without him.
A roving leg, forced to follow along a single path
to a single crematorium.
The rest of his body lasted three days longer.
      Three days. The phone call. Three days
        two days
           one day.
My father in his hospital bed, holding a conversation
with his dead sisters.
      With his mothers
        his fathers
           all the beings of humanity
           and *the light*, father, *the light*.

And you passed through another shining tube
with your leg, yours again at last—
because no one, no good spiritist,
has ever seen a being with just one leg.

Roving father, my mother hasn't told me
if you went away with longlegged strides
as you used to do.
There's lots my mother hasn't told me.

And when the sheets still breathe
in the form of your Cuban body

on the empty bed,
my sister speaks:
>   he had everything—flowers
>   first-rate care
>   intravenous drips
>   elegant last rites
>   a suit, a tie
>   his watch, a linen handkerchief.
>   He had everything—flowers
>   —don't you worry yourself so much.

Night settled on the Southwest side.
A bird of slender smoke
settled on the elevated tracks.
Sirens sounded in my ears,
machine noise from factories everywhere.

There was no burial. That had been his wish.
You can't be buried if you have no land.
What country made of earth for you,
unstable as the heart of an earthquake
felt round the world
that lifts and shifts the flowerbeds,
the furrows and the roadways of this earth?

Elemental, my father wanted fire.
Elemental, my father wanted water.

No memorial plaque in any cemetery
in the world.
No broken angel for a headstone.

My father, a warrior.
Father, the peace once more of watery tombs.

My father wanted the sea:
>   The sea has the rumbling roar
>   the wildness
>   the blues
>   the greens
>   the violets
>   the dolphins
>   the algae
>   the ships
>   the treasures
>   the fish
>   the reflections

The paths that lead back to the Isle.
And above all it has,

hidden in its soul,
>   other warriors.

Talking with My Mother in the Kitchen

Today it's nineteen seventy-nine.
Today it's December.
Today it's Cuba. Matanzas.
You've come back with a beige hat,
a tailored suit,
a gaze I rediscovered
within the crowd at the airport.
Through the shoulders, the heads,
the umbrellas they all carried.
That is to say: through, above, beneath, within
that crowd of my brothers and my sisters,
who were coming as I was
>   to wait (for you)
>   to kiss (you)
>   to weep with me.

Night has fallen, and by the bell tower
this borrowed balcony for you,
from which you can see the bay,
as silvery as a desert mirage
that's bound to split away.
To split, not knowing unsurely where.
To split your body, mine, in two
so we can live like two bitter better halves,
an orange divided to season others' plates.

And by the bell tower we speak about the dead.
And by the kitchen, the water,
saltwater, blue, pouring from the tap,
baptizing our conversations.
Saltwater, blue, the water of mermaids
and of drowned men.
Seawater pouring from the tap.
Seawater from the seawall.
>   And your lost half
>   and my lost half.
They make one body,
>   open,
>   alien,
>   strange.
Seabody, waterwall, where we see
>   sailing,
>   passing by,
>   dying,
the boats that had promised us so many things.

THE WALL

I am one more man,
one man split by a wall in twain.
In the part of me where I'm my mother
roams a rose-colored unconsciousness,
a pair of very tepid gloves
for clasping with forceps any excess viscera.

In this same side I am my father,
bringing home the bread,
roaring in the rigging without restraint.
Cursing and dying and even being resurrected.

And in this same side I am my sister,
and I sweetly sing a song of autumn
in my girlish dress: violet, scented,
covered with sparkles.

In the part of myself where I am me,
they come again to stay. I keep them company.

Rolando Estévez, *Un aire de familia, o, Feliz cumpleaños* (A feeling of family, or, Happy Birthday) (paper and ink)

CHAPTER 9

Other Roads to Santiago *and* *Other Poems*

Laura Ruiz Montes

(Translated by David Frye)

I. THE COIN

If I remained in this city always
it was not because I found the country's letters painted on the river.
Not for the fading city's beauty.
Not for the bridges or for the walls.
If I remained in this city always
it was because I tossed a coin into the air one night
and the way it fell chose the waiting life for me,
the certainty of every return.

II. THE OTHER SIDE OF THE COIN

If I remained in this city always
it was to await their returning.
The letters the photographs the postcards
—I negotiated them with my waiting.
I lived deliriously while all the others left.
I saw the walls tumble down,
the streets widen   the sea we once had grow small.

Now you're coming back all by yourself, coming back.
How old I have grown, how old.
You'll come rushing through, no time to peer into my eyes.
The city is demolished, no beauty here.
I'm just a pretext for you to hate returning,
for you to feel no unease, for you never to come back.

FOR RETURNING BEFORE THE SEVENTH DAY

Ay! If only I could find a chant, a word, a white dress for returning.
I would hazard anything. Day after day, without a pause.

First Day

I would bear my own nude body in my arms,
lift it to the level of my chest
and set it before you.
I'd stand there observing your gaze, your pallid grin.
If you don't lift your eyes to heaven, if you don't weep
I'll plant my body in the earth and walk away.

Second Day

I'll come smiling with my body healthy and clean, ready to embrace,
pretending I've forgotten all about your absence
and that your sorrows matter nothing, nor do mine.
If this does not work, if you don't smile,
in shame I will avert my face.

Third Day

I'll barely brush against your knife-sharp hand,
look nonchalant and keep on walking.
And if you don't touch the soft wheel of my white dress,
if you don't stretch out your fingers to reach me,
I'll disappear into the night.
I'll no longer be a contrail but a hideous white stain.

Fourth Day

Desperation will make me shout out loud,
blame you when I really want you to forgive me,
accuse you accuse you accuse you.
I'll stand there observing your gaze, your pallid grin from a fragile Isle.
If I don't move you, if you don't bend your lips into a scream,
I'll take off running and never stop.

Fifth Day

I'll have to take it back. Beg you to believe me.
I'll keep observing your serene smile, not knowing what it hides.
I'll have to interpret your silences, your ocean's roar, the sun that burns
me.
And if just once your incredulous gaze falls over me like a cloak,
like the very shadow of a falling cloak, I'll go.

Sixth Day

Silently and as if beyond hope I'll stand before you.
I'll show you the letters I did not destroy,
the faded offerings,
the sheathed dagger, the hands behind the back.
If you don't uncross your folded arms,
if you don't leave off your frigid gaze,
I'll shut my eyes and call on death.

Final Day

If only you could know that I made it all up—
the fleeing, the pretending, the exoticness, the distance.
I turned so far away from your certainties, your embrace, your peace.
If only you knew that I've lain prone on the ground
for fear of flying by your side, with you.
That I preferred the excitement of foreign tongues,
the abuse I suffered for all I thought I loved.
If you only knew...

If you could only realize, beloved body, Island, fragile land, my Country,
how faithless I've been to you, being here.
Ay! If only I could find a chant, a word, a white dress for returning
and if only you would understand.

OTHER ROADS TO SANTIAGO

for Teresa Melo,
Odette Alonso,
Damaris Calderón

What a pity that Santiago de Cuba is so far away
and that the Pórtico de la Gloria is also so remote.

What a pity that everything is so distant.
That's why it doesn't matter where we set off for:

                             Santiago de los Caballeros
                             Santiago de Chile
                             Santiago de Compostela
                             Santiago de Cuba.

What matters is not knowing anybody
                    and having no one recognize us.
Telling things we know by heart as if they were brand new,
making up things we haven't done,
smiling and believing that we speak an unknown language.
What matters is to be waited on like gods.

What a pity that Santiago de Cuba is so far away,
because when everything is distant
we almost always end up choosing wrong.

THAT WAS THE NIGHT THAT WAS

For Sigfredo Ariel

Life in the countryside wasn't like this,
it was much happier.
Life in the countryside wasn't like this,
it was much sadder.
Going back home wasn't what you expected.

You said you had been happy.
I knew it was the truth.
But the countryside can't be taken in now.
It doesn't care if you squint
or if you light one cigar after another.
The countryside doesn't care what you do, your flattery doesn't help it one
bit.

That night was innocent and heartbreaking.
A classical poet explained the classical Tchaikovsky,
not knowing that you and I were too:
            you were weeping into your black shirt
            and I was weeping into my white blouse,

as we were supposed to do, we both wept.

Heartbreaking was the night and full of noise.
We had the same ministers
and we read the same books;
we were the same, but we weren't.
You had already been to the Café Berlin
and you had said farewell to something called the 80s.
I still wanted to travel to Pompeii
and was pretending I had forgotten
            about the 80s,
            about the 90s,
            about Berlin,
and about the café, but I hadn't.

You came back to write about it later.
You looked like someone who felt at home
but from time to time you'd say *how strange it all seems.*
Strange, for you, meant *come join those who've left forever.*

It wasn't what you expected.
I wasn't ashamed or embarrassed.
I didn't feel I was up against a wall,
nor as grotesque as the ballerina with too much makeup
who tripped over the musician's foot.

It was the perfect night.
I didn't have to speak.
A night in the countryside made you understand:
            the silence

the anachronistic dignity
the stifling humidity
the naps taken on the side
—because the tortoise will never finish the race—
the bad habit of my remaining here
the deadly illness of my staying here still.

SECOND NATURE

...and the landscape crossed by a tragic stone horizon...
—Julia de Burgos

I don't want to be like myself either.
I don't want to be what I myself see in me.
Better the clouds of dust on the main street
when it is being remodeled.
Better the marble floor of the old drugstore
that brutish workers shattered.
I don't want to be my eyes
but rather what my vision sees.

I'd rather be the pieces of me
that arrive in the letters, the emails
        I get from those who are not here.
I want to be the abundance that they recall,
their melancholy memory lapse,
the white blouse I was wearing when they were about to leave
and I was turning into their own *stone horizon*.

DAMAGRAMA

for Damaris Calderón

Shouldering the burden of her broken bones
she walked toward the plaza,
like a sleepwalking guest
unaware she has not conquered all of Gaul

sitting in the center of the plaza
where she served as her own park bench
and the circle of shade under her feet,
she watched illegal vendors passing by,
                selling flowers
                selling bracelets with the images of saints
                and white socks for the schoolkids.
None of them was selling a city, a country,
                an island,
the God's green acre where they left behind
                the reels of string,
                the spools from the old Rayonera plant,
                the nylon fishing line

for tying up their tired articulations,
for reuniting snail with shell,
and for renewing the umbilical cord
on which to grasp and so to take
                —or take again—
their first step back to the country of their birth.

CHAPTER 10

"That's My Theme: The Human Adventure." An Interview with Ena Lucía Portela

Iraida H. López[1]

(Translated by David Frye)

Iraida H. López: Your latest novel, *Cien botellas en una pared* (One Hundred Bottles on a Wall), has been translated into seven languages, hasn't it? How do you feel about this achievement?

Ena Lucía Portela: That's right, seven languages. French, Portuguese, Italian, Polish, Greek, Dutch, and Turkish. Ha ha! I do feel happy about it, of course, and also a bit surprised, because my last... No, not last. Next-to-last. Because my next-to-last novel, as I was saying, wasn't written in international Spanish but rather in "Cuban," the slang of the back streets of Havana, which makes it pretty hard to translate. There was nothing easy about this. In France, sure, because my translator, François Maspero, knows loads about Cuba and Cubans. Maspero is a legend. But elsewhere...ick. The Netherlands, for example: the translators all ran away from it in terror. Fred de Vries was the only one who dared to grab the bull by the horns. But of course, he had particular experience; he had already translated Cabrera Infante. For the Portuguese, Marcelo Ribeiro and I worked together on it page by page, which was very instructive and interesting for both of us. And so on. I'm very grateful to all of them. Without a doubt, they contributed to this minor success. Because it is minor, you know? Let's not get carried away. And I'm not saying this out of any false modesty, because modesty, for me—yuck! Whether it's false or genuine. I'm saying this because in the real world—outside of our pretty little Cuba, I mean—this is no more than a good beginning, a good starting point, and also because my personal idea of success goes much farther.

IHL: You must have traveled to some of the countries where your novel was published, such as Spain and France. How did the Cuban emigrants there treat you? Did you run across any old schoolmates, or any writers or artists you hadn't personally met before, in those places?

ELP: Yes, over the past few years I've traveled to several European countries. As to dealing with Cuban emigrants...what can I say? For me, it's just as hard, or just as easy, as dealing with anybody of any nationality anywhere. I'm not a very sociable person in general, whether I'm here or abroad. I don't get off on patriotism or that nostalgic vibe of "remembering old times." I've met up with some old friends from Cuba, sure. As you might have expected, they've all changed. Some for better, some for worse. So far as my own generation goes, the experience of living under capitalism (formerly unknown) has led some of them to plant their feet on the ground, grow up, and stop being morons. For others, however, it has messed them up badly. They left because they couldn't stand living here, because of the poverty and lack of liberties, and now it turns out that they're the biggest communists around, and if you let them, they'll tell you right to your face without batting an eye that they've *always* thought that way. So why did they run away, then? And why don't they come back, huh? Let it be known, I respect every human being's right to hold whatever opinion they want, in politics or in anything, no matter where they live. But that doesn't mean I'm wild about sitting down to chat with schizophrenics and/or amnesiacs. And, yes, I've met on the side with a few Cuban writer exiles. I met Jesús Díaz in Madrid in 2000 when I was there for the book launching of my first novel, *El pájaro: pincel y tinta china* (The Bird: Paintbrush and Indian Ink), and I met Eduardo Manet in Biarritz in 2003 when he was a member of the panel that awarded me the Deux Océans-Grinzane Cavour Prize for the French version of *Cien botellas en una pared*. They were both very nice to me, which is nothing to be surprised about. After all, why shouldn't they have been?

IHL: Of course. Now tell me, what impact has the departure of so many artists and writers who have settled abroad, perhaps never to return, had on Cuba and Cuban culture?

ELP: Cuban culture, in my opinion, isn't just what is produced within the country's borders, geographically speaking. That is, on the island of Cuba, the Isle of Pines, and the adjacent keys. No. A Cuban, for me, is anyone who defines himself or herself as such by his own personal will, that is, anyone who considers himself inexorably fated to be a Cuban, no matter where he lives or what his passport says. From this perspective, the massive emigration, or the stampede, hasn't had any negative impact at all on Cuban culture. Quite the contrary. Being scattered around the world has also diversified it, enriched it, through its collision, even fusion, with other cultures. I don't agree with those who would like to limit it or constrain it, here or there, in the name of who-knows-what kind of purity that never really existed. Nationalism in itself seems like a stupid delusion to me, one of those monsters engendered by the sleep of reason, and as applied to culture I think it's fascistic.

IHL: One of the motives behind the emigration of artists has been the pressure not to transgress certain boundaries. Have you ever held yourself back when it came time to write? To what degree can we speak of censorship and/ or self-censorship in Cuba? Why is it that some writers, such as Leonardo Padura and yourself, can write a critical work without major repercussions (I think), but others can't?

ELP: No, I've never "held back" when it came time to write, nor when it came time to talk, no matter what the subject. Nor when it came time to live, for that matter. I was born in Havana in December 1972, and I grew up and went to school in Cuba, so that, by a matter of time and place, I am, or at least ought to be, a specimen of that human variety known—ha, ha!—as the New Man. "We shall be like Che!" went the slogan. Hardly anybody took it seriously, you know, but I did. And what was Che like? According to his own words: "a man who acts as he thinks, who has always been faithful to his convictions." There you go. Of course, *my* convictions are very different from those of Saint Ernesto of La Higuera. I feel no hatred toward anyone, nor do I have any interest at all in changing the world. I'm an individualist. But the principle of honesty at all costs still seems morally valid to me, so I carry it out.

As for censorship or self-censorship in this country...Well, that's what you might call an issue. I'll tell you about my personal experience. In 1997 I won the Cirilo Villaverde Novel Prize for *El pájaro: pincel y tinta china*, a prize given out by the UNEAC (Cuban Writers' and Artists' Union), better known as the UNEAC Prize. It was a minor scandal in the kolkhoz. For more than one reason, I was afraid they would censor my bird, wouldn't let it fly, and I asked one of the members of the panel what they thought about it. The guy told me, *nyet* censorship, the only thing that's forbidden here is slander against Fidel Castro. And the book was published. Even though many readers have seen my Dr. Schilling as a caricature of FC, the truth is that it isn't outright slander. I understood there was censorship, yes, but also that fiction was given much more free space than before the collapse of the USSR.

The free space does exist, but nobody is encouraged to notice it. Quite the contrary, they bring all sorts of pressure and coercion to bear, sometimes crudely and sometimes subtly, to make writers chicken out and censor themselves. You have to discover the free space for yourself, run the risk that any transgression implies, and of course accept the consequences, come what may. That's how I've published three novels and two little books of short stories over here, that is, almost all my works of fiction, and I'm about to publish my fourth novel, *Djuna y Daniel*, without my ever having deleted so much as a comma for reasons that weren't strictly literary. The consequences of all that cheekiness? Nothing serious: they've never awarded me the Premio de la Crítica (Critics' Prize), I've never traveled anywhere as part of an official Cubiche delegation, nothing I've written has ever been adapted for Cuban TV, there's been silence in the media, silence, lots of silence...I'm not complaining, I don't lose any sleep over any of this. That's all I need! I'm just describing a situation that might seem, and in fact does seem, a little frightening to other writers.

Well, that's about my fiction. But that's not all. Because I don't consider myself just a fiction writer, I'm also an essayist, and I'm just as enthusiastic about my work in essays, even though it is much thinner and less well known than my fiction. And while fictional literature can fool the censor's eye with relative ease these days in Cuba, the same isn't true of essays. That's where the space is really tight. Most of my little essays and articles are unpublishable here. My liberal principles are very obvious, if not explicit, and over here having liberal principles, which in other countries is considered leftist, or at least center-left, is just short of heretical. So I almost always publish those little pieces in Mexico. I hope to gather them into a book someday.

IHL: How do you think your writing and that of other young writers are affected by the emphasis on the ruins, the double standards, the hustling, the dollarization, the "every man for himself" attitude, and so on, that predominate in the discourse about today's Cuba? Is it possible to think and write about a different Cuba?

ELP: Ha, ha! Well, perhaps we should all get rid of this bad habit of always emphasizing the seamy side of Cubiche "socialism," not be so ungrateful, and devote ourselves to wholehearted praise for the extraordinary achievements we've made in the fields of education and health and who knows what else. Isn't that how it is? True enough, I notice a few items missing from your list: the racism, the homophobia, the drugs, the hunger, the delinquency, the witchcraft, the AIDS, the blackouts, the peasants in Havana, the totally unrestrained sex (homo and/or hetero, and if at all possible, sadomasochistic and with underage partners), the *balseros*, the shell-shocked Angola vets, the alcoholism, the suicides, the corruption and the police brutality, among others. Forgive my sarcasm, Iraida, okay? but when you asked me a question that's so…shall we say, naive, you were tossing me one of the most recurrent clichés about today's Cuban fiction. Or rather, the fiction of the 1990s, because I think the current fashion is to try and get a little bit away from all that and to move instead toward…who knows what.

But let me answer. This "emphasis" you mention does not affect, or burden, or harm my writing or anyone else's in any way at all. Because fiction cannot be better or worse on account of the themes it deals with or on account of the amount of optimism or pessimism it contains. Those are extraliterary criteria that in my opinion are not worth one bean when the time comes to evaluate a short story or a novel. It would never occur to a critic or a student of literature who respects himself and respects his profession, whether in the academy or not, to place a good fiction writer and a mediocre one in the same pigeonhole just because both deal with similar matters in their respective works. To do that would be, in my opinion, politic infighting, envying the success of others, mere, sheer nastiness, or at the very best, intellectual laziness. The avalanche of so-called dirty realism, which got started over here with the devastating economic and social crisis of the 1990s and which still continues (just as the crisis still continues—or do you think it has ended? Please! Sometimes I wonder if the people who would like a different

Cuba in fiction shouldn't also hope for a different one in real life), must be understood in its own context. On the one hand you have the crisis, euphemistically entitled the "Special Period." On the other, you have the lack of transparency in the mass media. I was telling you earlier that fiction has a lot of free space these days, which grows very tight when you're dealing with essays. As for journalism, there is no freedom whatsoever. No response is ever allowed, and the alternative press is illegal, because there's no freedom of the press either. So, it is natural that the content that properly belongs in journalism be diverted, successfully or unsuccessfully, into fiction. The main causes of the proliferation of dirty realism lie *inside* Cuba, not abroad. Is this literature generally pretty low in quality? Sure, it generally is. Just like most of the rest of Cuban fiction on other subjects, inside our enchanting little Cuba or abroad. Because literary quality does *not* depend on its themes, I repeat, but on the talent of each writer.

IHL: When I asked you whether it was possible to write about a different Cuba, I was thinking about a film like *Suite Habana*, which seems to contain other plans. For example, your novels are dominated by characters who are young, nonconformist, and rebellious, while the characters in Fernando Pérez's film are practically their opposites, with their impassivity and stoicism. How representative of your generation are the characters in your novels?

ELP: I don't think either the characters in my novel or those in *Suite Habana* are representative of my generation. In spite of the New Man experiment, my generation is as diverse as any other generation in any time or place. There are all sorts of people with all sorts of mentalities and attitudes toward life, from the most rebellious to the most brownnosing, from the noblest to the basest, from the most sincere to the biggest rascals, who are wonderful at fooling the idiot foreigners who ardently desire to be fooled, just so long as they don't have to let go of their illusions about Cuba and Cubans. It is the creative artist who chooses from this multiple and variegated reality what best serves him for telling his story. It will be up to the audience to decide which story is most convincing.

IHL: Your novel *Cien botellas en una pared* (One Hundred Bottles on a Wall) seems to contain an implicit critique of hardcore nationalism. Linda Roth, whose family is Jewish, from Austria, states that she was "a young writer . . . from a marginal country, yes, marginal, underdeveloped, primitive, wild, because she was Cuban even if her passport said something else, since you can put anything on a piece of paper. . . ." What does it mean to be "Cuban" today?

ELP: I don't think I'm responsible for Linda's opinions, or for those of any of my other characters, about anything. That's a question that you really ought to put to Linda (that is, to your own imagination), not to me. And the truth is that I don't have any idea what it means to be Cuban today, supposing it means anything at all. For me, with apologies to the patriots, all this rigmarole about nationality is nothing more than a bureaucratic formality, and a pretty screwed-up one sometimes. I see the Cubans in Cuba, I've seen them in the United States and in Europe, in fictional literature, in history, in the arts, in music, in film, and so on, and I find them to be so very, very diverse that I could never think up a definition for "being Cuban" that would be more specific, more narrow, than the same definitions that would work for "being human."

IHL: In other words, there's no Cuban "essence," in your opinion, despite the countless pages that have been written on the topic. And your new novel *Djuna y Daniel* doesn't even take on a Cuban theme, does it? How is it different from your earlier books? When and where will it be published?

ELP: Come on, Iraida, the fact that countless pages have been written on something doesn't necessarily mean that it exists. Look at what happens with God. You have the Bible, Patristic and Scholastic "philosophy," the works of all those theologians, exegetes, and preachers, and ...what? In the final analysis, it all comes down to a matter of faith. Behind the alleged Cuban "essence" there have always been economic interests and political ambitions of all stripes that have manipulated as they've seen fit the need that so many people feel to belong to something unique, exclusive, original. If believers want respect for their beliefs, the first thing they should do, I think, is to respect the skepticism of the unbelievers. Which is exactly what they don't do, calling you eccentric, nutty, a traitor, an iconoclast, and other petty things.

About *Djuna y Daniel*, it's by far my longest novel. The manuscript is about 400 pages long. Unlike my earlier novels, it's written in international Spanish, without a single Cubanism. That was really hard for me, a real challenge, especially in the dialogues, because up to now I've always expressed myself in Havana street slang (more or less stylized, but slang when you come right down to it). Of course, in this case it was necessary, even indispensable, to "delocalize" the language, owing to the novel's theme. It deals with the turbulent and ambiguous relation that took place between Djuna Barnes, the North American writer, and Daniel A. Mahoney, the guy who served as her model for creating the character of Dr. Matthew O'Connor in her novel *Nightwood*. The bulk of the story takes place in the Latin Quarter of Paris in the 1920s and 1930s. But there are other settings, too: New York, San Francisco, London, Berlin, Munich, Vienna, Budapest, Tangier, the French Riviera, and so on. Not Cuba. The word "Cuba" doesn't come up once in the whole book. There are no Cuban characters and no Cuban cultural references. If someone drinks a Cuba Libre, the rum came from the cane fields of Guyana. Ha, ha! I know people are going to ask me why on earth I did this—yes, I can see them coming!—because there's the cliché (ugh, another one!) that we Cuban writers can only write about our scrumptious little Cuba, present or past tense, or about the Cubiches living around the world. Our lettered city is more Cubist than Braque and Picasso put together. But let's not put the cart before the horse.... *Djuna y Daniel* will be published in January 2008 in Spain by Random House Mondadori.

IHL: You've admitted that you're very interested in the theme of violence, as can be seen in your fiction. What, apart from the extreme situations in which you sometimes place your characters, interests you about the theme of violence? And what other themes interest you?

ELP: Oh, Iraida, when you say "You've admitted," anyone would think that I've confessed to a crime or something. Violence interests me as a manifestation of the dark side of human beings. Note: by "dark," I don't mean "evil" but "irrational." A critic once observed that *La sombra del caminante* (The Shadow of the Traveler), my "darkest" novel, deals with the nature of Evil. Like that, with a capital E, a metaphysical vibe. Well, that might also be a valid interpretation, given that it is absolutely true that, in order to understand a thing, or even try to understand it, we each start from our own philosophical premises. But as far as fiction goes, I'm not too interested in general theses or ideas. I'm not trying to convince anybody of anything. My characters don't symbolize anything and they don't represent anything…except, perhaps, our species, which in the end is what I care most about, what most motivates me. Our desires, sadnesses, joys, conflicts, evasions, dreams, nightmares, lies, frivolities, heroic deeds, ridiculous acts, beliefs, disguises, cruelties, paradoxes, misunderstandings, vengeances, madnesses, victories, defeats, nostalgias, guilts, mirages, idiocies, prides, impulses, jokes, larcenies, rages, prejudices, faults, contradictions, learning experiences, fears, and tremblings. That's my theme: the human adventure.

Note

1. The interviewer wishes to thank Luisa Campuzano for facilitating the initial contact with Portela.

Bibliography

Barnes, Djuna. *Nightwood* (London: Faber and Faber, 1936).

Pérez, Fernando, director. *Suite Habana* (Havana: Instituto Cubano del Arte e Industria Cinematográfios, 2003).

Portela, Ena Lucía. *Alguna enfermedad muy grave* (Madrid: HK, 2006).

———. *Cien botellas en una pared* (Madrid: Debate, 2002).

———. *Djuna y Daniel* (Barcelona: Random House Mondadori, 2008).

———. *El pájaro: pincel y tinta china* (Havana: Ediciones Unión, 1998).

———. *La sombra del caminante* (Havana: Ediciones Unión, 2001).

CHAPTER 11

From Havana to Mexico City: Generation, Diaspora, and Borderland

Rafael Rojas

(Translated by David Frye)

Like many Cubans from the Generation of the 1980s, I went into exile in Mexico early in the Ambiguous 1990s. I arrived in the DF. while the Soviet Union was falling to pieces and Cuba was entering the complex postcommunist period that has dragged on, through openings and closings, to the present. For two decades now, I've observed the tensions and encounters between the Cuban immigrant community in Mexico and the rest of Mexican society. Mexico and Cuba, as has been said, are geographically close but historically far apart.

I would like to help reconstruct the moment of "beginnings" in the late 1980s and early 1990s, when a portion of Cuba's youngest intellectual generation left the island and settled in cities across Latin America, Europe, and North America.[1] After framing this movement within the "Diaspora of the 1990s," I will describe some of the distinctive elements of the Cuban cultural émigré colony in Mexico. Given its prominent role in the origins of that diaspora and the importance of some of its better-known members in Cuban cultural life, it would be hard to write the history of recent migratory waves from the island, including the virtual emergence of a transnational Cuba, without paying close attention to the capital of Mexico.[2]

Neither Here nor There

Much smaller than Mexico, Cuba has a less glorious prehispanic past and achieved its incomplete sovereignty almost a century later than its neighbor, yet it shares the experience of having lived through a twentieth-century social revolution and the dilemma of bordering the United States. It is that borderland experience, a characteristic of two distant neighbors, that distinguishes the community of Cuban immigrants in Mexico—some 6,647 Cuban-born citizens according to the official 2000 Mexican census (unofficially, perhaps tens of thousands), the majority of whom are professionals (59 percent have university degrees), women (53 percent), and young people (more than 80 percent are under fifty).[3]

The act of emigration or exile always involves an uprooting from one nation to another, and, in more radical cases, from one language to another, one culture to another. In the grand tradition of exile in Western culture, which Edward Said critiques in his *Reflections on Exile and Other Essays* (2002), change in language represents drama, and has led—as in the famous cases of Conrad, Kafka, Beckett, and Nabokov, which Milan Kundera and Orhan Pamuk have recently recounted—to some of the most sublime writing in modern literature.[4] Exiles who move between countries that speak the same language and whose cultures share historical roots, like the Spanish Republic exiles who settled in Mexico in the 1930s, may find a familiar symbolic universe in the new country, but they cannot help drawing distinctions between what is theirs and what belongs to others, or obsessively listing the differences between their home country and their refuge. Feeling different in a familiar country is a complex experience of alterity, akin to the processes of estrangement that occur in a family.[5]

In *Variaciones sobre tema mexicano* (Variations on a Mexican Theme, 1952), Spanish poet Luis Cernuda celebrated his reunion with his native language after fourteen years wandering in the universities of Great Britain and the United States. Crossing the border to Mexico, Cernuda said he felt he regained his symbolic life in the external world. The language that "had never ceased to sound within" now sounded "without interruption" all around him. But Cernuda couldn't help noticing the differences between the Mexican Spanish that redeemed him from the "Protestant industrialists who only utter words for business or necessity" and the Spanish of his distant Andalucía.[6] Though he expressed this difference by idealizing Mexico, "a land made to the measure of dreams," "a quiet corner of Andalucía" whose "delicate" language "without vulgar idioms or plebeian intonations" was closer to him than the English of Glasgow or South Hadley, the Spanish of Mexico was still not entirely his own. Feeling like an outsider when you are in a family or neighborhood setting can seem more painful than when you are in a completely foreign culture. This sense of the strangeness of the familiar is what leads, in exile discourse, to the theme of the impossibility of return or inheritance that are seen as irretrievable or unattainable.

Said, in the title essay of his book *Reflections on Exile*, refers to a poem by Wallace Stevens in defining exile as "'a mind of winter' in which the pathos of summer and autumn as much as the potential of spring are nearby but unobtainable."[7] Here exile is a vital uprootedness, a border crossing that intensifies the subject's relationship with his identity and his legacy. But unlike Said's uprooted exile, or Cernuda's Atlantic crossing, the migration of Cubans to Mexico is less a border crossing than a passing from one end to another of the same borderland. Cuba and Mexico are, as Jorge Mañach has argued in his unfinished posthumous *Teoría de la frontera* (1961), distinct versions of a single state: the state of being neighbors of the United States. Moving from one to the other is somehow a way of rehearsing a migration to the other side of the borderland; a perhaps futile way of shielding the subject from a worse transgression.[8] The Cuban immigrant in Mexico, as the singer David Torrens might say, is a floating subject who feels *ni de aquí ni de allá* (at home neither here nor there), but who gravitates, inexorably, toward the spaces of the island and of exile.

MEMORIES OF *PAIDEIA*

Zygmunt Bauman's book *In Search of Politics* includes a passage, "Memories of *Paideia*," that seems written especially for Cuban intellectuals of the Generation of the 1980s.[9] Here Bauman sums up his ideas about the difficulties that modern intellectuals face in achieving autonomy and critical political agency within a public sphere overtaken by two powerful spiritual currents of modernity: the totalitarian, which tends toward annulment by the state of all that is private, and the nihilist, which cultivates the individual's refusal to deal with anything public. Reading Bauman, we see his intellectual kinship with the people behind the *Paideia* project in Havana in the late 1980s. That idea, conceived by writers Rolando Prats, Radamés Molina, and Ernesto Hernández Busto and at first backed by the great majority of artists and intellectuals in the Generation of the 1980s, was the only effort to introduce a postmodern cultural politics in Cuba.[10]

The *Paideia* project's postmodern nature derived not only from its peculiar concept of autonomy—in a country whose cultural sphere was completely controlled by the State, the creators of *Paideia* had no intention of setting up a private enterprise, nor did they claim to be an extension of any official institution, as some of the most important publications of the revolutionary period (*Lunes de Revolución, Casa de las Américas, El Caimán Barbudo, Pensamiento Crítico*) had been in their moment—but also from its language, from the classic manner of speaking about politics that predominated among those who promoted this intellectual alternative most actively.[11]

Paideia, the Greek ideal of culture, was delineated in the work of the same name by the German philosopher and philologist Werner Jaeger (1888–1961), who dedicated his life to the study of classical Greece and wrote several extraordinary books on ancient philosophy. *Paideia* (1934) was the last book he published in Germany before he left his beloved Berlin forever and went into exile in the United States.[12] In the Havana of the 1980s, Jaeger's *Paideia* was one of the most widely read books among young people interested in the history of Western thought. This text, and perhaps Alfonso Reyes's essay on the pre-Socratic philosophers,[13] served as a literature of initiation into the art of rhetoric and discourse—basically oral rhetoric and discourse, given the lack of training for writing and the scarcity of publications on philosophical themes. Reading books like Jaeger's, some intellectuals in the Generation of the 1980s decided—even before they read

Foucault and other postmodern authors—that their calling was something as pretentious, pointless, or frustrating as thinking Cuba.

What was *Paideia*? Not a movement or a group; rather, a project and a space for intellectual conviviality. A proposal, as we used to say, for an autonomous cultural politics, designed by a handful of writers, and shared during the brief moment that it lasted by the majority of the artistic and intellectual community of Havana in the second half of the 1980s. This proposal consisted of offering an independent platform, not subordinated in any way to the cultural institutions of the State, for the most youthful, avant-garde Cuban creations in theater, music, dance, fine arts, poetry, fiction, criticism, and essays.[14] The driving forces behind *Paideia* managed to convince the authorities at the Alejo Carpentier Center in Old Havana to offer them a salon for carrying out the project. This salon became an exhibition space for the artistic and literary poetics of painters such as Flavio Garciandía, Arturo Cuenca, José Bedia, and Consuelo Castañeda; writers such as Reina María Rodríguez, Marilyn Bobes, Omar Pérez, Victor Fowler, Antonio José Ponte, and Emilio García Montiel; and playwrights, musicians, and choreographers such as Victor Varela, Carlos Varela, Caridad Martínez, and Marianela Boán. All of the *Paideia* sessions ended with an interchange with the audience, in which such critics as Gerardo Mosquera, Desiderio Navarro, Osvaldo Sánchez, and Iván de la Nuez frequently took part.

The first thing one notices about the project is its generational nature. The works that *Paideia* worked to make public were created by people born between 1950 and 1960, who had not been fully recognized by the official cultural institutions, whether on account of their youth or their avant-gardism. The generational range of these writers and artists was nonetheless very broad, as they went from published and award-winning poets, such as Reina María Rodríguez and Osvaldo Sánchez, to very young writers, such as Radamés Molina and Ernesto Hernández Busto, each scarcely more than twenty years old. *Paideia* was therefore an alternative project for cultural politics and conviviality that set out to act on the margins of official institutions, for the most part, as a gesture that would make obvious that artistic and literary production on the island could not be assimilated by the State. That gesture of *Paideia*, which was in tune not only with postmodern philosophy but also with the *perestroika* and *glasnost* campaigns that were then transforming the Soviet Union and the socialist bloc, made explicit the message that the culture being produced in Cuba in the mid-1980s could not be represented by the state institutions designed along Soviet lines in the 1970s. But *Paideia* and other cultural projects of that decade such as Castillo de la Fuerza did not insist on an abrupt break with the State, but rather a negotiation for autonomy through "complementary" or "helping" work arrangements that would teach the State how to administer culture.[15]

Politically, *Paideia* embodied the paradox that any cultural policy faces under a totalitarian system. Within a state-run public sphere, cultural autonomy is always relative, and the promoters of *Paideia* were quite aware of their limits. Nonetheless, they were looking for as much independence as possible, as illustrated not only by their distant relationship with the authorities of the Carpentier Center but also by the brief but intense experience of their literary magazine *Naranja Dulce* which, though issued as a supplement to *El Caimán Barbudo*, the official publication of the Asociación Hermanos Saíz, set forth a repertory of ideas and obsessions that were quite foreign to the regime's demands for ideological legitimacy.[16] The project, as its name suggested, aimed at what Bauman called a "search for politics" from the starting point of culture. Its leaders bore in mind the history of turbulent relations between intellectuals and power in the decades before and after the Revolution. They knew that the "commitment" or "neutrality" of writers vis-à-vis the political reality of the island had been a topic for debate in Cuba since the 1950s and 1960s. They knew that intellectual projects such as *La Gaceta del Caribe*, *Nuestro Tiempo*, *Ciclón*, and *Lunes de Revolución* had criticized *Orígenes* for its literary self-absorption.[17] But they also knew that the "neutrality" of *Orígenes* could be taken as an oblique form of "commitment"— with the culture, with the nation, but not with the society or the State.

Paideia thus called for the revival of the Greek ideal of culture, with its quintessentially democratic values, in order to formulate, in Lezamian terms, "another manner of governing the city": a politics of the spirit. In this literary conception of politics, with its slight overtones of nihilism, lay the strength and, at the same time, the weakness of the project. Curiously, it was its highbrow literary nature that gave *Paideia* an air of subversiveness in the late 1980s. At a time when the cultural politics of socialism was just beginning to transition from a demand for commitment to a demand for neutrality, the latter was taken by those in power as a show of oppositional apathy, as a shrug of the shoulders. If *Paideia* had been produced a decade later, after Abel Prieto and his UNEAC and Ministry of Culture had carried out his strategy of depoliticizing the intellectuals and canonizing Lezama and *Orígenes*, it surely would have been abetted and manipulated by those in power. But in the Aldana years, when the paradigm of art as an arm of the Revolution was in full force and the island's literary tradition was still narrated along the lines of Marxism-Leninism and revolutionary nationalism, the official canon of Cuban letters revolved around Nicolás Guillén and Alejo Carpentier, not José Lezama Lima or Virgilio Piñera.[18] *Paideia*'s literary nature moved those in power to oppose it. Cuba's ideological and cultural institutions joined forces to tear it apart. At the moment when it was being neutralized, the project could defend itself with a *cultural politics* that was better defined in intellectual terms than that of the State itself, but it lacked a *political politics* and the institutional resources to sustain it. An affective and generational community acted in favor of *Paideia*, but conspiring against it was its beardless sociability and its lack of experience in the wiles of autonomy.[19]

WHY WE LEFT

Twenty years have passed since Mikhail Gorbachev introduced the *perestroika* and *glasnost* reforms that led to the fall of the Berlin Wall, multiparty democracies and market economies in Eastern Europe, and the disintegration of the USSR. It will soon be twenty years since *perestroika* and *glasnost* began to be felt in Cuba and since the symbolic readjustment of the Cuban regime began with the constitutional reform of 1992. Among the many Cuban chapters in the history of this process, one would have to include the "scattering"—in the chicken-farming metaphor used by poet Reina María Rodríguez—of a good part of the Generation of the 1980s, and the adaptation of the island's political culture to the demands of postcommunist nationalism.

The culturally intense decade of the 1980s, which began with the *Volumen I* and *Cuatro por cuatro* and concluded with *Arte Calle, El Castillo de la Fuerza, Paideia, Naranja dulce, Credo, Memorias de la postguerra*, and *Albur*, drew in intellectuals and artists who are today between thirty-five and fifty years old, born shortly before or after 1959. This generation's last intellectual performances on the island were those of the group *Diásporas*, headed by Rolando Sánchez Mejías, and Reina María Rodríguez's *Azotea* and *Torre de Letras*, a tenacious project of autonomous conviviality.[20] At least half of this intellectual generation has left Cuba.[21] They form a more scattered and often less visible half than those who remained on the island, but they still constitute half of their generation. While we are waiting for the studies in historical sociology that will delineate the features of this exodus, we might venture a few notes on the reasons behind the exodus of so many intellectuals, though their aesthetic and political diversity resists any generalizations.

Only a handful of these exiles—María Elena Cruz Varela, Rolando Prats, César Mora, and a few others—left as open opponents of the Cuban political system and members of alternative organizations.[22] Most, though critical in their last years in Havana ("dissonants," to use a favorite term of Iván de la Nuez), only became opponents after they had left. This political radicalization—vehement in some cases, veiled in others, and inhibited in the rest—was shared by almost all, despite the wide differences in how they have projected it publicly. The political diversity of the diaspora of the 1990s can easily be read in a journal such as *Encuentro de la cultura cubana*, founded by Jesús Díaz in Madrid in 1996.[23] In essence, this generation left because they rejected the isolation and the rigidity of the ideological and political controls that were imposed on Cuban culture. They also left because they wanted better lives; that is, because they wanted to reproduce their lives under better market conditions: to sell their labor force, as described by the Revolution, at higher prices than what socialism could offer on the island. The contrast between freedom and well-being, between justice and comfort, which the government of Fidel Castro had for so long exploited, seemed unnatural to them: being free and equal also meant being more prosperous, or at the least more autonomous in their poverty.

The Generation of the 1980s is the only one formed entirely under communism. The subjectivity of this Generation is unique and unrepeatable, and best embodies the dream or nightmare of "the New Man."[24] Earlier generations fell under the Soviet order after living their youth, or at least their childhood, under the old republic; later generations were formed under the postcommunist moment—the time-out of the revolutionary period that began in 1992 and continues today, this lost era between a totalitarianism that struggles to endure and a democracy that hasn't come into being. In the post-Soviet Havana of today, you can be Catholic, Jewish, Santero, or Protestant; a fan of rock, jazz, salsa, or rap; a nihilist, liberal, conservative, or Marxist—just so long as you are not a public opponent of the regime or a dissident. In the Cuba of the 1970s and 1980s, when this generation was being formed, such diversity was inconceivable, because the regime was much more doctrinaire and institutionalized. Any ideological, moral, or sexual heterodoxy was tantamount to political sedition.

The members of this diaspora have diverse ways of relating to Cuban culture (of the island and of the exile community) and politics (of the regime and of the opposition). It could be said that, rather than sharing a public position, this generation practices a set of personal politics that converge in the diasporic gesture of having left the island and having remained abroad. It is this gesture, rather than a miserly measuring of the degree of one's critical intensity or an absurd demand for loyalty to one political tendency or another, that identifies this as a generation in exile. Some members of this generation publicly oppose the government of the island; some write editorials, make public declarations, or sign letters of condemnation; some do not reveal their rejection of the system, though they feel it intensely; some hide what they think for fear of reprisals (not being able to travel to the island, losing their space in Havana culture, suffering official demonization) or because they loathe the idea of speaking out in public; some do not criticize the government because they share socialist values or don't want their arguments to be used by one of many political movements in the exile community.

Some travel regularly to the island and some oppose traveling there. Others travel because they can't live without visiting their families, or because they aim to get something out of their ties with officialdom, or because they believe (ingenuously or not) that they can contribute to regime change through their contact with reformists in the government or with activists in the opposition. Some do not travel and do not care whether anyone else does; others do not travel and consider those who do to be "traitors" and "accomplices."[25]

In many emigrants' experience it is possible to shift from one attitude toward returning to another, depending on the greater or lesser degrees of flexibility in the politics of the island, the exile community, and Washington, or on the emotional and economic demands of each family. For example, I traveled frequently to the island from 1991 to 1994 while I was a graduate student in history at the Colegio de México. In 1995, when I started working for *Encuentro*—a journal often disparaged in official publications—and began publishing the essays that are gathered in my book *El arte de la espera: Notas al margen de la política cubana*

(Madrid: Colibrí, 1998), I stopped visiting Havana. Mine has been a personal decision, motivated by the political tension that characterizes my academic work, not one I have taken from a position of moral superiority or ideological purity.

Relations have been tense between this diaspora and earlier exile generations. For a long time, going into exile in any city in Latin America or Europe, according to those earlier generations, meant that you hadn't really gone into exile. The only conceivable place of exile was Miami, and anyone who lived in Mexico City, Caracas, Buenos Aires, Madrid, or Barcelona was suspected of complicity with the regime. This is no longer the case: important institutions in Miami, such as Ediciones Universal, *The Miami Herald*, Florida International University, and the University of Miami, are becoming more and more open to the new exiles, no matter where they live and no matter how they think.[26] With rare exceptions, the mentality that ascribed a genetic defect of authoritarianism to those who had been born and raised under the Revolution, keeping them from fully embracing the condition of exile, has run its course. The diaspora of the 1990s constitutes, properly speaking, the last generation of Cuban culture in exile, and its contribution to the democratic future of the island is plain for anyone who has the eyes to see it without prejudice or spite. With the biological clock running out on the first exile generations, it is in this diaspora that the greatest territorial tensions of Cuban culture are beginning to accumulate.

BETWEEN BORDERLANDS

From 1989 to 1992, from the fall of the Berlin Wall to the final disintegration of the Soviet Union, Mexico became a way station for dozens of Cuban writers and artists who left the island with plans to set themselves up for a time in the United States or Europe. Why was Mexico the gateway to the world for the diaspora of the Generation of the 1980s? And how was Mexico viewed by that generation—a destination, a bridge, an obstacle?

Mexico was nearby geographically and historically it had good relations with Cuban socialism. From the early 1960s, it was the only neighbor to oppose Cuba's expulsion from the Organization of American States and the embargo imposed by the United States. As the Socialist bloc fell apart, Mexico became an accessible alternative for mending the island's cultural relations with Latin America. Some Mexican institutions, including the National Autonomous University of Mexico (UNAM), the Colegio de México, Ninart (Nina Menocal's gallery of Cuban art), and the opinion journals *Plural*, *Nexos*, and *Vuelta* closely followed the changing reality on the island, whether as supporters or as critics.[27]

By 1995, when *Encuentro de la cultura cubana* was first published, a small intellectual community of recent Cuban exiles had gelled in Mexico City. This community, which withstood the call of the United States and Europe, produced a body of important, even indispensable works within the diaspora of the 1990s. The books they wrote in Mexico between 1995 and 2005 include (to mention only a few) *Informe contra mí mismo*, *Caracol Beach*, *La fábula de José*, and *Esther en alguna parte* by Eliseo Alberto; *Enciclopedia de una vida en Rusia*, *Livadia*, *El tartamudo y la rusa*, and *Treinta días en Moscú* by José Manuel Prieto; *Pan de mi cuerpo*, *Te devolverán las mareas*, and *Voyeurs* by Andrés Jorge; *Los laberintos de la imaginación* and *La transición invisible* by Velia Cecilia Bobes; *El enigma de Jicoténcatl* de Alejandro González Acosta; *Muerte y resurrección de Tokio* by Emilio García Montiel; *Los hijos de Saturno: Intelectuales y Revolución en Cuba (1959–1971)* by Liliana Martínez Pérez; *Dfe y otras erratas* by Osmar Sánchez Aguilera; and *Insomnios en la noche del espejo*, *Diario del caminante*, and *Cuando la lluvia cesa* by Odette Alonso. Mexico is an evanescent presence in these texts, but also a cultural contact zone that filters into the writing in subtle ways. Could these books have been written in any other exile city? Could they have been imagined and edited in the same way, without the experience of migrating to Mexico? It isn't a matter of creating a hierarchical contrast between "better" and "worse" places of exile, or of aestheticizing Mexico as a diasporic space for its supposed "neutrality" or for offering a "third way" between the more politicized cities of Miami, Madrid, or San Juan.

The Cuban exile community in Mexico is not depoliticized—just as the intellectual community on the island itself is not depoliticized, either. But it is quite true that in Mexico the Cuba question is politicized in a different way than in cities with large exile communities, with their social ties and their publications, their issues of visibility and their compulsions. Their integration into the realm of Mexican intellectuals, not as a "minority" or as a "lobby," but as a constitutive subjectivity in the historical Latin American immigration to Mexico, is clearly perceptible in the archive of community representations that have gone into these works and in the institutional presence that their authors have achieved. Cuban scholars and intellectuals have set down roots in the most important academic institutions in the Federal District and other Mexican cities, such as Monterrey, Guadalajara, Morelia, Veracruz, and Puebla.

The incorporation of Cubans from the Diaspora of the 1990s into Mexico's cultural and academic institutions is, naturally, less visible—but no less representative of Cuba's new migrant subjectivity—than the consolidation or the beginning of several careers in the world of television and entertainment. Over the past fifteen years, actors César Évora, Francisco Gattorno, Pedro Sicard, Zulema Cruz, Niurka Marcos, Julio Camejo, and Aylín Mujica, and musicians Pancho Céspedes, Amaury Gutiérrez, David Torrens, and Jorge Hernández have become established figures in Mexican public life. These artists' Cuban identity is incorporated into their projected media images, with all the associated frictions, in a climate of fierce market competition and facile reproduction of cultural stereotypes.[28]

Mexico has become a destination for young and professional emigrants who are generally flexible in their relations with a transnational Cuba.[29] The subjectivity reflected by this kind of community is removed from the more territorialized politics of the island's diaspora, and it constitutes a different migratory place, one where it is possible to relate comfortably with both the island and the exile community, both Havana and Miami. The keys to this subjectivity are not to be found in the affirmation or denial of one or another of the spaces in contention, but rather in uprootedness, in a ready acceptance of the greatest possible mobility in the face of the binary conflict in Cuban politics.

One of the paradoxes of contemporary Cuban culture is its reproduction strategy, given the politics of the island and the exile community. While its culture is structured as a fragmented sphere, deterritorialized and inhabited by diverse civil and migratory spaces, its politics keeps its poles in binary tension and affirms the identities in conflict. The experience of the Cuban diaspora in Mexico helps us understand this diversity of subjects and this multiplicity of communities as they reproduce themselves under the drama of a divided nation.

NOTES

1. On the idea of "beginnings," see Edward Said, *Beginnings: Intention and Method* (New York: Columbia University Press, 1985), pp. 40–42, and Arcadio Díaz Quiñones, *Sobre los principios: Los intelectuales caribeños y la tradición* (Buenos Aires: Universidad Nacional de Quilmes, 2006), pp. 19–63.
2. Cuban studies of transnationalism continue to concentrate on the emigrant experience in the United States, and pay little attention to other important Cuban diaspora communities in countries such as Spain and Mexico. See Sarah A. Blue, "From Exiles to Transnationals? Changing State Policy and the Emergence of Cuban Transnationalism," in Damián J. Fernández, ed., *Cuba Transnational* (Gainesville, FL: University Press of Florida, 2006), pp. 24–41.
3. I have taken these data from the interesting research project "Sociedades en movimiento: Causa, procesos y consecuencias de la inmigración internacional en América Latina," headed by sociologist Liliana Martínez Pérez of the Facultad Latinoamericana de Ciencias Sociales (FLACSO), Mexico. See also Velia Cecilia Bobes, "Cubanos en México," paper presented at the Guadalajara International Book Fair, December 2002.
4. Milan Kundera, "Die Weltliteratur: What Use Is a National Style?" *The New Yorker*, January 8, 2007, pp. 28–35; Orhan Pamuk, *Istanbul: Memories and the City*, trans. Maureen Freely (New York: Knopf, 2005), pp. 20–35.
5. Élisabeth Roudinesco, *La familia en desorden* (Mexico City: Fondo de Cultura Económica, 2003), pp. 10–24.
6. Luis Cernuda, *Variaciones sobre tema mexicano* (Mexico City: Fondo de Cultura Económica, 1952), pp. 20–35.
7. Edward Said, *Reflections on Exile and Other Essays* (Cambridge, MA: Harvard University Press, 2002), p. 186.
8. Jorge Mañach, *Teoría de la frontera* (San Juan, Puerto Rico: Universidad de Río Piedras, 1970), pp. 61–77.
9. Zygmunt Bauman, *In Search of Politics* (Oxford: Polity, 1999), pp. 85–99.
10. Liliana Martínez Pérez, *Intelectuales y poder político en Cuba: La "intelectualidad de la ruptura" y el "proceso de rectificación"* (Masters Thesis, Facultad Latinoamericana de Ciencias Sociales-FLACSO, Mexico City, 1992), pp. 160–185.

11. Velia Cecilia Bobes, *Los laberintos de la imaginación: Repertorio simbólico, identidades y actores del cambio social en Cuba* (Mexico City: El Colegio de México, 2000), pp. 150–175.

12. This history is laid out in the introduction to the Spanish translation of Werner Jaeger, *Paideia: Los ideales de la cultura griega* (Mexico City: Fondo de Cultura Económica, 1957; English trans., *Paideia: The Ideals of Greek Culture*, New York: Oxford University Press, 1939), pp. 15–23. Several years later, Fondo de Cultura Económica issued a Jaeger reader entitled *Cristianismo primitivo y paideia griega* (1965; English trans., *Early Christianity and Greek Paideia*, Cambridge, MA: Harvard University Press, 1961), which synthesized the thesis of his magnum opus and which also was read in Havana in the 1980s.

13. Alfonso Reyes, *La filosofía helenística* (Mexico City: Fondo de Cultura Económica, 1959).

14. See the "dossier" on *Paideia* compiled by Rolando Prats-Paéz and Idalia Morejón for *Cubista Magazine* (Los Angeles), Summer 2006.

15. Iván de la Nuez, "Más acá del bien y del mal: El espejo cubano de la postmodernidad," *Plural* (Mexico City), July 1991, pp. 7–10.

16. Ernesto Hernández Busto, "Paideia: Fotos fijas," *Cubista Magazine* (Los Angeles), Summer 2006.

17. *Orígenes* (1944–1956), founded by José Lezama Lima and José Rodríguez Feo, was the premier journal of the Cuban avant-garde in the 1940s and 1950s. *La Gaceta del Caribe* (1944), founded by Nicolás Guillén, and *Nuestro Tiempo* (1954–1959) were cultural journals linked to the communist movement in Cuba before the Revolution. *Ciclón* (1955–1959), founded by José Rodríguez Feo, was in many ways a successor to *Orígenes*, though publication of the two journals overlapped in its first year. *Lunes de Revolución* (1959–1961), edited by Guillermo Cabrera Infante, was the avant-garde weekly cultural supplement to the newspaper *Revolución* until it was suppressed by Fidel Castro's orders in 1961. (Trans.)

18. Jorge Ferrer, "Una escaramuza en las líneas de la Guerra Fría (ya finalizada ésta)" and Victor Fowler, "Limones partidos," *Cubista Magazine* (Los Angeles), Summer 2006.

19. Reina María Rodríguez, "La desbandada," *Cubista Magazine* (Los Angeles), Summer 2006.

20. José Quiroga, *Cuban Palimpsests* (Minneapolis, MN: University of Minnesota Press, 2005), pp. 115–143.

21. An incomplete list of exiles from the Generation of the 1980s includes poets María Elena Cruz Varela, Osvaldo Sánchez, Emilio García Montiel, and Ramón Fernández Larrea; fiction writers Zoé Valdés, Daína Chaviano, Luis Manuel García, Rolando Sánchez Mejías, José Manuel Prieto, and Andrés Jorge González; essayists Iván de la Nuez, Emilio Ichikawa, Madeline Cámara, and Ernesto Hernández Busto; artists José Bedia, Arturo Cuenca, Consuelo Castañeda, and Glexis Novoa; and journalists and critics José Antonio Évora, Wilfredo Cancio Isla, Camilo Egaña, and Alejandro Ríos. This diaspora also includes filmmakers Ricardo Vega, Marco Antonio Abad, Rubén Medina, Ernesto Fundora, and Lorenzo Regalado; scholars Velia Cecilia Bobes, Alejandro de la Fuente, Alejandro González Acosta, and Osmar Sánchez Aguilera; musicians Oriente López, Gonzalo Rubalcava, Albita Rodríguez, Pavel Urquiza, Amaury Gutiérrez, and Xiomara Laugart; actors César Évora,

Lili Rentería, Pedro Sicard, and Francisco Gattorno; dancers Rosario Suárez, Rubén Rodríguez, and Caridad Martínez; and producers Federico Wilkins, Alexis Núñez Oliva, and Miguel Cossío.

22. Omar Pérez, "Picheo duro" and César Mora, "Patria y soledad: a propósito de Tercera Opción," *Cubista Magazine* (Los Angeles), Summer 2006.

23. See, for example, the first five issues of *Encuentro*, dedicated to Tomás Gutiérrez Alea, Gastón Baquero, Eliseo Diego, and José Triana, from Summer 1996 to Summer 1997.

24. Rafael Rojas, *Tumbas sin sosiego: Revolución, disidencia y exilio del intelectual cubano* (Barcelona: Anagrama, 2006), pp. 428–465.

25. Two divergent political approaches within this diaspora generation can be read in Eliseo Alberto, *Informe contra mí mismo* (Mexico City: Alfaguara, 1997) and Zoé Valdes, *Los misterios de la Habana* (Madrid: Planeta, 2005). See also José Quiroga, *Cuban Palimpsests* (Minneapolis, MN: University of Minnesota Press, 2005), pp. 115–143.

26. See the dossier "Miradas sobre Miami," edited by Wilfredo Cancio Isla for the journal *Encuentro* (Madrid), n. 33, Summer 2004, pp. 160–200.

27. Rafael Rojas, "México y Cuba: Cercanía y diferencia," *Nexos*, n. 332, August 2005, pp. 40–47.

28. Jossianna Arroyo, "Lo veremos todo: Imaginarios transnacionales de la cubanía en la televisión latina estadounidense," paper presented at the 6th Conference of Cuban Research Institute, Florida International University, February 6–8, 2006, pp. 1–15.

29. Damián J. Fernández, ed., *Cuba Transnational* (Gainesville, FL: University Press of Florida, 2005), pp. xiii–xviii.

CHAPTER 12

Josefina the Traveler: Ceremony for a Desperate Actress (*Monologue*)

Abilio Estévez

(Translated by David Frye)

[The play opens on a brightly lit, empty stage. "The sound of the ocean is mixed with ship horns and the noise of swiftly passing trains." A spotlight shines on the sole character, Josefina Beauharnais: "this woman is coming from far, far away; she is clearly exhausted. She is wearing old, strange clothes, a jumble of articles from various eras and different countries; a stained dress that has not held up well to time and distance. On her head, a sweaty straw hat like the ones peasant women wear, tied with a blue ribbon. She is a vagabond, though a high class one, no doubt about it." Josefina's monologue is sometimes directed at the audience and sometimes at the image in the mirror she holds.]

I wanted to travel. (*Points to the mirror.*) She claims to be a martyr of my wandering ambitions, and she announces that she would have preferred, *thank you very much*, to have stayed in the Oriental mountains—the mountains of Cuba's Oriente province, I mean, I'm not talking about India yet. But the problem is that she is just an image. The real person here is me, and I wanted what I wanted, and here you have me.

(*Transition. Fascinated.*) The Orient! India, sure; China...But Cuba's Oriente! That's where I was born. As you can see, I'm not Indian or Chinese, but I am an Oriental, from Cuba. Oriente: my home province, my *patria chica*, as they say. I've always been an enterprising woman. But as for her— screw her. To console her, I tell her that woman proposes and God disposes. God, or whoever. As we all know, God isn't just God. (*Contemptuously.*) Oh, God! God be with you! (*Raising her voice for the image to hear.*) Did the women who're hiding around and eavesdropping hear me? Yes, I'm talking to the diabolical spies.

(*To the audience.*) Listen closely: woman proposes, and God disposes! (*She pulls a handkerchief out of the sack. Displays it. Confidentially.*) In this case, I have to admit, God is me. Little old me. My god. And it's amazing, this business of praying to yourself, begging yourself for favors and lighting candles to yourself, because you're the only one who has anything to do with deciding your vocation. . . . Besides, when you're young, you believe everything you're told, and as for her. . . . (*She points to the mirror. Waves the handkerchief.*) In front of the mirror, I'd repeat, I'd insist: "Girl, the world is a handkerchief."[1] (*Smiles ironically.*) Right, a handkerchief. . . And what a handkerchief! I had to convince her, didn't I? (*Rips the handkerchief apart and places the tatters on the cross.*) This is what I do to the world. [. . .]

(*A brief pause. She moves, with a searching gaze, onto the proscenium. She scrutinizes the members of the audience, one by one.*) You must be wondering: what is this poor old woman doing here, preaching this sermon to us? As tired as you all look. You seem wiped out! I can see it now—*all* of us are exhausted, fed up! You can see it in me, and I see it in you: we've come from far away! "Long is the journey and rugged the road."[2] Exoduses, peregrinations, emigrations. . . like the swallows. Our faces even look like swallows. (*Knocks on her face.*) The roads stay here! And in many other places, too. (*Points to a woman in the audience.*) Look at her: wearing her makeup, her perfume, well dressed, as if she could fool anyone. Forget it, girl, don't pretend. You, too: totally exhausted. (*Pointing to a man.*) And you: nice suit, tie, hair gel, nicely combed hair, like a good Cuban male. . . Cuban men may be dead tired and dead impotent, but their hair—gel it and comb it! And then they walk around like, "I've had success in my life, I've got a full wallet, an account in Chase Manhattan Bank, and a Porsche waiting for me at the curb." Look, son, no matter how Cuban you are, no matter if you live in Coral Gables, nobody can ignore the uncertainty of the way forward. Go ahead and laugh, all of you! "The world is a handkerchief!" And what a handkerchief!

(*Speaking to the image.*) And you, vulture, leave me alone, let me live! It isn't my fault that your vocation and mine are so closely linked, that I turned out a wanderer and you a stick-in-the-mud. (*To the audience. Change in tone.*) Oh, sorry, did I forget to introduce myself? Unforgivable! Josefina Beauharnais, at your service! An empress's name— Joséphine de Beauharnais, remember, the wife of Napoleon I? Don't try to get any clues from my name, son, none at all. I'm not an empress, and I'm not French. Unfortunately for me—and it is an unfortunate thing—I'm Cuban, a *cubanita* from Oriente, from where all those mountains stand. I imagine the mountains, at least, are still there? (*To a member of the audience.*) Life changes so fast, it's so vertiginous, it wouldn't surprise me if you told me they had run out of mountains in Cuba's Oriente. If you tell me, "Now there's a big desert out there," I'll believe you. My family's origin? French! Totally French. And I'm not bragging, either, let me tell you. (*Points to the mirror.*) Unlike her. She thinks she's better than anyone else, because of her French ancestors. My ancestors—and hers, they're the same ones—fled Haiti for fear of the blacks. From what they told us, they owned a coffee plantation there in Haiti, near Pic Macaya. When Toussaint L'Ouverture's blacks started killing the whites, my relatives didn't stick around, they slipped off to Cuba and tried to start up another coffee plantation. No doubt they thought, "Better to live as poor people in Cuba with our heads on our shoulders, than as headless plantation owners in Haiti!" They were sort of right. A head isn't the sort of thing you'd want to lose.

(*Transition. Cheerful.*) Alto Songo! The mountains of Oriente. The chosen land. As you all know, even though you left Hialeah for Coral Gables long ago, Alto Songo is, or was, I'm not sure, very near La Maya, just north of Santiago de Cuba. The coffee plantation was large, and they called it, as you might have expected, *Emperatriz*, "The Empress." But little by little, after all the wars, all the devastation, all the anguish, the empress finally ended up without a crown—a mountainside and a few sacks full of coffee that wasn't much good. They were ruined, like everybody else; ruin means the end of everything, except that, being French Creoles, they never lost their sense of aristocracy. (*Points at the mirror.*) Especially her. She really believed the bit about the name. The motionless empress.

(*Transition. Pulls an old doll from the sack.*) We were born on the seventeenth of February, 1885. Father, who was none too happy to see a baby girl—and he didn't even realize there were two of us—planted himself in front of my mother and said (*Imitating the father: solemn, somewhat ridiculous.*): "Her name will be Josefina Beauharnais, after Marie Josèphe Rose Tascher de la Pagerie, Empress of the French." Poor Father! The fact of the matter is that Mother, who had never left Songo-La Maya, much less learned who Joséphine de Beauharnais was, said, "Oh, of course, Josefina Beauharnais, Empress of the French." Even though my last name had nothing French about it by then. My full name? (*She lovingly places the doll somewhere on the cross. Speaking to the mirror. Scornfully.*) I am going to tell them my full name. And screw you! Josefina Beauharnais Pérez González, of the good old Pérez and González families!

(*Listening to what the image has to say. Slightly angry, she lifts the cloth from the mirror. Speaking to the image.*) I know, you old fool! Traveling was my idea! How could I forget it! Just like I can never forget your damned harassment! Telling them who I am, who you are, is a an act of basic human communication. Don't you think, dear? Or would you rather have them think we're a couple of madwomen? I don't know about you, but I'm not crazy. Old and vagabond, yes; crazy, no. And if I tell them my life, which is also yours, it's for a reason, not just because I feel like it, or to get it off my chest. [...]

(*Brief pause. Pulls a Cuban flag from the sack. Hoists it.*) This is what's to blame. Yes, sir. This ensign, this old lady. Everything that happened to me has been because of the flag. Because I'm a patriot.

(*Brief pause. Quietly playing in the background: "La Bayamesa" by Carlos Manuel de Céspedes and José Fornaris. The light dims, but Josefina and the Cuban flag remain in the spotlight, in imitation of the famous image Liberty*

Leading the People by Eugène Delacroix. Silence. The image dissolves. Josefina places the flag somewhere on the cross.) We're sixteen years old. Think back. A sunny, cool day. Early 1902.[3] The wind is coming down off the mountains with a smell of damp dirt and palms. Someone bellows, "The North Americans are gone! We're a republic!" You cry from sadness, I from happiness. Out in Havana, that Babylon on the Gulf coast, as you like to call it, they say they are going to raise the flag. I say nothing. To anyone, Not even to you, vulture of bad omen. It's my secret. If you know it, it's because you keep an eye on every step I take. Early morning. In the countryside. I'm riding Marie Taglioni. In spite of the name, he's a stallion, not a mare. Off I go. We go. First we tussle. Josefina tries to stop me. (*Grabbing an imaginary figure by the neck.*) I'll kill you, you bastard, if you get in my way, I'll kill you. In spite of you, Fefa, I have to get there, to Havana. I can't miss the miraculous moment. The flag finally rising to the sky, at the mercy of all four winds... To hell with everything! Home and family. You'd have rather seen the Spanish flag, the French flag, even the North American flag flying. You never had faith in Cubans, you bitch. You used to say that we were soft, immature, envious, debased. That we couldn't govern. I don't agree and I don't disagree with you, but you should have respected me. I also had a right to an opinion.

(*She removes from the sack a stole in the colors of the flag and drapes it over her shoulders. She picks up the sack. With great solemnity, she walks to the proscenium. She looks defiantly at the audience. Her expression is mocking.*) A patriot, right? I never got there. We never got there. (*Points at the mirror.*) She won. She always knew how to win. We never made it to Havana. [...]

To run away from the coffee plantation, I grabbed this (*displays a crook*), and this (*displays a bundle of clothes*), but I forgot the most valuable thing. I don't know whether I forgot it or whether it was a plot by this harpy. I bet the little viper works it out so that I forget exactly what I need the most. (*To the audience.*) What is the most important thing, when you go traveling? Anybody? What is it? (*Points to someone in the audience.*) No, son, no, not a passport, and not a camera either. When I was young, neither of those things existed: a passport was a piece of paper, sometimes called a safe-conduct; a camera was a huge, heavy contraption. Besides, the Japanese were still in the Meiji period, locked up inside their imperial archipelago. (*Points to someone in the audience.*) Yes, you're right, a pair of comfortable sneakers are very useful. But perhaps they aren't the most important thing. (*To someone in the audience.*) This lady said it, under her breath. She's a little timid, but she said it. I read your lips. Indeed, gentle countrywoman, you know more than a thing or two. I can imagine how you must have wandered around this good earth! My condolences! (*Pulls a compass from the front of her blouse.*) Of course, ladies and gentlemen: a compass! (*To someone in the audience.*) Don't look at me like that! Inspire pity, me? Never! I run away from home and it doesn't occur to me that, without a compass... (*Energetically.*) Never—listen to me!—never leave your compass at home! Better to go naked and shoeless than do without a compass. When north gets confused with south and east with west, no doubt that will be a centipede's joy, I won't argue with you there, but it's as if the planet had turned on its head and you were heading out into infinite space. A cosmonaut *avant la lettre*, as she, the Frenchified one, would say.

(*Change of tone.*) I was mistaken, like Alberti's dove.[4] Instead of following the road south to Santiago de Cuba, we went north and ended up in Nipe Bay, where the Virgin of Caridad del Cobre appeared, they say, to three impoverished fishermen—and that's the good thing about virgins: they never appear to the powerful. (*A ship's horn sounds.*) A ship. Of course, it's a ship, I tell Josefina. And Josefina makes an intelligent reply: "Every ship carries a compass." (*From the front of her shirt, she also pulls a knotted handkerchief that holds a few coins.*) I pay the passenger fare with the little bit of money I've stolen from home. And what happens next? The ship isn't even going to Havana. She knew it, and she wanted to annoy me.

(*Pause. Change in lighting. Josefina leaves the sack on the cross. Looks at her face in the mirror with a mixture of disgust and nostalgia, touches up her makeup, adjusts a few details in her clothing. Pause. She admires the results. To the image. As if in a trance.*) We've been a thousand things, Fefa, too many things. We've been aristocrats; lady companions; weavers in Lyon; nurses during the First World War, just like in *A Farewell to Arms*; models and "Jane Does" for Man Ray in the Paris of the 1920s; spies for the Allies during the Second World War; singers in a bar in Jalisco; widows in India; dance teachers in Rio de Janeiro; slaves in Algeria; cowgirls in Asunción; beggars in New York; barbers in Canaima; night guards in a seaside cemetery; nuns in the north of Poland; comrades in Siberia; tuberculosis patients in the Balearic Islands; flamenco singers in Andalusia; black rights activists; Peruvian communists; psychoanalysts—in Buenos Aires, of course; fur traders in Alaska; fortune tellers in Tunisia...

(*Brief pause.*) Nostalgia? What are you talking about, Fefa? Nostalgia for what? (*To the audience.*) Do any of you know what nostalgia is? (*To the image.*) The dictionary, to be sure, Madame de Staël, the dictionary! I forgot how cultured you were. So let me tell you: if you would be so kind as to look it up in the dictionary, you will find three definitions there. Should I tell you what they are? Here you go. One: sorrow at finding oneself away from one's country or friends. Two: grief caused by recalling some lost good. Three: memories of the past. What the dictionary doesn't mention, distinguished persecutor, is that in order to feel nostalgia, homesickness, yearning, dejection, or whatever you want to call it, you must first have a moment of idleness. Idleness! If only for one minute. An armistice in the midst of this battle. A short little truce, to sit down in the rocking chair, give yourself over to memories, and weep about what awaits you and what you've left behind.

Translator's Notes

1. A common Spanish phrase; roughly, "It's a small world."
2. A reference to the line "Fue largo el viaje y áspero el camino" in the long poem "Elegía a Jesús Menéndez" (1951) by Cuban poet Nicolás Guillén (1902–1989).

3. Early 1902: the United States occupied Cuba from 1898 until the inauguration of Tomás Estrada Palma as the first elected president of independent Cuba on May 20, 1902.

4. "I was mistaken, like Alberti's dove": referring to a poem by Spanish writer and painter Rafael Alberti (1902–1999), "La Paloma," which begins: "The dove made a mistake, / it was mistaken. / To fly north, it flew south; / it thought the wheat was water."

CHAPTER 13

Letter to Enrique Saínz, or, On Imaginary Conversions

Jorge Luis Arcos

(Translated by David Frye)

I

Dear friend, now that I've reached the season of imaginary conversions, of the
  most unsettled dreams
I can set the cinders of hate and the ghosts of hope aside
For isn't this the season of the end of days?
Days of wrath, Tertullian called them, cited the sybil of Málaga
Now that the senses are looking back, I may invoke you
ancient White Goddess, and give myself over to the confessions that tedium
  dictates
legendary sweat, like an overthrown Oedipus or a Virgil in death throes
with the peace of the scribe, an obscure chronicler, an ancestral dreamer who
  longs for the shade of flowering mango trees
First off: the country at issue, the inconceivable isle of my orphanhood
I had a friend who read through Nietzsche and went mad, like John Nash, the
                  Emperor of Antarctica
Is it possible to read Nietzsche unscathed in your youth? I was born on an
  island
Nietzsche is another island. He taught me the value of distance, the little
  broken bridge, the
                  faraway mountain, the eternal return
How can you listen to Bach and at the same time feel the Dionysian banging
  on the piano?
Shouting, *Ariadne, I love you.* And signing, *The Crucified*
Ah, love as limit, threshold, impossible dream
And his wounded name. And Nietzsche, his pseudonym
                  I was born on an island

And kept a shell collection in popsicle boxes. Ah, the perverse treasures
the reclusive relics, hushed labyrinths. The entire Milky Way
Shells or stars. I wanted to be an astronomer, a castaway, a crusader
Reality—obscene. Friendship—clandestine. The outdoors—unspeakable
(They lost my toys. They expelled me from the garden)

I was born on an island

I was always the exile, the madman, the impossible lover
The one who gazed avidly at Gustavo Doré's prints in *The Divine Comedy*
I felt the world so ugly, my world, my sinister isle
You never were my homeland—how can there be a homeland without a
    Mother?
I always was the exile, always longed for a return
Once I wrote, with the heartrending melancholy of youth:
Our farewells are so provisional that time returns them, trembling
But: *Therefore you replied to him, swineherd Eumaeus*[1]
And I repeated the sacred words like a monologous drone

Later on I missed the Three Kings, the sad Magi. The little star, way over there
The baby in the manger. The cattle's steaming breath. And the soul in the
    stable
It was Twelfth Night, Night of Kings, my night, my secret

But

it was time to fall, again, helpless. All broken down and far away
(They booted me from the fiesta. They broke my heart)
And to be born—be reborn?—*The sin without guilt, eternal suffering....*[2]

I was born on an island

But then, dear friend, how can one be born again in some other dark
    homeland?
The age-old dark night, the yearned-for homeland of Juan Clemente and
    Casal[3]
Two homelands have I..., said the castaway on the narrow beach of
    Cajobabo[4]
So I searched for some face, another's touch, any certitude
something unknown, *the dancing figures under the lake*
And skipped stones on the sea, the dark mausoleum, searching for its
    reply
I didn't know then that *if nothing is sought, the return will be unforeseen,
    unlimited*[5]
But there you were, Triple Goddess, terrifying, unforgettable Medusa
I didn't understand your lessons. And I searched the faces, the beloved
    faces, for
a message, some kind of sign, a distant language: the word—lost;
    reality—without

a name

(without pity, without sin). Ah, the iridescence of those faces buried in the
    sand, their

indefinable anguish

the original sex, a bridge to erase this terrible separation, this damned
                    dualism
Neither angel nor devil. Polo Febo and Celestina?[6] One whole. Something
    like that

I was born on an island. What were you seeking, María, on this strange
    island?
It reminded you of Málaga, of your father with his white alpaca suit. Ah,
    María
if this was your prenatal homeland, your childhood, your secret, and your
    fullblooded attachment
for me it was hell, the prairies of the damned, with a Sun in the center
light erasing people's faces, blurring their secrets
the site of expulsion, the place of shipwreck, the loss, the loss

Dear friend, you always knew it. It's hell, clear enough. The region of the
    children
The children of the night. And the unborn children. The eternal sensation,
    the brazen
                    abandonment
All split, broken. And the drop of laudanum. The candles fluttering out. It's
    hell, clearly

And then the temptations. Can any hell be clear? Life is an essay. You knew it
                    always
The dendrites encompassing you. The bitter circumstances. The country, so
    far off
Profaning the thresholds. Attacked by insomnia. Making your neighbor suffer
And looking off afar at things that are incomprehensible, reclusive. Entering
    the hidden park
The reliable pistol shot. Delirious pounding in your temples. And the fish's
    mouth
The autumn leaves falling slowly like a sacred mantle.

But what am I writing here, beloved victim? Everything is craggy, mute
And the dog's tooth coral. Perhaps. Yet nonetheless
there's one clear mirror. The eyes of your dog, like distant stars
Perhaps. I was born on an island. Quite close to the borders
to the edges. *My son, where have you hidden yourself? For I have sought you,
weeping.* Are there islands of forgiveness? In Solaris? Slowly
very slowly I look at the conversions, the tough simulacra
(How poor is Power. How pathetic the Tyrant). There is an entranced
fountain in the center of the patio. There, all music and splendor
pouring forth into the silence a clear alphabet
There, the Buddha, perfect. There, silence. Dear friend
can't we return to the secret fountain?
(*Alánimo, alánimo, la fuente se rompió*)[7]
I was born on an island. An island in the amnion

As you well knew, Raúl. Because we're just passing through: glowworm,
    firefly, green flash
eternal minotaur watching the stars. There is no clear hell
Dragonfly. At nighttime (and every night is gloomy)
                an eclipse appears. Staying there, dreaming
surrounded by the sea and the night and your hand
Your hand, like a forest. Your sex, like a meadow
Watching the lights, far off. And me, falling asleep in your hand
Like a small dry leaf, peony, cilantro

But...

                I was born on an island
                        And there is no clear hell

What's left to us are memories like fables, songs
like enchanted kingdoms, and *those green eyes*
as tranquil as a lake,[8] the lost moments, and all those visions
the incredible sense of being touched, the distant music, the strange smells,
    and at bottom
impossibly, an unforgettable taste
                        I was born on an island
I cannot imagine it
                        January 15 and 16, 2003

2

contritely praying paternoster and ave maría

                              R. Darío[9]

Dear friend, when was it that the gloomy dons arrived
dark emissaries of another night, another island, another possible
    homeland?
When was it they arrived? I cannot say. They were like the night
the night of my panicking. The claw that thrust into the smooth sheet
(under it, me, contrite, with my cold lantern). They were the giant puppets
the frenzied clowns, muddying everything with their enormous clown shoes
(Trompoloco, Bob Gray, alias Pennywise the Clown).[10] I couldn't write. I
    couldn't write
There was something of the ragdoll, the ghost, the worm about them[11]
Just as Lorenzo saw them on his unbelievable night
But *always the lead-fisted slap,* as you said, Lezama, in your melancholy way
                There are creatures of the mountains, creatures of the valleys,
                    and creatures of the swampy bogs and quagmires[12]
wrote the little gentleman in the giant overcoat
I don't know, but in my night, my secret hideaway
night of nights spent on empty beach
those creatures did not prosper. And I could write

collect seashells, imagine the world a different place
a vaster place, turn off the lantern and pull down the sheets
feel the cool floor tiles, the rustling of the pages
like waves, and the warm, dark sex of the night
by my side. Another island, another's touch, like a clearing in the woods
bonfire in the center, planets whirling past
like a chill up your spine. And all the sleepless night
of your eyes trembling like an impossible limit
like a dark essence. Ah, what vast regions
I discovered by your side, strewn with the landmines
of turbulent beauty. It was the gulf of visitations
of imaginary conversions. And you were the pauper
the outsider, the poet, the lunatic. All the marginalia
(alcohol and marijuana and a strange splendor
in every mirror)
     Dear friend, once more the world was
bitter and divided. Reality—crude; prophecy—wayward
the light—dubious, inane. Hope—childish, and the beast in the center
usurping the space of any initiation.

What is it about landscapes that they don't refresh the soul. Their
  enthusiasm
is so brief, their innocence so sparse.
          Dear friend, landscapes
discomfort the soul: bonds misplaced, abundance
lost, its foam forgotten, its color washed out. And a suicidal
anxiousness, and a strange dew seeping into everything. I don't know
perhaps, who knows. there are two races, two nights, two islands
that are enemies. The ancient line of Cain and Abel. And
     We only live, only suspire
     Consumed by either fire or fire[13]
          But
As the Prophet also said: *The end is where we start from*[14]
          January 21 and 22, 2003

         3

(...and then I sought to efface my reclusive, solitary, exhausted face in another, in the abyss of sex. To decant it into otherness, unheard-of beauty. To seek a feeling, a touch, a knot. Something closed and hard. The hand outheld, the eager gaze, the distant music, a clandestine scent, a memorable flavor. In the eternal girl of the opulent purple, a dewy basin, a secret spray. Ay, muck, becoming should commingle with being. And being born again: stone, palm, another river. Something mute, empty. An obscure point, impossible. And the bonfire in the center...)

         January 22, 2003

4

and to Miguel Angel Castro Machado

Dear friend, the flat roofs remain immutable. In the mountains of Baracoa
time does not pass. A certain person has never disembarked on these shores
The island exists only in the imagination. There only are heartbeats
The present does not exist. Nor past nor future. Beginning and end—
aren't they the same? We're like a splinter of the sacred chaos
We can't see your face because everything is your Face
That girl in the throes of death, that active volcano, that distant star
that battered rowboat, those caravels at dawn, that shattered cross
the Hurakán, the Cemí, all the little idols, the pictographs, the ceramics
the areítos, the blue tobacco smoke, and more, the desert island, and more,
the eve of the island
of the planet, of the Sun, of the Milky Way, of your brazen and beautiful eyes,
carousel, merry-go-round, labyrinth, spiral, and the shells in popsicle boxes
Silence. Triteness is all. *Why do platitudes exist in life?*
wonders the lucid monk. And the great-grandson of Nietzsche replies:
"We are only on intimate terms with life when we pronounce—*with all our
    hearts*—a platitude"
I must return the *polymitas* shells to their sacred place of origin. And the
    sigua nacre
from my cane, and its precious wood. Even the shiny pebble from the little
    beach at Cajobabo
And these clothes, these skins, these incredible minerals. All is naught. All
like an incredible piece of music, like a shower of golden ears of corn. Like
    you

January 22, 2003

5

Bolichán says: That's life . . .
Trío Matamoros

But, dear friend, down here, in the incredible jungle
the dense gloom closing over the last island
the sky falling heavy as a prophecy
the shadows chatting on the cold bleak plain
and us, gaping in the lowering night
remembering the scum, the sacred ghosts
the books, the bonfires, the melancholy ruins
the versions of ennui and the beloved faces
and the idle time like a blue sky, the inaudible music
the fountain like a stream of impossible splendor
the meager dying light and the empty house
and us, looking at the solitude at the end

January 26, 2003

6

Do the moments alone make up for the road? Is everything lost
everything, even those moments? Is that why we dream them?

I was born on an island

Once upon a time there was…

I cannot

I cannot imagine it

January 27, 2003

Translator's Notes

1. Eumaeus: the faithful swineherd who raised Telemachus during Odysseus's long absence.
2. *El pecado sin culpa, eterna pena*: A line from a sonnet by José Lezama Lima, in his *Poesía completa* (Barcelona: Barral, 1975), p. 59.
3. Juan Clemente Zenea (1832–1871) and Julián del Casal (1863–1893): two of the most influential Cuban poets of the nineteenth century.
4. *Dos patrias tengo yo: Cuba y la noche* (Two homelands have I: Cuba and the night), the opening line of José Martí's poem "Dos patrias," written in New York, which seems to prophesy his death shortly after he returned to Cuba (arriving at the beach of Cajobabo on April 11, 1895) to fight for Cuban independence.
5. *Si nada se busca, la ofrenda será imprevisible, ilimitada*: a line from María Zambrano, *Claros del bosque* (Barcelona: Seix Barral, 1977), p. 11. Born in Málaga, Zambrano (1904–1991) lived in Cuba from 1940 to 1953 and taught philosophy at the Universidad de la Habana. The poet directly addresses Zambrano ("María") in the next stanza.
6. Polo Febo and Celestina: characters in Carlos Fuentes' novel *Terra Nostra* (Mexico City: J. Mortiz, 1975) who join together and give rise to a new hermaphrodite form.
7. *Alánimo, alánimo, la fuente se rompió*: A line from a children's song (Come on, come on, the fountain broke!)
8. *Aquellos ojos verdes / serenos como un lago*: From the song "Aquellos ojos verdes" (Green Eyes) by Cuban composers Adolfo Utrera and Nilo Menéndez, written in 1929.
9. *y rezaba contrito páter y ave maría*: from Darío's sonnet "Los bufones" (The Buffoons).
10. Trompoloco was a well-known clown character on Cuban television played by Edwin Fernández (1928–1997). Bob Gray and Pennywise the Clown are manifestations of an evil force in Stephen King's horror novel *It* (New York: Viking Press, 1986).
11. *Tenían de peleles, de espectros, de gusanos*: from Darío's sonnet, "Los bufones."
12. *Seres hay de montaña, seres de valle / y seres de pantanos y lodazales*: José Martí, "Ismaelillo."
13. T.S. Eliot, "Little Gidding," *Four Quartets* (New York: Harcourt, Brace, 1943), p. 36.
14. Ibid., p. 38.

Nereyda García Ferraz, *Vivo yendo* (I live going away) (painting)

PART III

Regresos: When We Return

She feels a certain mutual indifference, a loss of meaning, a disillusionment, a falling away, a veil covering over spaces, the distance that separates her from almost everything, from an arrested time that has never ceased moving forward. A cloud, a reverie, a déjà vu. Everything is unchanged, but it isn't the same. A presence of a past. And the future?

—Nara Araújo

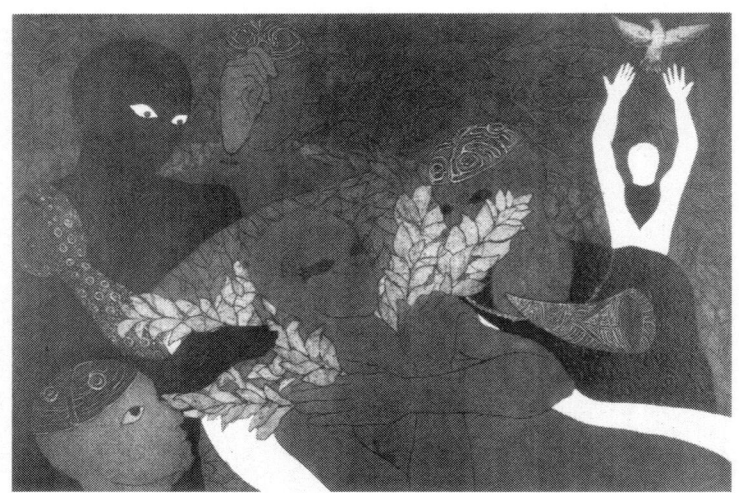

Belkis Ayón, *La dormida* (Sleeping woman) (collograph)

CHAPTER 14

In the Middle of Nowhere

Nara Araújo

(Translated by David Frye)

On the plane, I'm seated next to our young daughter. She's taken the window seat, and I've got the aisle. Are we each sitting in the seats we wanted? Are we each going where we want to go? Flying to Mexico on a job-related trip: I'm none too confident about this move, but it seems like everything's going to turn out fine. We'll see. You never know. For the time being, it's a matter of getting settled and adapting. These are all the things I was thinking while we flew on the jet. So much has happened since then. Our daughter finished her schooling; my husband kept writing; and me, I continued my academic life, in spite of stumbling blocks and illness. We became well integrated, despite coming from a rowdy coastal culture.

All through that decade I never picked up the local accent or idioms, for fear of appearing ridiculous, not attaining the perfect mimesis: speaking organically, without affectation. I tried to learn with the girl, for she was able to change her vocabulary and intonation to match her interlocutor's. But in vain. And I also insisted on eating food without hot spices. A well-known writer, also Cuban by origin, once criticized me: How is it that you still can't eat chili peppers? As if accepting the gastronomic symbol were an indicator of my incorporation into the culture where I was now living. At home, we kept up the same old culinary customs, though my daughter had already adapted to the regional dishes. For me, this wasn't a matter of principles but of habits, of education.

Making a linguistic choice wasn't an issue for us, because, fortunately, we were in a Spanish-speaking country. I had no conflict over my cultural identity, because it was already fully formed, and wherever I went, I would be Cuban. The conflict passed through different coordinates. With a life project founded on my native soil, I was forced to make a decision to set out to reinsert myself as part of a different project. There were the family obligations: loyalties, and also responsibilities for an adolescent's future. But at the outset of this change, I sometimes felt I had lost my niche, lost my place, and that I must therefore maintain my presence in my country of origin. I never stopped publishing, never ceased going back frequently, to touch it with my hands, look at it with my eyes, feel it with all my senses. And to enjoy the sea, always beginning anew. The erect sea, penetrating the city; or the lake-like sea, lullabying it as they lie gently side by side. The smell of marshes and brine. I yearned for all I had left behind. I might have met the same fate as Lot's wife, but survival compelled me forward and my salt pillar did not remain behind in the desert.

At some point, there came an end to looking back. My new milieu became natural and I got caught up in exciting professional projects. But at last the time came to go back. It really wasn't a matter of returning to the void, because I still had multiple networks of family and friends. My house, though somewhat worn down by time, could still be recovered. Once more, the conflict I felt had nothing to do with matters of cultural identity. It passed through coordinates that had to do with family ties. But, if I had so longed for the past from the Mexican highlands, a future on the Island now disquieted me. Would I return to my old job? It *obviously* wouldn't be the same any more. Could I resume my former life? At what price?

Other issues would also have to be resolved once and for all. I would have to settle an annoying situation with my mother's house that had been taken over for the past few years by a relative who had lost my trust. I did not suspect, on the day when I arrived to take it all back, that the past would rise up before me and place my history before me, like a mirror, reflecting what I felt when I faced it, and also when I faced the panorama that my surroundings offered me. While my cultural identity remains intact (intact?), I've lost something, because, as the saying goes, *el que fue a Sevilla, perdió su silla*— leave for Seville, lose your place at the table. Therefore, I'd like to set down this encounter with my past now, inventing a protagonist for myself who is me and is not me. I want to live again, and have written these lines.

* * *

It's a winter day, the steam isn't suffocating. She is just getting used to the torrid latitudes, having to put up with the muggy climate that weighs her down and wears her out, the treacherous humidity of this land between Cancer and Capricorn. No one accompanies her. She must enter the labyrinth alone, without Ariadne's thread. Driving along the Malecón, she passes the hotel built above the caves of Taganana where the Spanish once deployed their artillery, walks by the gas station and El Carreño, turns at the Castillito, climbs the street up to Infanta, turns right, and drives back down to the avenue that follows along the water's edge. She finds the entrance and parks among the dirty buses. In the bar on Hospital street, mechanics and bureaucrats are drinking concoctions, stretching their break time as a way to escape the daily grind. Garbage piles up in a trash can by the service door. A banquet for flies.

She doesn't drive down to the garage where billboards are rented to the highest bidder, where maybe black market deals are going down or a clandestine gambling table has been set up. She closes the car door and locks it. Rusty wire fencing encloses what were once flowerbeds at the entrance, and she is surprised to still see the metal devices for scraping mud off the soles of your shoes, a forgotten custom. There is no janitor in charge of keeping the place clean, and no one cares. These are Difficult Times. She climbs the gray granite stairs that lead to a large door made of a kind of wood that stands up to this country, an ideal breeding ground for fungus and pests. Urine stains the worn stone steps, and mold spreads across the walls in the form of a fish, a tambourine, a dagger, enlivening this mural painted by no one. She steps into arrested time, into the island of sorrows and ghosts.

She ought to leave the house of her childhood and early youth, the dwelling that has been occupied by relatives ever since the lady of the house passed away. Finally free of politically correct types, it now belongs to a family that keeps their altars lit. Now she should leave it, forever. Say good-bye. Scratch one item off the to-do list, put a check mark next to it. And forget. Forget? The house is inundated by images that mount up like the papers filling its boxes and shelves. She should sort through the accumulated piles. She opens the worm-eaten windows because the dust is choking her, covers her mouth with a scarf, ties back her hair, and gets to work. She has time, all the time in the world. She opens cabinets, looks through bookshelves, searches in wardrobes, and gags when she touches the remains of an insect.

In a cracker tin she finds photos she has never seen before: her mother, smartly dressed in a black sequined dress, a feather in her chignon; wearing a dress with a gathered neckline revealing a hint of cleavage; in sunglasses, culottes, and high-heeled sandals; adorned with a Florentine brooch; or with the gold orchid with a pearl pistil that she inherited from her and lost. It's so stupid to travel with precious things! Nevermore. Judging from her mother's sleepy eyes, she might have been a daughter of Oyá; from her rectitude and strict bearing, perhaps she was protected by Obbatalá. Piled up in the living room closet, she finds the elements of her mother's private altar: a Cristo de Limpias image, a glass of water, and a stone.

At this moment a wave of uneasiness sweeps over her. She reconsiders her plan of having a relative live in this house. It occurs to her that she had been in the midst of some exceptional moment—her stepfather was dying, she was traveling—and had made a decision without thinking things through. She is tormented by the dissolution of the uterus, the fecund womb, the implication of giving something away in order to fulfill a promise. Has she properly defended her own daughter's rights? She feels responsible, because this was where she took her first steps, right in front of her mother, who took such good care of this house. A house filled with ghosts: that's another reason to transfer it, hard as it will be on her, much as she will have to relinquish; waiting can be destructive, the house could fall into worse ruin, the neighborhood might go further downhill, because there's no recovery in sight.

Past experiences assail her on this journey back. In a casual encounter with old students, she is astonished by other people's memories of her alleged exam questions: Was Phaedra a revolutionary woman? And her alleged pronouncements in class: When Balzac died, he was acclaimed by his people, unlike his king. Impossible, those aren't her words. It wasn't her. Are they dreaming, or are they lying? They swear to her they've got her words written down in their old notebooks. She's not carried away with vanity or egomania, but with bewilderment. Above all, a sensation of what once was and never more will be. A sort of void. A distancing, a letting go. She feels a certain mutual indifference, a loss of meaning, a disillusionment, a falling away, a veil covering over spaces, the distance that separates her from almost everything, from an arrested time that has never ceased moving forward. A cloud, a reverie, a déjà vu. Everything is unchanged, but it isn't the same. A presence of a past. And the future?

It is in this frame of mind that she has to leave the house. Protected by the scarf, she opens the closets. She climbs onto a chair to reach the boxes, which cascade down on her with a torrent of dust. In them she finds school and college diplomas, conservatory certificates, awards and medals, report cards. She discovers evening gowns, velveteen capes and overcoats, mantillas, hats and gloves, seventies-style bell-bottoms. She recovers her lace wedding dress, a princess-cut with a silk sash ending in a bow in front, which her daughter will later wear for her birthday. She unearths sets of dishes, silverware, and house decorations, inaudible LPs and inoperable machines, shoes, handbags. Bed linen stained with damp. Forgettable paintings and disposable treasures. Dust upon dust. Time upon time.

Suddenly an avalanche of academic and work IDs tumbles out. Portraits and missives. Musical scores. Snapshots of friends visiting a pyramid or ladies carrying babies. Photos of people without stories. Photos of her parents that she has never seen before. Visiting cards that she used from the time she was young. Blue stationery with her initials. A notebook she had written in on the day she gave birth: My daughter, sweet servitude. She is surprised by several packets of letters tied with pink ribbons. She reads them; they tell her nothing. The handwriting records a past that can be recovered, but only in part, because it still remains the past. The trace of a trace, the enigma of the referent. The universe of mute signs and speakers. A past that the present activates in a variety of ways: to miss it and yearn for it, hopelessly; to interrogate it, for its mysteries; to question it, in order to condemn it; and perhaps, still, in spite of all the years, to love it.

She goes through holiday postcards, tourist brochures, souvenirs of trips, museum entrance tickets, train tickets. From a pile of receipts she keeps only those that hold special meaning: the one that set up their fortunate rental of this house, the ones that register the debt on a paternal property on the beach. She files everything in boxes, which she then seals and marks for later removal. She unknots the scarf. She loosens her hair and shakes it out. She looks once more through the house. The ghosts withdraw, fade, and fall silent. The emptiness makes the house look bigger. The granite floor edged with baseboards has resisted the footsteps of the person who has walked through here. The house no longer belongs to her, neither literally nor symbolically. Silence. What remains here is Silence.

She rests. Breathes. Wipes her eyes and forehead dry. Opens the door, closes it behind her, and says good-bye; walks out through the great front door and descends the granite stairs that are ruined by neglect and destined to be replaced by some ignoble material or face a long and grueling death. The stairs, sullied by dogs and drunks. The façade, fissured by the humidity that has traced the forms of a sunfish, a tambourine, and a dagger, a mural painted by no one. Outside, parked buses line each side of the street, waiting for the uniforms to emerge from the nearby offices. She bids farewell once more to her dead. She enters the car with difficulty, her hands burdened with memories. She drives down the street of bureaucrats and mechanics, people who eat, gesticulate, and carry on—for here people talk by shouting, and no one could whisper in the middle of this deafening verbosity—competing against the music that unvaryingly blares from some loudspeaker; a loud-mouthed scene of prattling and groping, of hissing and flirting, the ancient Havana tradition from the days of Landaluze.

The way people talk in this country. Eloquence and verbosity. Words, words, words, as the Prince of Denmark would say. Volutes and virgules, lat-ticework and arabesques, tapestries and embroidery, textures and texts, vines and creepers, billows and waves that spread through the air in sustained cadences. Vacuity and meaninglessness. Time is wasted, all one's time, in a vicious circle where you talk because, in the end, there's nothing else going on. Clerks dealing with customers talk endlessly because it doesn't matter, there's no attempt at service because there are no incentives for serving. In offices, in hallways, on the telephone, you see employees turning to another desk, another counter, instead of attending to clients, because they find relief in dialogue for this spinning of wheels.

In the beginning was the Word. And it became the light, and the darkness shone. Rhetoric and Discourse. Lip and Beak. Chit-chat and Chinwag. Natter and Chatter. Prattle and Palaver. Gabble, Guff, and Gossip. Logorrhea. Murmurs. Shouts. Ecstasy. Fury. Running riot. Myriad tongues waggling ceaselessly in a concert of laryngeal and buccal organs, of papillae and fol-licles: muscular tongues, round or long, narrow or wide, red or whitish, smooth or rough, timid or aggressive, mellow or sharp, spoons or stilettos, truthful or lying. Saintly or Damned. The thousand tongues become one giant tongue, heard by the Ear, the totality of incessant listening. A Tongue that seems to take off from its base, rising convulsively and carrying off an entire nation, which it thrashes and beats and finally swallows whole in order to satisfy the ravenous hunger of Leviathan. In Leviathan's belly it will live forever on illusions: the cornucopia of abundance and the plethora of kindness. We are the Greatest.

The word is good for filling the vacuum of the object, the word becomes the object, the object of unsatisfied desire. The urge of the libido, the repeated urge, in the Word is the Act. The word maintains its hint of magic, but what if, after the words, the Word does not survive? Talking endlessly is a national illness that fills appetites and yearnings, that satisfies the hunger for events, that entertains and amuses, that gobbles up the air on the Infinite Plain of Boredom. She turns onto the Malecón that encircles the loudmouthed, bellicose city, that tightens round its sinuous, sensual waist. The eternal silence of its infinite spaces do not terrify her. The water held back by its cement wall is as transparent a blue as the celestial surface that it reflects.

To her right, the Tower of San Lázaro, where the Inquisitor's bonfire has been cold for centuries; Maceo Park, above the ancient cove; and in the distance, almost on the horizon, the Tower of the Three Kings, its building material indiscreetly revealing its youth by its difference from the original stone, impossible not to notice when you look at the city. To her left, the sea skirts the coast until lost to sight. She heads west. Ingenuous tourists expose themselves to the setting sun, sitting on the sea wall, gazing at the parade of cinnamon and sloe midriffs on bodies that are lean and hungry, elastic and tense, where what stands out is the curve of the backside, the signifier of a race and, in this country, an entire philosophical category.

Her car continues along the sea wall route up to the mouth of the Almendares, which is her Country and her Blood. She hears the bells of Ochún. The water laps against the little site that the English once trod upon, and joins up with the sea currents that spread along its wings: haban, avana; meadow, savannah; haven, port, havana, harbor. San Cristóbal de La Habana. Carenas Bay. Havana. Yemayá swishes her skirt, holding it out so that it barely grazes her hips, and dances as if rowing, as if grinding a pestle in a mortar. Amber necklaces shiver on her neck, bracelets jingle on her honeycolored arms, and a golden crown with five pendant jewels rests atop her hair.

The orange disk dips under the horizon and leaves behind its tender iridescence. A few little skiffs hustle to get out, weather from the north approaches. The car descends beneath the water, rises back up to the west along the tree-lined boulevard, the clock has stopped, and on the corner of La Copa one lion roars while the other, its paws hurt and its snout broken, meekly bows its mane. Purebred dogs are walked by their masters, and baseball is being played on the empty field. Across the cracked cement walk sweaty pedestrians who long for life eternal. As they walk, they talk with one another, endlessly, endlessly, endlessly. The way we talk in this country. And what if, after all these words, the Word does not survive?

She's worn out. Her chores have been exhausting. When she gets home, she puts the documents in order, looks through the manuscripts, and opens a few letters. She has outwitted Pandora's fate. She rereads some letters and contemplates the photos of her mother. It's time to turn back by looking to the future, to speak of the presence of the past. A ship in harbor after the storm, she's in remission, but you never know, a flaming sword dangles overhead and time is not negotiable, the countdown could come to an end. The flesh is sad, and she has read many books. The year is almost over and it is time to leap into the void. It's a matter of finding the signs that represent things, settling on the right tone, and deciding who you're writing for.

She now ought to make a performance of writing. Encode her traces in space. Repeat the unrepeatable. Become not a drifting floe but a ship that rocks its rigging in search of other climes. Weigh anchor without fear of shipwreck, without ten cannons on a side, with the wind at her back and under full sail, cutting through the sea, flying. From the balcony she sees a few seagulls soar over the sea, which disappears into the distance, a lake-like sea on which the sunlight beats and reflects across the city that sleeps tamely by its side. She wants to write a mirroring story that could give her back this river of experiences that rain down on her out of time, sparks of light and lines of flight from her object of desire.

*   *   *

The foregoing lines form part of a work in progress: an exercise in going back, and an attempt to recover the times I have lived through. They are an effort to set down in writing what I was, in order to attempt to be that person again. I have sensed, in this journey back to the land of my birth, that there is a before and an after, a lowering and raising of curtains, an empty theater. My resistance to the tropical environment is a symptom of estrangement (*It's so hot, so hot, so hot!*). And these have been contradictory encounters, with some who have held firm without giving in, and with others who are already defeated. How did they arouse passions? Why do they still seem so annoying? I am surprised, more than ever, to see gray hair, weight gain, wrinkles, protruding abdomens, as well as dark gaps between a few pairs of lips. I am assailed by a terrifying doubt: how must they see me?

I admit that, at this point in the game, I am afraid of decadence: orange-peel skin, rings on the neck, bacon strips on the abdomen, car tires on the hips, flabby inner thighs, double chins, and skin sagging under the arms. It's become impossible to wear short sleeves or plunging necklines, two-piece bathing suits or tight dresses, a blouse tucked into a skirt. Time to disguise these inveterate pieces of flesh that flop against each other to deadly effect. We, the women of back then, are no longer the same.

But rereading these lines, I have an insight: perhaps I'm wrong about the way, perhaps this distance that I make the protagonist feel, which is my own, is not a sign of absence but of presence. Perhaps it isn't a matter of not belonging but rather of going beyond the yearning for symbiosis that compels us to recognize that we form part of something. A drifting subject, perhaps, I am in the middle of nowhere, given that I no longer belong here, but I don't belong there either, a situation that calls forth in me not anguish but surprise. So, if the conflict isn't one of to be or not to be, but of being the same and being different, I understand that the question is tacking in a different direction: I'm someone who should continue growing more, as a human being, in order to carry out a narrative project and attain an object of desire: living in harmony, overcoming the anguish of what remains unfinished, of the time that is slipping through my fingers, and attaining peace. The flesh is sad, lamentably, and I have read many books.

In this frame of mind, I should get rid of this feeling of estrangement, or perhaps, staying within it, reinvent myself and move forward into this third stage of my life's passage. Concentrate, concentrate, concentrate. Breathe, meditate, and find the energy. And, above all: not judge my fellows, but instead understand and forgive. A hard task. But, if I am a survivor, if it has been almost a decade since I was on the edge of the abyss, I should make use of this opportunity that life has handed me. And this, perhaps, at least for me, is the question. And the lesson of a journey back to the land of my birth.

CHAPTER 15

The Woman Who Wanted Bridges

Ruth Behar

No era bueno quererla; por los ojos
le pasaban a veces como nieblas
de otros paisajes....
It wasn't good to love her; her eyes
seemed veiled at times by mists
from other lands....

—Dulce María Loynaz, "La Extranjera," in *Versos 1920–1938*

I am with Nena, Kaki, and Yoyi the first time I go to Varadero Beach. I feel myself returning to the time of creation as my feet sink into the mythical sand. It is supposed to be softer than satin, softer than the sand of any other beach in the world. Mami and Papi always spoke about the sand at Varadero with a kind of reverence. After leaving Cuba for New York, we spent every Sunday in July and August camping out on Jones Beach. The gritty sand had particles of soot that stuck to your toes, but freedom from communism came at a price, my parents declared. Once they had saved up a little money, they took my brother and me on their search for pristine beaches in Miami and Puerto Rico, but none had sand that compared to the exquisiteness of the sand at Varadero, where they'd spent their three-day honeymoon. Somewhere on that satin sand in Varadero I must have been conceived, for I was born exactly nine months after my parents' honeymoon.

But now it is 1992 and I am in Varadero with Nena, Kaki, and Yoyi. I love calling my new Cuban friends by their diminutive nicknames rather than by their baptismal names, María de los Angeles, Raquel, and Jorge Luis. Until then I hadn't known it was possible to keep being called by your childhood Cuban name in grown-up life. In their company I return to the name I had as a child, the name only my parents still use to call me. I am Ruti again.

Like the child I was when we left Cuba, the child who in old pictures is held by the hand by her Mami and Papi as she wobbles along the wall of the

Malecón, now that I am back in Cuba I still need to be led by the hand. My friends have brought me to the section of the beach next to the old Dupont estate. I would not have known to go there, but Kaki's grandparents had a summer house in this part of the beach and she has memories of her extended family gathering there, all the aunts and uncles and cousins, before they were divided by the Revolution. The moment we arrive I know why Kaki loves that strip of beach. It is wild and deserted and radiant. Spanish developers, she tells me, have their eye on this virginal territory. They want to line it with luxury hotels. When we were there they had not yet deflowered it. They would soon enough.

The three of us make a run for the ocean. Nena splashes into the water in delighted leaps. Yoyi follows. Kaki hangs back, watching me hesitate at the water's edge.

"Aren't you coming?"

"Yes, in a minute," I say. "Go ahead without me. I'll catch up soon."

Kaki glances at me again. "Are you sure?"

I nod and she laughs, "You'll get so hot, you'll have to get in the water."

She slips on her snorkeling gear and dives in. She moves with confident, sleek strokes. Her training long ago as a swimmer with the Olympic team of Cuba still shows. She's comfortable in the ocean, glistening like a fish.

I'm not sure why I take so long to go into the water. Maybe I need to take a moment to breathe, to stand there and feel the sand caressing my feet, to take in the fact that I am in Cuba, that I am in Varadero Beach. I have come prepared with a plastic bag and I bend down to fill it up with sand. A gift for Mami and Papi, though only Mami will accept it. Papi wants nothing from Cuba, not even honeymoon sand.

Kaki is right. The sun is burning and the water looks inviting. With careful steps I make my way into the ocean. The blue-green water is clear, so translucent I can see my feet. I am propelled forward by the waves. My body rises and dips, rises and dips.

Just before I reach the point where I can't touch bottom, I stop. I'm only a little bit afraid. I can sort of swim, as long as I keep my head above water. I've never liked to put my head under water.

Nena and Yoyi are a few steps beyond me and Kaki is much further out, barely visible on the horizon.

"Come over here, it's not that deep," Nena calls to me.

I tell her I'm okay where I am.

"*Te da miedo, Ruti?*" Nena asks.

Nena, who's been traveling to Cuba longer than I have, knows about my fears and she's trying to help me get over them. She and I have flown together to Cuba. She held my hand and steadied me when the plane dove toward the island and I began crying.

According to the Cuban government, we were both "taken away" from Cuba as child-immigrants. Since we didn't make the decision to leave, we're granted a certain immunity when we return to the island. Nena wants to use that privilege to open a critical dialogue with the Cuban government. *No tiene pelos en la lengua*, as the expression goes. No hairs clogging her tongue. I watch Nena confront Abel Prieto, at the time the president of the UNEAC, the Writers and Artists Union of Cuba, and now the Minister of Culture. She demands to know why esteemed writers who've recently left Cuba can't be invited back for literary events. She demands to know why Cuban Americans who are equally critical of the Castro government and the hardliners in the Miami exile community are denied the right to return.

She's so brave she scares me. Nena means "little girl" and I feel I need to protect her. Eventually Nena will cease going back to Cuba. She will grow tired of being brave. She, who others know as María de los Angeles Torres, will be done with her journeys of return to Cuba. Home isn't there anymore for her, she will say. But that will be years later.

For now she sees I am scared on that afternoon in Varadero and nudges Yoyi to return closer to the shore with her so I won't be alone. Nena and Yoyi float toward me and then we bob around together in the water like three corks, surrounded by an infinite sky.

Suddenly the water wells up beneath us so forcefully it almost knocks the three of us off kilter. Kaki appears, having soared under the water with such speed we hadn't noticed her approaching. She pulls off her mask and exclaims in her husky voice, "It's a marvelous day to go snorkeling. So many fish. So many colors. Just beautiful."

Kaki hands her mask to Nena and commands, "Go out deeper. Go see the fish."

Nena does as Kaki says and comes back exhilarated. "You're right, Kaki, it's unbelievable."

Yoyi goes next. He's thin as a rail, with the piercing eyes of a character from an El Greco painting and a thick salt-and-pepper beard that seems to weigh him down. As he swims away I worry he'll be swallowed by the sea. He barely speaks, he's a poet and measures his words. When he returns, he says in a low whisper, "*Vale la pena*." It's worth it.

It's my turn but I don't want to go.

"Let's leave it for another time," I say to Kaki.

"But what other time? There is no other time. Go, you won't see anything like this any place else."

I shake my head. "I'm sorry, I can't."

"I promise you won't drown," Kaki says. "I'll go with you. I was a life-guard for many years. I'll be there to save you."

I still say no.

"All you have to do is put your head under the water and open your eyes. Just for a minute."

"I can't. Sorry."

I could feel the sun burning my shoulders and back, but I was also burning with shame about my fears.

"*Lo que te pierdes, Rutica*," Kaki says, in a voice so gentle it shocks me. She liked to call me "Rutica," an even more tender diminutive than "Ruti."

I know I'm missing out on the chance to see something spectacular, something I'll only be able to see once in a lifetime in Cuba.

This feeling of being in Cuba and not being able to take it all in fully will come to haunt me later, on trip after trip after trip.

I can keep returning to Cuba till kingdom come.

But Cuba is lost on me.

Cuba is wasted on me.

* * *

I remember well that afternoon in Varadero Beach with Nena, Kaki, and Yoyi, when my fear kept me from looking underwater at the beauty that was begging to be seen. I remember because I got the worst sunburn in my life and winced from the pain for days afterward. But I also remember because it was there, or I want to think it was there, on that satin sand, that the idea of bridges to Cuba came to me, the idea that Cubans had been torn apart by politics but could be reunited through poetics, the poetics of bridges, of claiming a common language of history, culture, and memory.

I've never been good at politics. From the time I was a young girl I learned to fear politics. It was politics that had divided us as Cubans and it was politics that had led to tears and sadness in my own family when I expressed views that opposed the hardline position of refusing any contact with the contemporary island. The idea of bridges appealed to me because I didn't want to declare my allegiance to one side or another. I wanted to try to understand everybody, the revolutionaries, the exiles, those who stayed, those who left, and those who fell somewhere in between. I also didn't want to distinguish between exiles and immigrants. That's why I started referring to all Cubans living outside the island as forming part of a "Cuban diaspora," drawing on my experience of the Jewish diaspora and using that elastic term long before other cubanologists started using it too.

Could I call for bridges to Cuba and pretend Fidel Castro didn't exist? I wanted to believe such a thing was possible. The consensus among Cuban exiles was that they didn't want to return to Cuba because of Fidel Castro. Much as they despised him, his name was constantly on their tongues. I wanted to return to Cuba in spite of Fidel Castro. I'd never speak of him. But I was terrified he'd plant himself in my path. Reporters and celebrities visiting Cuba swooned for a chance to have their fifteen minutes of fame with the Comandante. My fear was that I'd be forced to look him in the eye. He was the Medusa who'd gaze at me and turn me to stone.

My dread of a face-to-face encounter with Fidel Castro gradually evolved into a different fear: of finding myself in Cuba on the day he takes his last breath. What would happen then? Would the insane of Mazorra, the madhouse that sits perilously close to the Havana airport, take to the streets and laugh and weep? Would blackouts envelope the island in darkness? And most worrisome of all, would the military roll out their tanks and not let anyone out, by sea or by air?

In the years following that afternoon with Nena, Kaki, and Yoyi, I would literally become a commuter to Cuba, traveling back and forth from Michigan as if it were the most natural thing in the world to do. Yet I always feared I might be trapped inside the island. I went knowing I could leave. I had a ticket out.

During my last moments at the airport in Havana, on every single trip, I still grow dizzy and faint while waiting to be cleared by Cuban army officers who always seem to scrutinize my papers with excruciating care. It's as if I feel a primal need to reenact the trauma of my departure from Cuba every time I return. But I should stop worrying. I've spoken about my fear to our former neighbors, Consuelito, who is my mother's age, and her daughter Christy, who is my age. They still live in the same apartment building where we once lived in Havana. Consuelito and Christy, who have no experience of exile or immigration or any kind of travel outside the island, say not to worry, they'll make sure I always make it back safely. To this day, they recite the rosary for me every time I'm leaving Cuba. And Christy always says the same parting words to me, "*No te preocupes, Ruti, vamos a rezar por tí, para que llegues bien.*"

So now you know: I, a woman who's afraid of putting her head under water, wanted bridges. I, a woman who selected the bridge as the metaphor for her quest to bring Cubans together, find that I'm petrified of bridges. I can't drive over a bridge without trembling. Even as a passenger, crossing a bridge like the Verrazano that seems to go on forever, I hold my breath and pray I'll reach the other side.

The fact is I have a lot of fears, all of them contradictory.

I love the ocean but, as you already know, I'm also deathly afraid of it.

I'm afraid of the dark, yet I'm happiest late at night.

I'm afraid of flying, yet I travel constantly. At least twice a month, I'm on a plane going somewhere.

The thing I most feared was traveling to Cuba. Yet after that afternoon in Varadero Beach I vowed to keep returning to Cuba and not need anybody to hold my hand. The repeating island became part of my life. I went back over and over. I found a voice in Spanish and wrote poetry that Ediciones Vigía published in beautiful artisanal editions. I learned the stories of the Jews who had stayed, each of them offering a window onto a parallel life that might have been mine. I was still afraid, but I learned to ignore the ghosts that followed me everywhere I went in Cuba.

*　*　*

Nena had told me that Kaki was a cousin of the artist Ana Mendieta, who had fallen to her death, or been pushed to her death, from a thirty-fourth-story apartment in New York City in 1985. Through an issue of *Sulfur*, a magazine published in Michigan, I had learned of Ana Mendieta's ethereal work, in which she used her own body to leave traces of her presence on earth, water, fire, and sand (she too had gathered sand from Varadero to bring back to the United States). After our afternoon in Varadero, we returned to Havana and I wanted to ask Kaki about her cousin, Ana Mendieta, ask how she remembered her, but I didn't dare.

Kaki intimidated me. She kept her hair crew cut short, accentuating the strength of her jaw. She didn't mince words. If she thought you were a fool, she told you so. She smoked Populares, which gave her the husky voice, and she had the tough stare of a boxer ready to pounce at the first sign of trouble. She was a *revolucionaria*, alright. But not a *fidelista*, she declared. She didn't intend to leave Cuba because of Him. Cuba was bigger than Him, much bigger than Him. She planned to stay until *el último capítulo*, until the last chapter was written by History. Nobody was going to push her out or silence her. She had a lot of attitude, as they say. When she raised her voice just a little, Yoyi would wilt. That's why, even though she'd understood my fear of the ocean, even though she'd called me Rutica, I was afraid of how she'd respond if I asked about Ana.

Somehow I got up the courage. It was late at night and we were at Kaki's house in Playa, an elegant house that had belonged to her mother's family, filled with art on the walls and books on the shelves. A bottle of rum was opened and shared among us, to forget that the refrigerator was empty. It was the moment of *el derrumbe*. Things had fallen apart, the last utopian ideals were unravelling. Blackouts and hunger, hunger and blackouts, day after day.

To hold on to their dignity, Kaki and Yoyi refused to succumb to the boredom of whining about *el tema*. That was the only thing everybody else wanted to talk about. Still, in the midst of conversation, Kaki and Yoyi let it slip that they appeased their growling stomachs by sipping water each morning sweetened with a spoonful of sugar. But they didn't think the grind of daily life was worth talking about and soon went back to discussing literature, art, music.

Kaki was astounded at my ignorance of Cuban history and culture. I didn't know anthropology had already been done in Cuba by Cubans of the caliber of Fernando Ortiz, Lydia Cabrera, and Manuel Moreno Fraginals. I hadn't yet read the works of the Cuban literary masters, José Lezama Lima and Virgilio Piñera. I wasn't familiar with the songs of Pablo Milanés. No one had told me that the lyrics of "Guantanamera" were verses written by our independence leader José Martí, a poet of delicate frame who tried hopelessly to become a warrior. Kaki laughed and shook her head. "*Ay, Rutica, pero tú no sabes nada.*" She was right. I didn't know anything. But the idea of bridges to Cuba had been floating around in my head and I guess I'd decided it was time to see if Kaki would laugh at that too.

I'm not sure how I phrased my question. I have a lot of respect for the spirits of the dead and I didn't want to invoke Ana's spirit in vain. I think I asked, "Kaki, would you consider writing something about Ana, your cousin? There's a magazine at Michigan, I want to put together a collection, something about bridges to Cuba." She looked back at me with her boxer's stare. And I thought to myself, What had I done? Why had I opened my mouth? I wanted to disappear into the night, as inconsequential as a moth.

Kaki stood up and walked over to a chest of drawers, an antique of carved wood. She opened one of the drawers and pulled out a few yellowed pages. "Here," she said, and handed me the pages. "I wrote this and never published it. It's about Ana. Maybe you can use it."

It was called "Silueta" and I read it immediately, breathlessly. "Years later you returned... You came with your Art, and we waited for you in the lobby of the hotel... You left and you came back several times. You were still the same little girl, passionate and argumentative. But now your soul was hard, as if covered with calluses... One day the news reached us: your silhouette had been carved, forever, indelibly, into a New York street."

This writing was a discovery for me. It was the bridge in the other direction, Kaki, writing from the island about her cousin and the impact of Ana's return on her, the one who stayed behind, the one who was there to receive Ana when she came back.

"Kaki, I must have this," I said. I held on to the pages tightly, preparing to fight to keep them.

Her gaze softened. "So you like it?"

"Yes. I like it a lot."

"You can have it. Use it for your *puentes a Cuba*."

*   *   *

Raquel Mendieta Costa, who I knew as Kaki, let me publish her piece, "Silhouette," in *Bridges to Cuba*. Afterward I invited her to the University of Michigan for the "Bridges to Cuba" conference, held in 1994. Much as we wanted to take pride in our bridges, we were in the midst of the *balsero* crisis. Cubans were plunging into the sea on flimsy rafts in a desperate effort to get to Miami while Fidel Castro allowed the floodgates to be opened. There was no bridge for the countless numbers who drowned and ended up buried in ocean graves.

Kaki was one of two Cubans from the island who'd come, all expenses paid, to be a bridge to the thirty or so of "us" who were "here" and could pay for our own travel. We wore fashionable black leather jackets as the autumn weather turned wintery. Our island guests stayed warm in borrowed parkas that were ready to be donated to the Salvation Army. Throughout the conference, they zipped up their parkas and went outside by themselves to smoke. None of "us" who were "here" had any need for tobacco.

I didn't know that Kaki wasn't planning to return to Cuba. Kaki had decided to use the bridge that I was offering in a way I hadn't counted on, to become one of "us" over "here." She kept her secret from me very well. I didn't get wind of her plans until after the end of the conference. Maybe she thought I'd have an existential crisis, or maybe she just wanted to keep up the illusion a little longer that the bridge really reached all the way to Cuba.

But later I learned that she'd broken with the island in two hugely dramatic ways: she split up with Yoyi, leaving him behind in Cuba, and once in the United States, she came out as a lesbian, entering into a relationship with a Cuban-American artist.

* * *

Jorge Luis Arcos, who I know as Yoyi, didn't attend the conference, but he participated in the book, *Bridges to Cuba*. His contribution was a letter-poem, "Epistle to José Luis Ferrer," addressed to a close friend who left Havana for Miami just before I met him and Kaki. In the poem, Yoyi shares scattered thoughts and quotations from books he's reading with José Luis, every so often breaking the flow of his narrative by inserting the refrain, "Diaspora, like death, interrupts all conversation." This reiterated line serves to remind the reader of the impossibility of maintaining a conversation with a friend who is absent.

Not even Yoyi could have imagined that one day, just over a decade later, he too would leave Cuba and write a letter-poem to say goodbye to Enrique Saínz, a friend who was staying, a friend that now he was leaving behind. No, that wasn't imaginable then, back in that moment in the early 1990s when Yoyi was unwilling to forgive those of us who'd left the island. We were the killers, we in the diaspora who dwelled in absence, we who left nothing but death in our wake.

Yoyi was still in Cuba, steadfastly in Cuba, and he wrote of a present moment that seemed enchanted, telling José Luis how he passed the time with Kaki: "In the shade of flowering mangoes or beneath inconceivable stars, Kaki and I play checkers, play Parcheesi, play Chinese checkers, roll and smoke a cigarette, drink coffee, herb tea, bitter orange, sometimes a bottle of homebrewed wine." There was happiness, vanishing happiness in Yoyi's letter: "This summer, in Varadero, we picked up many shells!" In the next line, sad again, he enclosed in a parenthesis words that would later be prophetic: "little bones in the sand."

* * *

Kaki stayed and really did try to become one of "us." She taught part-time in Chicago and then became a graduate student in literature at Stanford. She'd been a history professor in Cuba, but to be a professor "here" she had to get the degree from the United States of America. She called upon me to write a letter of recommendation, which I did gladly, but with embarrassment, remembering how huge was my ignorance of Cuban history and culture compared to her vast knowledge. It wouldn't be long, I thought, before Kaki made a big splash in the academic world—soaring up from beneath, forcefully, as she had done years before, in the ocean, in Varadero.

And then one day I was with Ester Shapiro Rok and Alan West-Durán in Boston, both of whom had been part of *Bridges to Cuba*, and the phone rang. It was Nena in Chicago telling us Kaki had taken her life in a public park in San Francisco. She had bought a gun, put it in her mouth, and blown her brains out. She was 49 years old.

The summer before, Kaki had returned to Cuba. She sank into a deep depression when she realized she was no longer part of the island, that her home there was gone. She had left her house to her only child, a son who'd married and sold her precious art and books in order to support himself and his wife. Had Kaki died because she'd lost Cuba and despaired of ever finding a real home in the United States? Had the martyrology of the Revolution and its proclamation of *patria o muerte,* sanctifying those who died for the country, scarred her psyche? Had she chosen to die outside of Cuba to demonstrate that the Revolution had failed her? Or had she died because of the withering of the passionate relationship that had led her to leave Cuba? Was she so brokenhearted she couldn't continue living?

Everyone thought they knew why Kaki had killed herself. But in truth all of us who knew her had no idea she was contemplating suicide. No one saw she was in danger. No one saw that she, the lifeguard, she, the prize swimmer, was drowning, and in need of a helping hand.

Kaki, who knew the history of Cuba better than anyone, knew that the freedom to die was the one true freedom we Cubans had always claimed as our birthright. She had died for Cuba, outside of Cuba. She knew that suicide was a path out of suffering that Taino Indians in Cuba chose in the early days of the conquest and that African slaves later also chose in the days of the colony. It is no accident that in Santería, or Regla de Ocha, as practitioners call the African religion that miraculously survived the brutality of slavery in Cuba, the dead must be called by name, one by one, before any ritual can begin. The deity of Olokkún, the one *orisha* closest to the Jewish concept of divinity because it can't be represented in images, being utterly unknowable to the human mind, lives at the bottom of the sea, watching over the multitudes who died in the crossing to the island and now die leaving the island.

Kaki had chosen to die on November 2, All Souls' Day, a sacred day in the Catholic calendar, when the living remember the departed in their prayers. She'd chosen to die asking for our prayers—all the prayers that we Cubans, an irreverent people who come from everywhere and have ended up absolutely everywhere, can possibly recite for her.

And that is why, even though I know I am not the person who should be telling this story, I am offering these words as a Kaddish for Kaki, a prayer for the peace of her soul. If the island reeks of death, then let us not forget that the Jews added their own grain of sand to the enormous beach that is the island of Cuba. Jews are a people who say Kaddish for the dead endlessly, who remember the dead for all time, and when they came to Cuba in the early twentieth century seeking refuge, they left their own obsession with death all over the landscape of Cuba, building cemeteries in tropical towns and villages that they filled with Stars of David that grew salty with the ocean breezes.

I wanted to extend a bridge to Kaki, but in the end it is this Kaddish I must offer, this uncertain prayer. I know I'm not responsible for Kaki's death, but I never forget that she came to the United States because of my bridge. She gave me her story about her cousin, Ana Mendieta, whose death she mourned, not knowing that she was foretelling her own death.

Kaki had died because she wasn't supposed to stay in the United States. She was supposed to return to Cuba, so that I could keep extending my bridge to her. But she had wanted to be part of "us" here. And "we" had welcomed her. She wasn't supposed to die. She was supposed to make good. She was supposed to take the "opportunity" offered her by the United States of America and become a "golden exile" like all the rest of us Cubans who shine with the luster of our success and fortune.

But no, Kaki had chosen to die. She had chosen to die in the year 1999, the end of the century. Kaki wanted to die turning her back on what the new century held for her, held for Cuba, held for humanity. Kaki burned the bridge. Eventually the ashes of that bridge, along with the ashes of her body, would make their way back to Cuba, to be scattered in that same ocean in Varadero where we had swum. In that same ocean brimming with the most breathtakingly beautiful fish that can only be seen by those who aren't afraid.

NOTE

Quotations from Raquel (Kaki) Mendieta Costa, "Silhouette," p. 75; and Jorge Luis Arcos, "Epistle to José Luis Ferrer (From Havana to Miami)," pp. 180–181; in Ruth Behar, ed., *Bridges to Cuba/Puentes a Cuba* (Ann Arbor, MI: University of Michigan Press, 1995). For background, see Louis A. Pérez, Jr., *To Die in Cuba: Suicide and Society* (Chapel Hill, NC: University of North Carolina Press, 2005).

CHAPTER 16

Piedra Jaimanitas

Rosa Lowinger

In the late 1990s, when Cuba was a popular destination for American cultural tour groups, I frequently led trips that focused on architecture and historic preservation. These weeklong tours would start with a three-day chronological meander through Havana. I'd spend the first day touring the old colonial city and Spanish fortifications of the sixteenth to eighteenth centuries; continue the second day on buildings from the early years of the Republic located in the vicinity of the Parque Central; then begin the third day visiting several key buildings—the Hotel Nacional, the Bacardí Headquarters, the López Serrano apartment house, and the Italianate mansion of Julio Lobo—that were all built around 1930, and finish with the brash and fabulous 1940s and 1950s, when Cuba's architects began opening their buildings to the tropical climate, making them as light filled and sensuous as the breeze off the Straits of Florida. The rest of the weeklong trip was spent visiting Cienfuegos and Trinidad, two of the island's loveliest rural colonial cities, and offering travelers a sampling of the island's music, dance, cigars, Afro-Cuban religions, and, of course, politics.

Because I am an architectural conservator, I always tended to give detailed descriptions of building materials—iron grillwork, stained glass, terracotta tile, and, inevitably, the craggy local limestone, called Piedra Jaimanitas, that since the sixteenth century has been used to construct everything from Havana's buildings to its city wall. My tour groups liked this type of information, and at some point one of the travelers would remark something like, "What beautiful stonework!" or "I never expected this place to be so rich in architecture!" when I got into details about the shell inclusions in the limestone, or explained how it had once been covered with a coat of stucco.

Often this realization about the richness of Havana's architecture was expressed on the second day of the trip—either when we were inside the Hotel Sevilla's elaborately tiled Moorish revival lobby, or on Hotel Plaza's rooftop, at eye level with the glazed terracotta mural on the upper registers of the Bacardí building's façade. For me the best moment in the trip was when someone in the group would realize finally that spectacular monuments were only part of the story—that Havana's real architectural magnificence lies in quantity. "Here is a city that contains every major international style of the last 400 years," I would explain. "You can read the entire story of the Western hemisphere in Havana's architecture."

A few years back, I asked a Cuban architectural historian friend of mine whether that was in fact true. He gave me a long and complex answer, but the bottom line was, yes, Havana was like a pop-up book that told the history of the hemisphere. I was glad to hear it, for in my tours I'd often slip into this type of bravado about Cuban history and the far-reaching influence of our music and art. I didn't make anything up, of course; but my delivery definitely tended to tip toward the dramatic. I knew that many other tour leaders, including some of my Cuban counterparts, sounded more scholarly and measured, but I couldn't help being so enthusiastic about my delivery, especially when it came to talking about materials. Piedra Jaimanitas—that local stone whose tiny shell inclusions make it particularly resilient to the local climate—seemed to me the perfect metaphor for Cuba's sovereignty. Sometimes I'd get embarrassed listening to myself talk this way. But I couldn't help it. Havana's architecture, dilapidated as it is, made me feel as passionately patriotic as the men who crowd the *esquina caliente* of the Parque Central, arguing about baseball. Even when I talked about our troubled political history, I used architecture to redeem our self-importance. For example, when I showed the group the Palacio de los Capitanes Generales, the massive Jaimanitas stone building that served as the administrative seat of the colonial government for Spain and was completed in 1776, I'd usually make some comment about how our colonists were hunkering down for the long haul at the same time the Americans were throwing theirs out. "We are a country rife in contradictions," I'd say, "but make no mistake about it, even the Revolution has served us, for if not for the fact that all real estate development ceased once private property was confiscated, we'd be looking at a lot less Art Nouveau and Art Deco and many more glaring office towers."

During these lectures, not everyone connected with my point of view, but those who did would pepper me with questions about the future: "So what's going to happen when Fidel dies? Is everything going to be torn down for developers? Could I buy an apartment here now? How can I get a jump start on investments in post-Castro Cuba?" I'd smile graciously and shrug, hoping that I wasn't revealing my feelings on the subject, which was a sinking dread in the pit of my stomach, and a sincere hope that someone somewhere was considering all these questions and coming up with answers to prevent a real estate feeding frenzy if and when the country changes back to capitalism and help preserve all that has lasted thus far. Not that I thought that all foreign investors—and particularly not the historic preservation-minded people in my groups—were going to pose the ultimate problem for the country. Indeed, much like me, who found it easy to see Havana's splendor past the peeling paint and rusting grillwork, I'd usually catch my travelers staring, with a trance-like reverence, at half-flayed murals, pink terrazzo floors, and details like a Philadelphia manufacturer's stamp on a cast iron staircase. "This was an amazing country," someone would invariably comment at those times. "It's still amazing," I'd reply.

During those years, I took a lot of heat from people who thought it was wrong to lead tours to Cuba while Castro remained in power. Interestingly, my parents, who fled in the middle of the night on January 6, 1961, losing a 1952 Vedado apartment building with black terrazzo floors and a curved staircase that my grandfather had financed with money he'd earned first with a pushcart then with dry-goods stores in Camagüey and Havana, were not among them. On the other hand, Ofelia Fox, widow of the Tropicana cabaret's owner Martin Fox, and my collaborator on a book I wrote about the night-club, clearly felt that my trips were at best misguided, and at worst a method of, to quote the cliché, "putting dollars into Castro's pocket." In our long interview sessions, held several nights a week at her Glendale, California home around a bar that, despite its location in a suburban den, somehow managed to retain all the cheer and spirit of her husband's famous outdoor nightspot, there would always be a point when the conversation would turn to my travels. "We saw shocking pictures the other day, of buildings collapsing after rain-storms. It's really criminal," she remarked one night as she prepared martinis. When I explained that it's precisely because of this that I like to travel to Cuba, take photographs, offer my Cuban conservation colleagues my twenty-plus years of experience in architectural conservation, she laughed in a bemused fashion, like she was humoring my claim that anything apart from personal adventure was the real motive for my travels. In a way, she was right. I liked going to Havana. I liked the clang and music of the streets, the rough scent of the air—a mix of salt, heat, frying onions, pungent unfiltered cigarettes and cigars—and the artists, writers, tour guides, bus drivers, and architects whose lives had become twined with mine. Though the agencies I worked for were willing to pay for a hotel room for me, I chose, instead, to stay in a friend's two-bedroom Vedado apartment, whose layout was almost identical to the place my parents had abandoned in 1961. I shopped for fruits and vegetables in an open-air market in the shadow of a building with curved Art Deco bal-conies and had my nails done in a house where the 1920s tile pavers formed complicated patterns. So, yes, Ofelia clearly had a point; but I had a book to finish, so I carefully avoided taking the bait when she challenged me on the subject of travel to Cuba. Frankly, one of the main points I was trying to make in *Tropicana Nights: The Life and Times of the Legendary Cuban Nightclub* was that Cuban culture and history is something we can all be proud of—no matter where we live and what political beliefs we hold. So even when Ofelia plainly stated that it was wrong to travel to communist Cuba for any reason but perfectly fine to vacation in communist China or Vietnam, or implied that I was a Castro-apologist for suggesting that the Cuban government's use of Tropicana as a major revenue source had at least kept the buildings well preserved and the grounds nicely manicured, I held my tongue.

Shortly before our publication date for *Tropicana Nights*, when Ofelia was already ill with the cancer she eventually succumbed to, I learned how deeply she and one of her closest *comadres* actually resented my position on travel to Cuba and preservation of its architecture. "We are sick of hearing you make excuses for Fidel Castro by saying that thanks to the Revolution we have la Habana Vieja or la Catedral," wrote a friend of Ofelia's to me in an e-mail that accused me of everything from being a "pinky with obviously pinky friends" to a "leftist *comemierda*" to a "liberal fool." That three-page diatribe, written a year and a half after the United States Treasury Department's Office of Foreign Assets Control had banned all cultural trips to Cuba, was the product of stress over Ofelia's terrible illness—she had stage four colon and liver cancer. Still, it was disheartening to realize that even three years of close collaboration on a book in which I took great pains to balance the political positions of Cubans who stayed, Cubans who left, Cubans who travel to Cuba under the communist regime, and those who do not, could not bridge the gap between us.

*　*　*

In 2003, shortly after the Bush administration announced that by year's end all cultural tours to Cuba would be abolished, there was a mad rush to send groups out for the last few weeks of sanctioned travel. That winter I led something like eight groups in two months. Every Sunday morning I would find myself in the Plaza de Armas, gathering my dazed and jetlagged group before the Castillo de la Real Fuerza, the oldest Spanish fortress in the Americas, recounting the story of Columbus and Diego Velásquez, Hernán Cortés, and the hemisphere's conquest.

The last time I began that lecture—I believe it was December 29, 2003—I found myself struggling for content. Maybe it was because I knew that this was going to be my last tour for a long time—I don't know—but I couldn't come up with a coherent historical narrative. Instead, I found myself only able to talk about materials. In front of the Castillo de la Real Fuerza, for example, I began to describe the fortress's perfect proportions, its Renaissance sensibility, its history first as a garrison, then as the residence of the first Captains General who administered the island government, when I switched into a lengthy and overly effusive narrative about the coastal areas where Piedra Jaimanitas was quarried and the evils of cleaning it by sandblasting.

I got stuck on the same tack in the Cathedral Plaza. Shouting above the bustle of musicians who played on the patio of a mansion-turned-café where a palm reader once told me I'd find true love only when I stopped traveling so much, I couldn't say much about the history of the Jesuits in Cuba, or the moneyed families that built mansions around the plaza, but instead spent the entire time talking about the casting of the bronze bells that grace the Baroque cathedral's asymmetrical towers, and the difference between true stained glass and the brightly colored fanned windows that are ubiquitous above the doorways of Havana's oldest mansions. By the time we headed down Mercaderes street toward the Plaza de San Francisco, I felt like I was taking elemental slivers of the city, inspecting them under a microscope, and committing them to memory. Iron forging, wood carving, concrete casting, and glazing tile—these were the only things that seemed to make sense to me at that moment. Unlike the influence of the Spanish, the Americans, or the Fidelistas, these were tangible, irrefutable occurrences. One could not argue whether they'd been good or bad for the country.

Of course, that's me thinking of this in retrospect. At the time I was just trying to construct a story that made sense. Once we emerged onto the Plaza de San Francisco—a broad open space flanked by a colossal red-roofed customs house, a Renaissance revival stock exchange from 1909, and a sixteenth-century Franciscan church, even that line of discourse dissolved. I grew lightheaded. Unfocused. It was a bright, windy day, so I attributed my reticence to loss, and my dizziness to dehydration and the blinding whiteness of the pavement and the Piedra Jaimanitas in the plaza. I led the group into the dark, cool church. My eyes adjusted and I quickly recovered my composure. I took another tack, this time beginning with a lecture on the hurricane that destroyed the church's nave in 1828. In the middle of my talk someone in the group said, "Holy cow, I'm seeing things. I think that plaza blinded me!" I, too, had been seeing occasional pale wisps of air floating among us; but thought this was a trick of light produced by going from a sun-drenched plaza to a dark interior. But now I clearly saw something— amorphous human shapes, moving through walls and out into the courtyard. My heart raced. I was overcome by a powerful euphoria. I started following these figures up the stairs, but then our tour group leader—a friend from Los Angeles with whom I'd worked for years—remarked that we had only five more minutes before we had to move on to lunch.

Later that afternoon, after we'd visited the fortresses across the harbor (where I recovered my ability to lecture), I went back to the Convento for another look. The wind was up and birds were flying through the vestries of the second cloister. I spent more than an hour climbing the stairs from level to level, walking from courtyard to courtyard, and seeing nothing out of the ordinary. But that unbridled joy returned—a joy mixed with a desire to weep.

On the last two days of the trip—the last times I would be in Cuba for at least two years—I went back to the Convento de San Francisco several times each day, hoping against hope that some personal truth was going to be revealed to me before I left the island. Nothing was, of course. But I expect someday I'll get some further clarity on the subject. And though I'm not really sure if what I saw was real, or if it (whatever "it" is) was especially tied to the convento itself or to the city in general and its materials in particular, I sure hope those buildings will be standing when I get a chance to go back.

CHAPTER 17

Going Home Via Africa and
Cayo Hueso

Alan West-Durán

Cayo Hueso is a poor neighborhood of Havana, mostly but not exclusively black, that holds a unique place in Cuban lore, especially Afro-Cuban culture. Many great artists hail from there, such as Omara Portuondo and El Tosco (José Luis Rodríguez of NG La Banda). The streets are treacherously pockmarked, the dust swirling about could choke a horse, and the poverty is noticeable, but not crushing. The running joke is that Cayo Hueso is where Superman came, took off his cape, and wept in desperation. It is here where my *padrino* Félix lives, a block and a half from the Parque Trillo. I first met him in November of 2003, through a mutual friend and photographer, Héctor Delgado.

Over the years my interest in Regla de Ocha (also known as Santería) went from being cultural curiosity to impassioned quest for knowledge to vital necessity, launching me to direct research that eventually immersed me further in its philosophy, rituals, and practice. The curiosity was aroused many years ago, in the late 1970s, when I first heard Yoruba chants and *batá* drumming that left me breathless. Something stirred in me despite not knowing a word of Lucumí, but this commotion stayed on hold as I became a political activist during most of the 1980s.

My interest in the religion as an integral part of Cuban culture never vanished, resurrecting again in Puerto Rico, where I was lucky enough to go to a *tambor*, taken there by friend and author Mayra Santos Febre. At the *tambor* I was standing next to a man in his thirties who suddenly became a vessel for Yemayá. The orisha of the oceans inhabited him for over an hour, during which he twirled around and danced like her, his voice changing pitch to that of a woman, and he went around offering advice and admonitions to those present (and willing to listen). Later, he was placed in a white and blue dress, Yemayá's colors. Exhausted from the experience, he still agreed to speak to me afterward, where I realized he had not remembered a thing about his movements, his voice change, or his words of advice.

Similarly, at another *tambor* in Puerto Rico I saw Ogún mount someone, whereupon the *santero* proceeded to down two bottles of rum in less than half an hour. When he came out of the trance he was impressively sober and had not a whiff of alcohol on his breath. Both these experiences were exhilarating, troubling, and of course, inexplicable from a rational point of view, and left me with a deep respect if not an incomplete understanding of a realm of belief that would need much greater attention and study.

When my family left Cuba I was seven and a half years old. Baseball, not Santería, was my passion and I was a Cienfuegos fan, my older brothers *fanáticos* of Almendares and Havana, respectively. There is a framed photo of all three of us in the uniforms of our teams, with my pants slipping below my waist, in a sort of avant-la-lettre hip-hop fashion. We arrived in Puerto Rico—after brief stays in Houston, New Orleans, and Panama—when I was ten and a half.

Puerto Rico was more than welcoming, and interestingly these formative years made me both more Puerto Rican and more Cuban at the same time. More Puerto Rican because I found it difficult to identify with Cubans in Puerto Rico, who tended to be extremely clannish, snobbish, and dismissive of Puerto Ricans, not to mention their politics which, as I grew older, I did not share in the least, be it Vietnam, Puerto Rican independence, the Allende government in Chile, or the Young Lords, whom I joined briefly when they came to organize (disastrously) on the island. So my new baseball hero became (and still is!) Roberto Clemente, my political inspirations Albizu Campos and Juan Antonio Corretjer, my cultural icons Clemente Soto Vélez, Willie Colón, and Eddie Palmieri. This exploration of *boricua*-ness led me to examine my Cuban roots too, embracing the likes of Martí, Maceo, Pablo Milanés, Fernando Ortiz, and Los Van Van. The only times I saw these loyalties as divided was when Puerto Rico and Cuba faced each other in sports. On principle, I always rooted for Puerto Rico because they were the underdog. It helped that I also knew the boricua players, sometimes personally.

In Puerto Rico I also was a member of the Antonio Maceo Brigade, even though I never went on any of the trips and thus was not featured in the film *55 Hermanos,* nor did I become overly involved in Brigade politics, despite supporting its aims and goals. My first trip back to Cuba was as a translator and group leader for a Health Psychology conference in 1984. Again, despite my politics, I wanted to experience Cuba as independently as possible for the times. Being involved with the Brigade in Puerto Rico allowed me to *recuperar* a Cuban identity that was quite distinct from that of most of my compatriots who lived on the island. I was not alone; many Cubans in Puerto Rico were straddling those identities, combining the catch phrases for Puerto Rican identity (*boricua, jíbaro*) with their Cuban equivalents (*cubano, guajiro*) to invent new terms for themselves as *BoriCubas* or *guajíbaros.*

Soon after the *tambores* in Puerto Rico, in February 1996, I gave a talk on Ocha at Brown University as part of Black History Month. The first question I was asked at the end of my presentation was: are you a *santero?* I asked why, and several students chimed in that I presented it so convincingly that they just assumed I would be. That should have been a sign—and, of course, it was—but I didn't completely own up to it at that moment.

Barely two years later, in fall of 1998, Cuban photographer Héctor Delgado came to Northeastern University to show and speak about his excellent work on both Ocha and Palo (in black and white, predigital days). One of his more striking images was of a *palero* with his eyes closed and an open outstretched hand. His other hand held a candle that had dripped considerable hot wax onto it, again reflecting how the spiritual realm can defy the limitations of our physical world.

Delgado visited a few more times (obviously before the pre-2003 clamp-down) just as I started to visit Cuba more often, taking groups. I finally decided to have a *registro* (a reading of the cowry shells) done. I found out my *ángel de la guardia* was Yemayá, which I had suspected, but the *diloggún* often suggests otherwise. A Yemayá necklace was going to be prepared for me, which I had to come and collect at the end of the day. I had an interview with the rap group Obsesión in, of all places, Regla. (Yemayá is syncretically linked with the Virgin of Regla, who protects this important Cuban port city.)

On the way back from Regla, I asked Héctor if the shells could be read again to see whether I should become a *santero*. Then the idea stopped me cold, but as we drew closer to Félix's house to pick up the Yemayá necklace, I thought, why not? I asked Héctor, what if the reading says I should *hacer santo* and I don't want to? He looked at me and said, "That's between you and the orishas, don't look at me!" So the registro was again performed and sure enough the orishas said I had to become a *santero*, but there was no rush, that I should do it before I died. I prayed that this was not a sign that I was going to die soon.

The first *registro* of the day had predicted that even though I looked strong and healthy I would become ill. Six months later I was detected with fairly severe arthritis in my back and knees. The registro also said I would be facing a huge amount of paperwork. Tenure was around the corner. I thought: this *padrino* was good, considering that we had just only met. I felt I was in good hands, and truly believe that much of what makes an initiation relationship work is the level of trust that is built between *santero* and initiate. Sacred and human realm bleed into each other. The day of the reading proved to be the beginning of a new family that I would be part of. Despite the familiarity and deep bonding between us, we refer to each other in the *usted* form, very un-Cuban: I because he is my *padrino*, to show respect, but since I am a university professor, *un profesional*, he also wants to show respect.

After 2003 travel to Cuba became difficult, and I did not go again for almost two and a half years. I submitted a research proposal to investigate and document Regla de Ocha in late 2005, particularly its use of space as one that defines Cuban modernity. As I waited for an answer in April, my mother fell ill, was hospitalized, and then died in early May of 2006. When

I visited her in the hospital I brought some candles to light in her room, one being of the *Siete Potencias Africanas* (Seven African Powers). Right after I lit them up one of the male nurses walked in and saw the candle. He looked puzzled, and then smiled. It turned out he was a son of Changó. Five days after my mother passed I heard about the grant, which would allow me to travel to Cuba three times within a year.

On the first trip (August) I received the necklaces, the *guerreros*, and Olokun, all while documenting two different santos, one Elegguá and the other Changó. This all happened in about seventeen days, ending with a celebration to Yemayá, since my last day in Cuba was September 7. In that period I personally saw or lived through almost every major ceremony in the life of a *santero,* from necklaces to *misas blancas* to *asiento*, and even the truly amazing *cajón al muerto* ceremony.

I received the necklaces and *guerreros* while the Elegguá was being initiated, which meant that I was getting some extra *aché* from this initiate. A fortyish theater director from the island who now lived in Madrid, he looked half his age and was truly the living incarnation of Elegguá: youthful, playful, a real trickster. His transparency in being Elegguá made me think about the archetypes that the orishas embody and how each individual is enmeshed (or not) with said archetypes. So in some ways orishas can be a complement to what is missing in our soul. I adore Yemayá, but am I the embodiment of maternal traits? Do I follow her stern demeanor in meting out justice? Not exactly.

We could neither be with him nor document his Día del Raspado (the day his head is shaved and the *aché* is administered), but I shared fully with him on his Día del Medio, where I sat on the mat with him, eating the seven types of meat that had been offered in sacrifice the day before. At first I felt shy, as if I were crowding his moment, but then I remembered the story of Eleguá as being the great purveyor of *aché* and how he reacted when Oloddumare appointed him messenger to all of the orishas. Instead of bragging or puffing his chest out in pride, he threw a banquet and invited all of the other orishas to share his good fortune. *Aché* breeds generosity and this Elegguá was generous to a fault.

Several things came to the fore during these intense days of observation and experience: an amazingly subtle use of space that went from sacred to profane effortlessly, a truly collective sense of work and worship woven around the different ceremonies or rituals, as well as a revelatory and empowering sense of what it meant to enter into conversation with the orishas. I must qualify the word conversation by invoking its ancient meaning of "inhabiting or dwelling among others." Of course, the most immediate sense of conversation happens indirectly through the *registro,* where the orishas speak through the shells, the *diloggún.* However, it is not a matter of the orishas speaking through the shells while the initiate merely listens and obeys. As an initiate, you enter into a dialogue with the orishas, the *oriaté*, and yourself, and you even talk back. This is even truer on the day of the Itá reading, where someone else (not your *padrino* or *madrina*) interprets the shells for you, and you enter into a conversation with the orishas, the *oriaté*, your *padrino*, as well as friends or family members present who might know something about you. It is a supremely moving and thoroughly democratic and spiritual conversation about your past, present, and future.

The most interesting case of "talking back" I witnessed was in a *cajón al muerto*, an extraordinary ceremony where the rumba *cajones* are played in a religious context. A young *santero-palero-espiritista* brought down the spirit of a sixteenth-century Haitian slave named Francisco. In a broken Spanish that combined elements of *bozal* (Spanish as once spoken by recently arrived Africans) with what seemed like Haitian Kreyol, Francisco started to reveal very personal—and unflattering—information about one of the people present. The person spoke back to Francisco and said "This is not the place to discuss this, especially in front of others." Francisco obliged and turned to someone else. In my case, Francisco told me that I had to undergo initiation as soon as possible. My *padrino* Félix interceded to calm Francisco down and then said, don't worry, I will consult with Yemayá and explain that that was not possible, at least not for a while.

My second trip was planned to document San Lázaro (or Babalú Ayé), whose feast day, December 17 (also my wife Ester's birthday), was characterized by hundreds of thousands of pilgrims who go to the church in Rincón, a little beyond the town of San Antonio de la Vega. Some believers go on their knees all the way from the center of Havana, a distance of nearly fifteen miles. This was both thrilling and exhausting, with huge crowds, lots of walking, and an extraordinary outpouring of faith and hope in this tiny church. The Rincón church has one of the most beautiful St. Lazarus images in the world, as well as niches with La Caridad del Cobre (Ochún) and Yemayá (the Virgin of Regla).

But the true revelation happened when we were walking in Old Havana near the intersection of O'Reilly and—what else?—Calle Cuba. I heard the batá drums about half a block away, unmistakable and relentless in their drive and poetic modulation. We headed over to the apartment building in question. There were people hanging out on the balcony. I called up and asked what was happening. All I heard was the word Yemayá. When I said I was a son of Yemayá they waved Ester and me up.

After making my offering and prayer to one of the most spectacular altars to any orisha I had ever seen, we realized that it was really a *tambor* for three *iyawós*, or initiates: Elegguá, Ochún, and Changó. In the *tambor* ceremony, one of the most beautiful rituals of Ocha, the *iyawó* is presented to the sacred drums amidst a group of *santeros* who dance and chant. Since I was dressed in white they invited me into the circle of dancers and chanters and fortunately they began with Elegguá, whose chant I knew. They were surprised I knew the words, this *cubanito de afuera* who looked like a *yuma*, a guy from the United States. On occasions, someone will be possessed by an orisha. The drums are splendidly decorated with flags, sequins, shells, cloth, bells, banners and the like. The *iyawó* lays down before the drum, then kisses it, and finally places his or her head on it (on all three drums). The sound of the drum going straight into your head is the closest thing to heaven on (and in) earth that you can imagine.

I look at the photo taken of me on my Día del Medio, from the top of my open Yemayá crown, revealing my shaved head painted in blue patterns. I go back to that moment where I'm in the *igbodú* (the sacred room where the initiation takes place). The bath with the *omiero*, the cutting off of locks of hair, and the shaving that is accompanied by the most elegant chanting I've ever heard by the *obbá* who is shaving me along with my *padrino*, two young male *santeros* and seven women *santeras*, almost all of them initiates of Yemayá. All of this intense activity, followed by the placement of the *aché* into my head, happened with my eyes closed.

When I opened my eyes an hour or so later things indeed looked different. The *aché* in my head gave off an incredible warmth that lasted for about three days; the room had a strange glow that you could feel but not see, the sweat dripping off the *santeros* glistened in the ninety-seven-degree heat of mid-July: all this was coupled with a feeling of exhaustion and relief. But that was soon followed by animal sacrifice, *la matanza de animales*, which happened with an admirable velocity and efficiency.

Every single creature was presented to me and positioned at different parts of my body. Having my head pressed to a goat's forehead, looking into its eyes, then briefly placing it between my legs before handing it over to the knife was extremely moving, as I simultaneously experienced both a sense of unease and true calm. I had witnessed and documented this ritual on camera several times, and perhaps the detachment necessary to do so kept me at a safe distance. This particular ritual is always shaped by strong emotions and sensations: the heat of the room, the smell of blood, feathers, entrails, the different people moving about, the sound of live animals that will be offered next, cigarette smoke, and the absolute focus of the *santero* wielding the knife create an intensity that often borders on the unbearable. But being the *iyawó* imbued with me an eerie calm, helping me understand more fully the Yoruba notion of sacrifice. Aside from the obvious (the blood is for the orishas; the meat, cleaned and cooked, is for the *santeros*), one sees a dynamic steeped in spiritual concerns. The consumption or killing of an animal is not something proper to you, but an act that entails an equilibrium of cosmic forces, also creating a community that brings forth *aché*. All sorts of rules govern this act: unknown to me one of the goats died before it could be offered. That goat could not be part of the ceremony, so a mad scramble ensued to find a new and live one while the ceremony was in progress. The goat was delivered by bici-taxi to the *padrino*'s home just in time. While symbolically there is a death and rebirth in the *raspado* (shaving of the head), the *matanza* grounds the *raspado* in a literal sense without losing any of the philosophical or spiritual dimensions.

I have been asked how have I changed since becoming a *santero*. This is not an easy question to answer. My friend, photographer Héctor Delgado, claims that I am calmer, more relaxed, and exhibit a kind of spiritual serenity that was not there before. I feel this also as well as a strong connection to both ancestral spirits and a more intense relationship with Yemayá. But at times I grow impatient, drink too much wine, get stressed, act selfishly, and can irritate other people. I remind myself that I am still an *iyawó* and have nine more months of wearing white and being especially observant. This further reminds me that initiation is just that: a beginning. A new beginning, of course, but still a beginning, one that I cocreate with my orisha, as in the song by Gema y Pavel:

> Elewa te enseña el camino
> pero no te enseña el andar
> cada día se hace el destino
> la suerte no se sienta a esperar
> . . . .
> y ponle una vela a los santos
> pero no te acueste' a dormir
> si tu mismo no te la juega'
> no hay nadie que lo haga por ti.

> [Elewa shows you the path
> but not how to walk
> destiny is made day by day
> good luck does not sit and wait
> . . . .
> and light a candle to the saints
> but don't lie down and doze
> if you don't lay it on the line
> no one will do it for you.]

Am I now more Cuban because I am the child of Yemayá? The simple answer would be yes, but what could be more universal and less bound by territory than the ocean? I know Mexican, Colombian, Jewish, Puerto Rican, and Italian *santeros*. Are they more Cuban and less Mexican (Colombian, etc.) because they have become *santeros*? Maybe, but in their cases their initiation represents a different kind of homecoming (spiritual) while my own is one that is plainly rooted in family and past in a visceral and physical sense that I carry in my body at all times, like breath.

Describing some elements of this spiritual journey—which is now just beginning, despite the lengthy period leading up to my *asiento*—has led me to a Cuba I knew about and had studied, but had not actually lived. In a sense, going back to Havana from Boston to Cayo Hueso meant taking a detour through Africa. A Cuban Africa, but Africa nonetheless. In my own fashion, I have geographically, culturally, and spiritually traced the contours of Gilroy's "Black Atlantic," one of the great engines of modernity. During this process I have witnessed how Regla de Ocha is a true expression of Cuban modernity, not a quaint remnant of African tradition that lingers in current Cuba. I could offer anecdotal evidence for the modernity of Ocha, such as the time when Héctor Delgado sent daily e-mails with photographic attachments to my wife Ester in Boston, a kind of blow-by-blow (image-by-image?) account of my initiation. Her favorite photograph is of me on the throne, dressed as Yemayá, all in blue, with the crown on my head with her trademark fan in my left hand. But that is a superficial image of the religion's modernity, which, of course does not invalidate its millennial roots. If we see how Ocha modifies and redefines space, if we examine its philosophical subtlety, its pragmatism, its capacity to syncretize with other religions, its ability to heal and how it does so, its fluidity in bridging technology with artisan traditions, its uncanny way of bridging the world of the living and the dead, the visible and the unseen realms, then Ocha's modernity becomes much more apparent as an exhilaratingly creative example of Cuban modernity.

Let me return to the *cajón al muerto*. When I listened to Francisco, the sixteenth-century Haitian slave, I was witnessing a voice of history speaking. There was nothing scary about it: this was a spirit speaking, not a ghost. Ghosts haunt. Spirits speak. In Cuba, modernity speaks through tradition, in the magnificent, comforting, belligerent, irreverent voices of the orishas.

CHAPTER 18

Writing from Babylon

Pedro Pérez Sarduy

(Translated by David Frye)

For a Cuban poet, especially one of African descent, living in London might seem heretical. But, despite her unsettled and volatile weather, her rich mix of sobriety and extravagance, elegance and slovenliness, entertainment and crime, indiscretions and scandals among royals, parliamentarians, pagans, and swindlers—all connected to the overwhelming vitality of the media that thrive within its formidable urban anatomy—London is one of the most exuberant cities of the modern world, one that always holds some surprise to discover.

Among its attractions, since 1966 London has offered a Caribbean carnival that draws nearly two million fans a year from across Europe during the August Bank Holiday. Exotic rhythms and their followers abound here, with an impressive dollop of specialists in capoeira, tango, and salsa. Notable among these are the self-proclaimed "Cuban salsa masters"—much sought-after instructors of that popular hybrid dance, who are not necessarily Cuban, much less "masters." Not that it matters. The bottom line is being able to say, "Made in Cuba."

The weekly *Time Out* tells us that more than 2,000 London restaurants offer "ethnic food," drawing on the cuisines of the world. London's voracious ethnic appetite is supported by groceries and open markets that sell foods, spices, and ingredients from many distant lands, including Cuba. Here we find Cuba Libre, Cubana, and the two latest additions you mustn't miss. One is La Bodeguita del Medio (La B del M)—translated as the Little Bar in the Middle of the Block—a restaurant located in a cozy alleyway in the posh borough of Kensington. It is named for the emblematic bar located in Old Havana, established in 1942 and famed as the home of the Mojito cocktail and favorite haunt of many Bohemian artists and writers including Cuban National Poet Nicolás Guillén and American writer Ernest Hemingway. The other one is Floridita, named for Cuba's signature bar-restaurant, where Hemingway adopted the famous Cuban cocktail named Daiquirí for a lovely white-sand beach near Santiago de Cuba. London's Floridita, in the lively central neighborhood of Soho, and La Bodeguita del Medio both offer a wide variety of supposedly Cuban dishes that are actually cooked up by a medley of chefs from other regions, each recreating the Creole taste in their own way. Here, for example, they serve grilled chicken breast marinated in hot sauce—even though any Cuban will tell you that our sauces avoid hot spices, due mainly to the strong influence of Spanish cuisine, which is rich in sauces based on onions, tomatoes, and only the mildest of peppers. Nonetheless, among the amenities offered by this Floridita are a good selection of the best music groups direct from Cuba, Cuban drinks, and even a Cuban cigar emporium, La Casa del Habano, with a resident cigar maker temporarily imported from the island.

London was not always like this.

A quarter century ago, restaurants and supermarkets that offered such products labeled them, almost pejoratively, as "ethnic food," while the musical rhythms that went along with them were generically described as "world music." In short, we were "the other," exotic and anodyne.

But yesteryear's "alternative" is today's common denominator. London is no longer a purely English city, properly speaking, and not even a strictly European one. Due to her perfidious past as the capital of the empire on which the sun never set, she remains a crossroads of sorts, a meeting place for diverse cultures, though she has never pretended to be a "melting pot." With a population of eight million, plus commuters from thirteen counties, London has evolved into a multitude of small cities incrusted in a sprawling megalopolis of low-rise buildings, where the colors of architecture and flora from various periods harmonize tastefully. In this way, each lucky Londoner can have the pleasure of constructing, bit by bit, his or her own London, around private or collective housing, well-preserved old houses (ours was built in 1895, the waning days of the Victorian era), or apartments built atop the ruins left by World War II bombing raids in several areas of the city.

It was here that I came to live with my English partner and our two children in 1981, and here where, three years later, I conceived the idea of writing an impressionistic fresco of short vignettes that I entitled *Diario en Babilonia* (*Journal in Babylon*), using the name bestowed on England by the followers of Jamaican reggae.

Back then, you could count the Cubans living in London on your fingers, and few of the locals had a very clear idea about where Cuba was located. There were none of today's clubs and restaurants with allegorical names from the largest island in the Caribbean, just a few danced to the rhythm of the *son cubano*, Virgin Atlantic didn't fly to Havana, and Cubana de Aviación didn't provide the direct flights to London that since then have built an uninterrupted and almost daily human bridge across the Atlantic from various cities in the United Kingdom.

A quarter of a century back, Cuban emigrants had little reason to look for anything they could identify with culturally. Those were confusing times for anyone who decided to move from Cuba. If emigrating is an act replete with complexities, emigrating from Cuba multiplies those complexities, especially given the inherent political implications of the act. Besides, Europe in general and Britain in particular have never been the Cuban emigrant's destination of first choice.

Anyway, I began to like this city, perhaps because my ties with it, and with this island, are different. And just as the British took Havana for a few months in 1762 without ever occupying the entire island of Cuba, I set myself the goal of "taking London." I imagine that if the British had colonized Cuba, my relationship to Britain and London would have been different. It is here, in this fabulous city that I have learned to make my own, that refugees and political exiles, philosophers, writers and artists, revolutionaries, patriots, legal and illegal immigrants, virtual and fictitious dissidents, dilettantes, and accidental snobs have found shelter. All told, a healthy contingent of voluntary or forced exiles from almost every corner of the world.

In this same city, more than a thousand Cuban men and women thrive today, few of whom require the protections extended by the United Nations Human Rights Council. Take me, for example, a mere poet, born and raised in the city of Santa Clara under the watchful gaze of my paternal grandmother and a host of aunts and uncles, then transplanted in the early 1960s to a one-room tenement flat in the working-class Havana neighborhood of El Cerro, where my divorced mother was trying to rebuild her life, and from where I set forth daily to defy the culture of poverty at the School of Letters in the University of Havana.

I shared my life in that crowded building with Jean, a young English graduate student who had arrived in Havana in 1968 from a rebellious and psychedelic London that was sheer literary fiction for me. Joined together in matrimony (mainly to avoid institutional harassment), we lived in various Havana hotels from 1970 to 1977. During this period our two children were born. First our son Ilmi, then our daughter Sahnet.

Moving back to El Cerro, for three years we enjoyed the comfortable use of a modest apartment in a building set aside for "microbrigades," until we finally decided to emigrate, moving of our own free will to London without the stigma of having reached the "point of no return." Our children graduated from university and have become successful professionals in their respective fields of applied arts: Ilmi is an animation illustrator, and Sahnet a fashion designer. Since 1990 my trips to Cuba have become more frequent.

Today, racially mixed couples in Britain are very common. Cubans are not exceptions.

From the point of view of exoticism, this mixing affects me personally. It stood out more in Havana in the mid-1960s, and to a lesser degree over the next several years, than it did here in London. What's more, I can testify that, ironically, I have rarely felt here the kind of racism expressed against us as a couple that I have in Cuba, especially in Havana, a city distinguished above all by its fantastic hybridity. During the 1960s and 1970s, in response to the Afro-American initiative to affirm that "black is beautiful," many of us young Afro-Cubans also let our curly hair grow out gracefully. I was a student at the University of Havana's School of Letters, which the commissars of the day had branded as a lair infested with extravagant, alienated youth with Western and therefore decadent tendencies. (By the way, one of those rule-enforcing party members was the late author Jesús Díaz, our professor of Marxism, a course one had to pass at all costs. His Stalinist homophobia together with his leftist extremism was beyond ridiculous.) Our pseudo-intellectual pretensions were rebuffed by the entire conservative and racist spectrum that had ruled the Cuban subconscious since the very failure of the Republic. On top of this, very few people of African descent had chosen the field of humanities. Thus, our heresy was multifaceted.

Eventually, I got my first good job in Havana in the mid-1960s, shortly before I finished my university studies, at the Instituto Cubano de Radiodifusión, which later became the Instituto Cubano de Radio y Televisión. The norm of "good appearances" demanded by my profession as a journalist meant I had to be smartly dressed (in Sovietized proletarian clothing), close-shaved, and with neatly trimmed hair. Rejecting these demands stigmatized me once more as a "conflictive" and "problematic" individual, earning me gibes, rebuffs, and even a few academic reprimands at the university and sanctions at work. That's how things were in those years of my youth.

Nothing of the sort happened to me years later, when I worked in the same profession as a journalist for the BBC World Service, the famous British radio network that is as closely monitored by the British state as Cuban radio is by Cuba. Making me even more exotic, I was the only Cuban (of African descent, at that) in the entire Latin American bureau, though I had many colleagues from African and Asian countries in the other foreign services. For many of my Latin American colleagues, this was the first time they had worked closely with a Cuban of African descent, and several of them hardly knew (or accepted) people of African descent in their own countries. In short, after twenty odd years of socializing in Britain with people of varied social classes and ethnic groups, there was only one occasion, not in London, when I have been the object of racial insult, which is now treated as a crime and is subject to penalties. And this in a country where racist crimes have regrettably been making the news in recent years. Despite the well-intentioned efforts of British authorities and institutions to counter racist outrages that might incite racial hatred, many British nationals persist in defining themselves, at least privately, as instinctive racists, given to a taciturn sort of violence.

In Cuba, during those years from the mid-1960s to the late 1970s, loud insults were frequently hurled from bus windows when some passenger or other saw me strutting down La Rampa (the well-known Calle 23 that empties into Havana's Malecón) on my way home from work. "Negrooooooo! Afrooooo! Get that nappy hair cut!" It pains me to have to describe it so graphically, but that's how it was. Though this kind of verbal insult might be considered part of the Cuban folklore we so love to celebrate when we attribute it to our much-trumpeted *choteo cubano,* our "Cuban humor," by any lights it is politically incorrect. But what could you expect, given the impeccable credentials that we Cubans as a people, and Cuba as nation, have held as the most racist nation in the Spanish Caribbean? It is true that no serious racially motivated crimes have been carried out in Cuba, yet many of the old esthetic and cultural norms remain in force in many of the country's institutions.

Altogether, I feel that, as an Afro-Cuban or Cuban of African descent, I have been more exotic in my native land than here in the United Kingdom that took me in as an immigrant, and where racial fraternizing and mixing continues to be concentrated in urban spaces due to its nature and social structure. I recall now that my first impression of England, upon my arrival one freezing cold January morning in 1981, was quite different, as I have reflected in a chapter of my *Journal in Babylon,* entitled "If white folks hadn't existed. . . ."

This is how it all began. A fragment:

When it was my turn at the customs desk at Gatwick International Airport, a pale blonde woman, working half time, absolutely uninterested in pretending to be sympathetic in the attention she paid to "aliens," meticulously examined my passport, arching her thick eyebrows and staring at me coldly to verify whether the face on the photograph was mine. She inspected my visa, of course, and keyed some input into her computer to indicate that I was coming from a "Communist country," but I think it must have replied, "All in order." Finding no obstacle to letting me through, she let out, "So you people are allowed to travel with this?" "You people" were the Cubans, no doubt. "This" was my plain passport, whose equally plain gray color didn't help much, to tell the truth, given that Cuba is a sunny country almost 365 days of the year and is surrounded by a bright bluegreen sea. I, too, would have imagined that the color of my passport should have been magenta, amber, turquoise. She was right. But. . . was she really referring to that detail, the implications of that connotation? It wasn't worth just then to give her the reply I imagined she deserved. I wasn't yet trained in responding to the British sense of irony. That would take long and constant on-site training, which of course would mean learning their culture. "Of course I can travel with it, ma'am," I said suavely, accompanying my statement with my best prefabricated smile. She returned my passport after stamping it with the proper stamp, while pointing out some of the official regulations I would have to comply with over the next seventy-two hours at the police station nearest my place of residence. Leaving the climate-controlled space of the airport, I confronted for the first time in my life the natural air conditioning that kept the air around me at about four degrees celsius below freezing. My tropicalized long-sleeved safari shirt and the wool sweater I wore over the shirt immediately became jokes.

It isn't just that London has changed since my first visit twenty-plus years ago, but that I've been a witness to how it has kept in step with the times, even in this epoch of tribulations in which we live. Over time, I have also come to respect the behavior of this enormous, welcoming, walkable city adorned with beautiful parks and gardens. I think I've also made a modest contribution to insuring that Cuba's artistic culture is no longer invisible, or seen only sporadically as an exotic display. In spite of the scant hundreds of Cuban nationals who have moved to Britain over the past two decades, the Cuban presence can be felt in one way or another in almost all the arts, whether theater, the fine arts, cinema, literature, dance, or music, in all its ubiquitous varieties. From being a rare bird in the early 1980s, Cuba and its arts have today become prized consumer goods in this stout capital city, as they are in cities across the country. Products "made in Cuba" can be enjoyed here without trouble, harm, or obstinate hostility, and Cuban culture has become a talisman to ward off ill omens. Naturally, Cuban music is the finest balm for the soul, and fortunately it is played here by its best performers, Cubans of African descent.

Several airlines connect British airports with Havana, Varadero, Holguín, and other cities and resorts in Cuba, affording most of the Cubans who live here the possibility of traveling there fairly easily if their immigration status is clear and legal, especially now that emigrating no longer means having to make a definite break with the country. Others can get a tourist visa that costs £15 and an airplane ticket, and ten hours later they're landing in the largest island in the Caribbean. Britain has nothing like the "Cuban Adjustment Act" enacted by the United States Congress, which permits the Attorney General, "in his discretion and under such regulations as he may prescribe," to "adjust" the immigration status of Cuban refugees who find themselves in the United States to that of permanent residents. The only law of its kind in the world, this act offers privileges to Cubans who reach the United States by illegal means that are not given to would-be immigrants from any other nation. This arbitrary U.S. policy against Cuba has provoked three great migratory waves in more than four decades: Camarioca, 1965; Mariel, 1980; and the so-called balsero crisis, 1994.

Since the 1990s, the governments of Britain and other European states have become more wary of allowing people to enter and remain in their countries under the status of political refugees. Cubans are no exception. Recent parliaments lean, instead, toward setting immigration quotas. The United Kingdom already has too many headaches caused by relations with its own "aliens." The pot is so full of exotics (the most recent Home Office estimate suggested in 2006 that there could be between 310,000 and 570,000 unauthorized immigrants in Britain whether Cuban or others, black, white, or yellow) that some even foresee an amnesty for the illegals.

When a couple of Cubans happen to run into each other here, one never asks the other how he or she made it. At most, they ask a routine question to break the ice: "So, how long have you been here?" or "When was the last time you were in Cuba?"

The great majority of us were not born in this country, and the first generation of Anglo-Cubans or British-Cubans is still in its infancy. In general, we do not suffer from any identity conflict in this country. We know all too well that, even if we have British citizenship, we simply are not British and do not claim to be, apart from the fact that English is not our mother tongue, even if we are fluent in it. In my opinion, the Cuban ethos inherently means, almost by consensus, belonging to a mestizo culture, even if such a category is thought to be indiscriminately manipulated and abused. For Cubans of African descent, such a social pact has taken on crucial meaning over the past fifty years, because it has been a matter of our own survival. All this must somehow be taken into account when the time comes to negotiate new strategies toward the nation and its citizens. We are no longer a minority, neither ethnically nor culturally. At last we Cubans of African descent have ceased to be invisible!

In this concert of conjectures, I believe that maintaining direct and constant contact with Cuba has been, and remains, fundamental for individual and group preservation. The old cliché about "recharging your batteries" with a transatlantic trip is, in my case, more than just a tourist's metaphor; the same can be said of many of the other Cuban men and women who live in this country and throughout continental Europe. The effect that the supposedly inexplicable magic of Cuba produces on the vast majority of us is a sine qua non, regardless of whether we have stuffed our carry-on bags with *dulce de guayaba*, or frozen *harina de maíz tierno* for making tamales, or "the colors of the strings of necklace beads, to keep my roots alive," as the poet Eloy Machado, better known as El Ambia, wrote in his poem "Soy todo" (I Am All). This is the result of the constant ebb and flow of suggestions that the great majority of us Cubans residing on this side of the Atlantic like to give the island, in our own fashion, every time we go back. We're an integral part of the island, and that is how we have insisted on being seen, which shows how things have changed in the past twenty-five years.

Though we are not numerically important as providers of remittances, we are important as providers of forceful and diverse projects, which have already had an effect and which, over the short, medium, or long term, will be felt more and more. As a 100 percent Cuban, and also as a person of African descent, I find it a great relief not to have to struggle with the ghost of identity. Any unpleasantness or quarrel that might happen can always be negotiated, but not my cultural identity—another integral part of what we persist in calling the great African diaspora.

Looking back, I am happy today to find myself living in an intellectual and therefore academic world away from my original "home," without a guilt complex on having been part of some brain drain. In the final analysis, it turns out that my exoticism did not come solely from my ethnic makeup or citizenship, but rather because in those years, anything that wasn't English was exotic per se, and was most often rejected with violent fury out of simple ignorance.

As a Cuban of African descent who lives in London, I consider myself privileged to have been able to contribute my grain of sand to the realization of positive change. It is equally gratifying to know that I can pass along this experience to my young students—which gets me out of any charge of heresy.

To sum it all up, the biggest beneficiary of all is the culture of our great green crocodile island.

CHAPTER 19

The Convergence of Time: Being Cuban in the Present Tense

María de los Angeles Torres

I used to return to Cuba frequently, and did so until a few years ago when I came to the end of a very long journey. It had taken years to return to the place of my birth in which five generations of my family are buried, to the place in which sunlight lingers and music is heard everywhere. And it took almost two decades to feel that I had completed my return.

I am not quite sure how it happened or necessarily what it fully means, but it did. I no longer have a burning need to recuperate a past that had defined so much of who I was. A past so abruptly interrupted by the forces of world politics.

THERE IS NO RETURN TO THE PAST

There had been a lot of pain. But a strange sense of sadness and peace is how I remember the journey's end. My last trip to Cuba broke my heart. Travel to Cuba has never been easy, as both governments have at one point or another criminalized our movements. For many years, we could only return to the island through official mechanisms. These had become so staged, so manipulative. I had become so aware of the political machinations behind them that it was impossible to continue to be part of a charade in which security officers paraded as academics, and American academics went along with it so they could have exclusive access to the island. So I had opted to visit family and friends and set out to enjoy the beauty of the island with my daughters and husband.

We packed our bags, including one huge duffel bag filled with clothes, vitamins, and medicines for my great aunt in Yaguajay, and threw in a copy of *Cigar Aficionado* that featured Cuba. We boarded an Air Jamaica from Chicago to Montego Bay where we transferred to another plane headed toward Havana. It was the easiest trip I had taken to Cuba.

The first night we stayed at el Comodoro, a hotel on Havana's seacoast. A magician charmed my daughters, and I sighed a deep sigh of relief, hoping that the rest of the trip could go so well. We traveled through the beautiful countryside of Pinar del Rio, took in the breathtaking views of a sunset, walked through orchid gardens and climbed the hills to see the falls of Soroa.

The illusion was abruptly shattered when we visited a cigar factory. Cuban cigar workers were proud and eloquent. They were the backbone of Cuba's War of independence from Spain. They pooled their money to have someone read to them as they rolled cigars. But here, they were performing for tourists and begging for money. I remember thinking that unlike other Latin American countries, our beggars worked sixty hours a week.

We drove to Meneses, the town where my mother had been born. Rumors had reached my mother in Miami that people were saying that her mother, my grandmother, had made several apparitions. She had been beloved and had died very young. We visited the cemetery only to find the marble angel of my grandmother's tomb gone. It had been stolen a few years earlier, just like the railings, to be used at the Coppelia at the center of town.

In Yaguajay, we stayed with my great aunt. We went through photos of our family, including ones from the early days of the Revolution. My great aunts celebrating, with wide smiles, and pedal pusher pants, side by side with *barbudos* carrying rifles. "I don't know if you know," she whispered to me, "we were revolutionaries."

I showed her the magazine filled with images of pristine hotel pools, and sumptuous close up shots of food buffets filled with pineapples, mangoes, papayas, lobsters, shrimp, and chilled bottles of white wine. She wanted to know where that Cuba was. Hers was lived in a wooden house, filled with colonies of termites that had created cavernous tunnels in the walls, rocking chairs, and picture frames. A thin, oily, black layer of pollen from the nearby sugar refinery covered the floor and wicker, rocking chairs in the house. She cooked her food in a wooden oven and bathed in the back patio with a hose rigged up as a shower and rain water collected in a steel tank.

I wanted to do something special for her. I felt that this could be the last time I would see her; indeed, she died a few years later. I couldn't take her to the beach to stay with us, since island Cubans were not allowed in hotels. There was a resort nearby in Mayagüez, and I had a beautiful picture of her and my mother when they were very young, sitting alongside a pond smiling, holding hands, their skirts neatly arranged in a semicircle. But when we arrived, the guards would not let us in. We had left our passports back at the house, and they were sure that my oldest daughter, who was thirteen at the time and was sitting on her father's lap in the front seat of the cab, was a Cuban from the island. It took me a moment to realize that they thought she was a *jinetera* with an American tourist. My obsession had to stop.

It was impossible for me to be a tourist. I knew too much about the political intrigues, the mirages, the manipulations, to be able to relax and enjoy the beach, chat with my friends, enjoy a weekend family visit with relatives.

When I was at the beach resort, I could not invite friends or relatives to join us for dinner. They were not allowed in. I was constantly torn. Unlike other tourists, I had ties to people who lived outside the secure walls of the hotels.

There was another important moment of closure for me on this trip. Unlike my mother, who had returned to visit her relatives, my father had never returned; in fact, he refused to talk about our trips at all. Yet for this trip, he sent me an old Esso map of the island and Matanzas, the city of his birth. He had carefully circled the places he wanted me to visit. The Teatro Sauta, the place of his first singing debut; his childhood home; the park where he played, and his school. The theater was easy to find. Friends from Matanzas were staging a play, *El Baño Público*, a poignant debate about who is entitled to enjoy public spaces. The others were harder to locate. The addresses he had given me had names like Vera that rolled off your tongue. Sometime after we had left, the government had removed the street names and given them numbers instead: Primera, Segunda, Tercera. After some searching we came to the house where he was raised. The neighbors still lived next door, and they asked about my grandmother Rita *la enfermera* and about my father. "Does he still sing?" They invited us in for a small cup of coffee and begged us not to show him pictures of his block. "He'll have a heart attack to see how run-down everything is."

In many ways, the past had been recuperated. In the process new relationships had been forged. But I could not continue to travel back. That part of the journey had ended. The next few summers we traveled to other parts of the world. We went to Italy with a close family friend who had lived there during the Pinochet regime. I started a research project in Rio de Janeiro, where we traveled the country with Mexican friends who had been thrust out of their country in the late 1960s. They, too, had lost homes. Political exiles, after all, have been so common in human history. We were no exception.

The physical distance to the island widened.

In Some Ways, the Future is Already Here

Fidel's imminent death has brought Cuba and its future back to the front pages of newspapers. It has been a strange time. Everyone I know, and everyone I meet who finds out I am Cuban, asks what will happen after Fidel dies.

For a year he has hung on, even though there are those who swear he is dead. We do have the macabre images of the ailing Fidel periodically appearing on television. In one video clip he is seen wearing a jogging suit, doing what looks like a slow moon walk. And once again, the media have managed to reduce the exile to a cliché. In summer of 2006, when the news broke that he was ill and at the brink of death, television images showed jubilant exiles in a moment of public euphoria over the possibility that the end was near. What they never said was that we had also cheered when he marched into Havana. He had promised social justice and democracy, but he never held elections.

In reality, though, anxiety and not euphoria is what characterizes the mood among the Cubans both here and there. Privately in Miami and Havana there is skepticism about dramatic changes. Fidel's death, whether it occurs this week or in a few years, will undoubtedly leave a power vacuum that many will compete to fill. Five decades have left multiple factions in the huge state bureaucracy each waiting for its turn to rule. Most importantly, selective party membership has left most people out of what Cubans call "Olympus." Short of all-out repression, some power-sharing arrangement will surely have to emerge. But even if there is a more open political system, indeed even one resulting from fair and honest elections, there are several constants that will limit the possibility for dramatic changes in the short run and that will continue to make a normal relation with the island difficult.

Regardless of who rules the military, Raul Castro or anyone else, it will continue to have a strong presence in the life of Cuba. We are not that different from the many other Latin American countries that had military regimes during the 1960s and 1970s. The military is an institution of political elites whose loyalty has been enticed with economic incentives that have included the best hospitals, houses, cars, schools, vacation homes, and travel abroad. This level of privilege is not easily dismantled. Adding to its political power are its economic enterprises. After the collapse of the Soviet Union and the drying up of its subsidies to the island, the military led the way to create a system of state capitalism, or market Leninism, mainly focusing on the tourist industry. It is widely known that the military's "mixed enterprises," coinvestment with foreign capital, are more economically successful than those run by the sloppy and inefficient Ministry of the Interior, the second most powerful repressive arm of the regime. Maybe they will liberalize the economy while holding onto political power.

Paradoxically, I think this will happen with the help of the United States, particularly if the present-day anti-immigrant hysteria continues to infect policy toward the island. For many it may be more important to shut the aquatic border that divides Havana from Miami than to have democracy on the island. The military is the only institution in Cuba that can guarantee that.

And then there is the question of the economy. Before the Revolution, Cuba's economy was one of the most prosperous of Latin America; what it lacked was a more equitable distribution of its resources. While the Castro government did a better job of distributing social services, its policies destroyed the economy. Factories that once produced textiles, dolls, or sulfur, to name a few products, have deteriorated beyond repair. Today Cuba imports even sugar, since the few refineries still working are dedicated to the production of rum for sale to tourists.

One of Cuba's top industries is tourism. Economies that rely on tourism do not encourage the kind of social structures that facilitate sustainable democracies in the long run—particularly the kind of tourism industry developed in Cuba, which has criminalized small businesses that could thrive from tourism. For instance, Cuba imports fruits from other Caribbean countries instead of permitting local farmers to produce and sell their products. Those in power fear that decentralizing the economy could also lead to political competition. This may change.

Most disturbingly, Cuba's main tourism is sex-driven. Men from all over the world come to the island in search of prostitutes. The state is the pimp and demands a payment for a permit to allow tourists to take Cubans into their hotel rooms. Cubans are normally prohibited from entering tourist facilities. While we may see changes in the exaggerated reliance on prostitution as the main lure for tourists, it has left a lasting imprint.

The exile community is already a major factor in the life of Cuba. Since the beginning we have helped relatives back home. Remittances have become the first gross national product of Cuba. However, both governments have criminalized our desire to visit our relatives, stay in contact with them, or send them aid. They have also exploited our hearts and our memories, making a normal relationship difficult.

Time has passed, and long gone are the deep political divides of the early days of the Revolution. Geography is no longer an effective way to define the politics of those who stay and those who leave. The recent arrival in Miami today was in Havana yesterday. The former political prisoner was an activist on the island, the rafter probably a farmer, and the artist who overstayed her visa, a professor at Havana's Art Institute. Few of us will be going back to live, much less to reclaim a house in which a relative is probably living.

The future of Cuba is already here. And it is no longer geographically confined to an island. Nationalism's promises in all its versions failed. Indeed, in many ways nationalism became a way to exclude and repress. In our case, the promise was to create a democratic, inclusive, and independent nation.

It did not come true. We now have the distinction of having had the longest-standing dictator in modern times, whose most glaring political failure has been his lack of viable succession plan, beyond turning the reigns of power to his little brother. The nation did not include; it produced wave upon wave of exiles, living testaments of the failure of the nationalist project. And as to the island, I am no longer sure of the viability of an independent island nation-state. How can one survive—for that matter how can any country survive—on one's own in the world we live in today?

THE EXPANSIVE PRESENT

By coming to terms with the past, I was able to situate myself in the present. Parts of my past were laid to rest as I understood the circumstances that led to my exodus, along with another 14,000 children, to the United States in the early 1960s. Through this research journey, I met others like myself who had come to the United States as children. Together we searched the past for answers about our exodus. We began working on projects to help children refugees. We lobbied not to let the United States put the children of Guantánamo Bay refugees in foster homes, leaving their parents behind vulnerable to the whims of immigration policy. We spoke out against using children as trophies in political battles. We bonded, and through one extraordinary woman, Elly Chovel, we came together in an organization that brought together individuals of all political persuasions, professions, and parts of the country, creating in the heart of the Cuban exile a more tolerant and gentle way of relating to each other.

Elly died unexpectedly at the end of the summer of 2007. I attended a memorial service at the Ermita de la Caridad organized by Operation Pedro Pan group, an organization she founded. She felt strongly that we had to talk about our experiences, the good ones and the traumatic ones. As deeply woven as we were to the myth of the origin of exile, that of the children saved from communism, our stories needed to be shared and a critical eye turned to our histories. Elly guided me through the historical journey, one that uncovered uncomfortable facts about our exodus. We discovered how a program that had started to bring a few hundred children of the underground to safety while their parents fought to democratize the Revolution, mushroomed into the largest unaccompanied exodus of children. Lots of people with good intentions helped the exodus, but many children and young people did not find a safe haven, instead some faced horrible physical and emotional abuse in the catholic orphanages and foster homes in which they were placed. Our parents were to join us within months. Mine did, but some 8,000 children were caught in the aftermath of the October Missile Crisis, as the United States shut the doors to incoming refugees and Cuba prohibited the return of those who had left. It was not until the Camarioca exodus in 1965 that the doors were reopened.

Elly helped us heal, to come to terms with the heart-breaking contradictions of our exodus. Dying in exile has been equated to the supreme sacrifice. I like to think that having our dead here, buried on this side of the Florida Straits, expands our borders, and begins to give us a narrative written in the present.

My sense of geography has expanded. It is not just the travels; something has shifted. I feel confined within the narrowness of nationalisms. Appeals for unity scare me as I wonder what is lost in conformity. Political rhetoric rings hollow and the spectacle of power fails to entertain.

Grand schemes make me suspicious. Nations are made of memories and desire, the past and the future so they can ignore us in the present. Our need to belong and to have a coherent social context can be so easily manipulated.

For many Cubans of my generation, our search for home led us back to the island. I suspect that in reality we were searching for more. We were searching for a time in our lives, a time when we were younger. We were searching for a context that made sense, that is, one in which we could belong. We gave the island this mystical quality of being the place of origin, the place where we belonged.

In many ways, those journeys did make us part of the island, part of its history, our history. We rewrote official history on both sides of the borders. Our experiences created a richer narrative of nations and home that expanded them beyond physical borders. We found that we had shared experiences, but there was no doubt that there are differences in our political cultures. To rephrase a quote by Eugene Ionesco, the founder of the theater of the absurd, maybe ideologies divided us, we found that dreams and anguish bring us together.

The island, however, no longer defined us. We were in Spain, Mexico, Miami, Chicago. Cuba included all of us who had left. My Cuba included the family and friends on the island as well. When possible, I saw friends outside of Cuba. Some even visited us here in Chicago until the United States once again shut the doors to travel.

Cuba became more personal. My Cuba was in books on my bookshelves, pictures in albums, letters form my aunts in Yaguajay, and images on videos; my Cuba is always alive in music. My Cuba stayed close. As it continued to live in the soft memories of childhood, incredibly poignant ones of young adulthood, and in the dreams and disillusionments I shared with friends from the island some who had left at the same time I did, others who continued to leave, many who stayed. My Cuba lives beyond the political rhetoric of the left as it does beyond the confines of the Cuban state.

Cuba, however, is no longer home, it is a point of reference. Home, my mother-in-law once told me, is where your children are born. I resisted her claim. Her world had been destroyed by World War II. She escaped the death of the Holocaust. And although she returned to Vienna and in some ways had a professional life in her home country, she had accepted that it was no longer her home. At the time I did not have children, and I was at the beginning of a journey that I thought I could recuperate my physical place of birth as home. Ignorant of the impact of time, I believed our home was still there, it was just politics that kept us out. We wanted to believe in the exceptionalism of our case, the uniqueness of our circumstances. But we are not exceptional. Dislocations, in so many forms, are common experiences. At the end, I have found comfort in the fact that we are not so different than so many other diasporas. This has allowed for a broadening of our experience and of the communities to which we can belong.

For now, my home is in Chicago. It is the place my two daughters were born, and it is also the birthplace of my husband. And thanks to the fact that I was born in Cuba, I am an exile and an immigrant in a city of immigrants, in a country in which the debate about immigrants has become a critical forum in which to struggle for the kinds of principles and attitudes I believe are necessary for us to survive in a global world: tolerance of difference and respect of everyone's basic human rights.

I have a voice in this debate, one which at the end may be drowned by hatred and ignorance, or ignored by the silence of politicians, but for now I can speak as a Cuban in the present tense.

Belkis Ayón, Sin título (Untitled) (collograph)

PART IV

Más Allá de Cuba: Now and Then We Try to Forget about Geography

There was my fascination with discovering a new world, but on the other hand, there was this other world, in which I was "The Cuban," a rara avis whom everyone mentally tried to return to her island. The worst of it was that they each wanted to take me to the island that they held in their imaginations, which for the most part had nothing to do with the island where I had lived.

—Karla Suárez

Rocío García de la Nuez, *Haiku: La ola* (Haiku: The wave) (painting)

CHAPTER 20

Citizen of a Certain World

Karla Suárez

(Translated by David Frye)

I arrived in Europe in 1997, the same year the Buena Vista Social Club CD hit the market. I arrived with my curiosity intact, with high hopes of traveling around the much-vaunted old continent, of seeing with my own eyes the museums and monuments I only knew from photographs, of forgetting the shortages and the transportation problems and the lack of electricity and the uncertain future and Cuba, Cuba, Cuba. I arrived with a huge pile of cassettes onto which I had recorded the musical soundtrack of my life in Havana—Silvio Rodríguez, Santiago Feliú, Frank Delgado, Carlos Varela, Gerardo Alfonso, and a few things taped off the air from Havana City Radio, the only station that would play songs by the *trovadores* of the "generation of the moles," who were never heard on television or in large concerts, and foreign singers, lots of Argentine rock and other bits from all over. I arrived with this haul, which I planned to share while talking about my friends and my life and my joys and my sorrows. I arrived in the hopes of becoming a citizen of the world in a continent without borders, hopes of being free of national shackles, of moving around like everyone else, of playing the lead in the film of my life. Except that, for some mysterious reason, as soon as I showed up anywhere, someone would announce the arrival of "The Cuban," and they'd put on the Buena Vista Social Club CD and ask me, "What's going to happen in Cuba after Fidel Castro?"

Whenever you show up in a place you don't know, you're a stranger, a foreigner from another geography, and people will always try to associate you with what little they know about your country of origin. Therefore, if I were to fit my nationality when I got to Europe, to Italy, I would have to dance to the Buena Vista Social Club and talk about Fidel Castro. Because that was Cuba for almost everybody: the new hit CD, which was beautiful, but wasn't the music of my life; and Fidel Castro, of course, though I was tired of his having to play the lead role. So my load of tapes and my stories could go back into the suitcase, because hardly anyone was interested. Everything began to seem very odd to me then.

On the one hand, there was my fascination with the unknown. Moving to Rome was almost like being born again, becoming like a child who has to be told how everything works, learning a language, having no reference points aside from literary ones, which in the final analysis are other people's reference points, because the new city had no marks of my own personal life. I had to learn how to walk and how to move and how to enter a different psychology. Understanding a sense of humor is rather different from understanding a language; grasping words is quite distinct from learning them. It was also difficult because I was coming from Havana, so it wasn't just a matter of a change of cities but rather a change of worlds, because Cuba is another world. Its social organization is unlike that of anywhere else. Back there, for example, you didn't buy things, you "resolved" them; the water wasn't on at all hours, instead, "the water was coming"; public telephones didn't work for making international calls (for the most part, they didn't work at all); you traveled by hitchhiking or on bicycle; you didn't have to pay anything to enroll in the university; there was only one party, with one everlasting party leader; and you could just show up at anyone's house without having to phone ahead. All this seems so trivial—the "underdevelopment syndrome," as we like to say—but at first it was a problem. So I had to start getting rid of old habits and learning like a child who watches how adults do things. Stumbling and bumbling, whenever I felt lost I'd listen to one of my old cassettes and travel back to Havana for a while and let my feet touch solid ground, or else I'd shout curses in my own language so I wouldn't forget them.

On the one hand, as I was saying, there was my fascination with discovering a new world, but on the other hand, there was this other world, in which I was "The Cuban," a rara avis whom everyone mentally tried to return to her island. The worst of it was that they each wanted to take me to the island that they held in their imaginations, which for the most part had nothing to do with the island where I had lived. Their imaginary islands were limited to a short set of topics. For some, I had come from the earthly paradise, a wondrous place where everyone enjoyed free healthcare and schooling. For others, I had emerged from hell, a horrid site where people couldn't say what they thought, and where only one political party exists. In reality, I had come from both places, but where I wanted to be was Europe. It surprised me to find, after living in a country where the individual is nullified by the amorphous mass of the collectivity and where we are theoretically all equal and have to do the same things, that here on this side I was being placed on my interlocutor's mental island, where we were all the same, according to a model of Cuban that existed in his head. We all danced to the Buena Vista Social Club, we all hated green salads and loved rice and beans, and we had to have everything explained to us, because we were coming from a place that was isolated from the rest of the planet. We were like a sort of friendly native tribe, raised under communism. It was okay if they wanted to explain to me how a phone worked, but when they asked me if I had ever heard of the Bible or if I knew who Michelangelo was, I thought that was going too far; this wasn't the "underdevelopment syndrome," it was the "loincloth syndrome."

Broadly speaking, I ran into two types who particularly annoyed me. One was the "Cuba specialist." Whether he practiced unconditional love or bitter hatred toward the Cuban government, he almost always considered that he possessed the absolute truth, and he'd talk nonstop, without the slightest intention of listening to anything I had to tell him. The other type was the "enthusiast," who would put on a salsa CD as soon as he saw me coming and ask me to dance. If I tried explaining to him that this wasn't exactly the kind of music I had listened to in Havana, that my music was rock and things of that sort, the guy would look at me as if to conclude, "but then you aren't Cuban, girl."

So began the process, a fairly conscious one, that could be called "growing distant out of exhaustion." I began to reject the Buena Vista Social Club and almost everything that came from the island. I want to leave you, Cuba, but they won't let me, neither here nor there. Of course, I kept on listening through my earphones to my own music on my old cassettes. That was when, for the first time in my life, I told myself, or perhaps asked myself: I am Cuban. When I was living in my country, being Cuban was something everyone around me had in common. Besides, being Cuban was part of the nationalist and collectivist spirit of the system, a kind of condition we took on from the time we were children, by dint of repeating phrases and patriotic songs. If I had never spent much time reflecting on my national identity, I did know I was Cuban; but in Europe, I wasn't in my place of origin, I was a fish out of water, and my water was an island about which hardly anyone felt indifferent. There are some countries that carry more weight than all the land they contain, and Cuba is one of them.

What happened next—and this actually was unconscious—was that over time the process became inverted. Distance is a double-faced monster: the closer I felt to this side, the more I needed the other side. Maybe this has something to do with the human need to seek balance by coming back to the place where you started out. Or with the human resistance to loss—because if I lose you, I get lost myself. The farther away you got, Cuba, the more I wanted to know you. I then grew interested in things from my country that I had never looked at before. I devoted myself to searching for history books, discovering authors who didn't figure in the official history we studied at school, reading the ones who had been proscribed by the system, listening to different musicians, reconstructing that distant country, and trying to understand it from its origins in order to know who I was and where I had come from. Because I didn't want to become the caricature of the Cuban that some people carried in their heads, I didn't want to fit their themes or start behaving like someone I wasn't. But I also didn't want to deny my nature by refusing to do things, and so become a different caricature, an invented woman, a sham. I simply wanted to know where I had come from, so I could know who I was.

A person is not her country, but a person carries her country inside herself. That is inevitable. We all carry scraps of our country around with us, and I think we are never so aware of coming from a land as when we're away from it. After Italy I moved to France, where I live today. Once again I had to learn another language and other norms, but the two societies were similar, so I had little trouble adapting. I almost belonged here, except that I felt more and more like I belonged over there, as I began to notice bit by bit, through small details. First, no doubt, there was my need for the sea, and my discovering that I was absolutely incapable of bathing in the cold water of the ocean on this side, my absolute dependence on that hot, clear bowl of soup, the Caribbean. Then came other things. One day, for example, I began to miss the fiestas, and to grow tired of the dinners where everyone eats and talks for hours without getting up out of their chairs. Another day, I discovered that I missed the rowdiness of my Havana neighborhood, in contrast to the silence of Paris (after having spent so many years criticizing the noise in my old neighborhood). Then there were the neighbors who formed part of your life in Havana, who knocked on your door and asked for things at all hours; in Rome I rarely saw my neighbors, and in Paris even less (only when they came to complain about the noise). I didn't realize how much I missed them until I had the good luck of getting a Peruvian neighbor in Paris who knocks on my door and whom I can ask for things. We talk with each other, and to me this seems like a gift, a huge stroke of luck. And so on, with many things, fragments of everyday life, the way people think, the way they laugh or touch each other, the men's *piropos,* how eagerly people tell their whole life stories the first time they meet. Things are so trivial that, precisely because of their simplicity, they mark our differences. And so I threw myself more deeply into it, wanted to learn more and more, to discover everything I hadn't understood about my country so that I could incorporate it. One of the funniest things happened recently. There's a TV show that plays peasant music in Cuba called "Palmas y Cañas" (Palm Trees and Sugar Cane), which as a child I thought of as a program "that grandparents watch." Well, it so happens that a concert of Cuban peasant music was announced here in Paris, and I went to see it with some friends. They were, of course, the singers from "Palmas y Cañas," with their *décimas, controversias,* and *seguidillas*—all very entertaining. My Cuban friends and I broke out laughing without exchanging a word. If anybody had told me a few years ago, at some rock concert in Havana, that someday I would be going to a "Palmas y Cañas" concert in Paris, I would have thought they were insane. But so it happened. I don't know if you can call it nostalgia, if it's because all this was part of the environment when I was in Cuba, or if, as the Pablo Milanés song puts it, "time goes by and we start growing old . . . ," but the fact is that now, in addition to that old pile of cassettes, my Cuban discotheque has a bit of everything, because music is ageless and because it all belongs to me.

So I really do feel that I have lost nothing. Quite the contrary, I think I have gained Italy as a country, and I hope that France will come to me in the same way. My world is divided among three languages, and each one has its place: I write in Spanish, drive in Italian, do my shopping in French, and so on. As for Cuba, the specialists and enthusiasts mentioned above bother me much less now, while the obstructions and restrictions of the system bother me much more. Perhaps I'm getting used to the former and unaccustomed to the latter. Cuba will continue to be my origin, my point of departure, but now I have the sensation that it is bigger for me. Now that I find myself in new waters, I can understand where it was I came from. It's as if, in my case, physical distance has already summoned the implicit opposite reaction. Mirror magic. So I'm Cuban, and even though I don't think that means anything special, that's what I am, end of story. I'll put on the Buena Vista Social Club CD now and smile. Care to dance?

My Repeating Island

Gustavo Pérez Firmat

De las islas no se despide nadie para siempre.

—Dulce María Loynaz

What sort of an exile is someone who has spent four-fifths of his life in another country and who has no intention of returning to Cuba to live no matter what the political conditions on the island? In exile he grew up and grew old. In exile he acquired a language, met all of his friends, married, had children, pursued a career, endured illnesses and separations. He's certain that he will die in exile. He's just as certain that he will die *an* exile. What sort of exile is this person, whose homeland is no longer his home?

*   *   *

In the movie *The Lost City,* Andy García's character, Fico Fellove, declares: "I'm only impersonating an exile. I'm still in Cuba." When Fico says this, he has just arrived in New York City from Havana. I wonder what Fico would say were he still in New York forty years later. Perhaps he would say this: "I'm only impersonating a Cuban. I've always been in exile." Time turns exile into a chronic condition, in the literal sense of the adjective: a way of being in the world inseparable from the experience of temporality. The chronic exile never says, I am an exiled Cuban. He always says, I am a Cuban exile: the noun, the substantive, is exile.

*   *   *

It is often thought that an exile spends his (or her) time in remembrance, but for the chronic exile, it's not quite true. Even when he was young and still had relatives who, unlike him, had spent most of their lives in Cuba, he was not the source of memories but the one who received them, and later, the one who relayed them. He was the executor of the nostalgia of others: his parents and grandparents, his aunts and uncles, all those members of his typically distended family that included people whom he barely knew. His own memories of Cuba, such as they were, seemed less urgent, less necessary, than those of the grown-ups around him. It still seems that way, even now that he is the only grown-up around him.

* * *

When the chronic exile longs, he longs for a time when the people around him still had memories. He longs for the days of temporary, rather than chronic, exile. Virgil Suárez, one of the chronic exile's heroes, writes in a poem: "How far do your roots extend? Far enough to do damage." That is, not far enough.

* * *

Years ago a Miami newspaper carried an item about a man who had been paralyzed as a result of a stroke. He would spend his days in a wheelchair by the window of his Miami Beach condominium, facing south, mumbling to himself the only word he was still able to pronounce: Cuba. The chronic exile believes that he is like that man. Rather than recollection, his exile involves iteration: Cuba, Cuba, Cuba. What is this Cuba that he iterates? What are the modes of his iteration?

* * *

Three ways of thinking about Cuba: as *país*, as *pueblo,* and as *patria.* Not living among Cubans (*el pueblo*), and not having gone back to Cuba (*el país*), the chronic exile thinks of Cuba as his *patria*, a personal possession, an imaginary homeland, a country he cannot leave or lose. This Cuba goes with him wherever he goes. It dreams with him. It wakes up with him. It gets sick with him. It will die with him.

To the three ways of thinking about Cuba correspond the three faces of Cubanness: *cubanidad, cubaneo,* and *cubanía. Cubanidad,* a word that goes back to the first stirrings of a Cuban national consciousness at the beginning of the nineteenth century, designates a civil status embodied in birth certificates, passports, naturalization papers. By contrast, *cubaneo* isn't borne out in documents or decrees, but in a loose repertoire of gestures, manners, customs, words. Rather than naming *un estado civil, cubaneo* names *un estado de ánimo*—a mood, a temperament, structures of thought and feeling: what used to be called "national character." Its frame of reference is not *un país*, a political entity, but *un pueblo,* a social and cultural entity.

The third face of Cubanness is *cubanía,* one of those rare words that actually has a birthday, since it was coined by Fernando Ortiz in a lecture at the University of Havana on November 28, 1939. *Cubanía* is not accident of birth, or a menu of manners and mannerisms. According to Ortiz, *cubanía* inheres in *la conciencia de ser cubano y la voluntad de quererlo ser.* Unlike *cubanidad*, which requires external verification, *cubanía* demands an act of the will. Unlike *cubaneo*, which requires the society of like-minded people, *cubanía* requires only a willingness of the heart. It does not find expression in a nation, *un país,* or in a people, *un pueblo,* but in something more abstract and ineffable—in a homeland, *una patria.*

Cubanía doesn't depend on place of residence or country of citizenship; it has little to do with language or demeanor; and, perhaps most importantly, it cannot be granted or taken away. It is the expression of Cubanness most available to those of us for whom Cuba itself remains an unachievable blend of *ser* and *querer ser*, a redemptive form of wishful thinking. If *cubanidad* is political and *cubaneo* is prepolitical, *cubanía* perhaps should be described as postpolitical, as the nationality of those without a nation.

Touched by *cubanía*, the chronic exile no longer feels like a stranger in his own skin.

* * *

Iteration begins with memory fatigue. Like seeing childhood friends too often, after a while—years, decades—repeating the same stories over and over becomes unpleasurable. Worse: it becomes unpainful. The memories have lost their sting as well as their savor. Like a museless museum, or a house with closets but no skeletons.

* * *

Or iteration begins with memory loss, which is what happened to the paralyzed man. Unable to remember Cuba, he could only utter "Cuba." After the memories fade, what remains is the impulse to address, to point and name. Iteration is deictic, directional. Looking south, the man in the wheelchair could not see the island from where he sat, but his head was turned that way, one could say he was headed that way, though he would never reach the place toward which he was headed. This turning toward Cuba, as distinct from returning to Cuba, is the chronic exile's mode of iteration. An invalid's apostrophe.

* * *

In the 1930s Xavier Cugat recorded "Miami Beach Rhumba," a song about a young woman who, on the way to Cuba to learn how to rhumba, found what she was looking for in Miami Beach:

> I started out to go to Cuba, soon I was at Miami Beach.
> There, not so very far from Cuba, oh what a rhumba they teach.
> Palm trees are whispering "yo te quiero," what could I do but stay a while?
> I met a Cuban caballero, we danced in true Latin style.

> So I never got to Cuba, but I got all its atmosphere.
> Why even Yuba and his tuba, they played a night right here.

Like the girl in the song, the chronic exile makes do with atmosphere. Almost anything can create it: a riff, a whiff, a word, a gesture, a smoke. Atmosphere cannot be seen but it can be felt. Rather than a sense of place, the chronic exile is trailed by atmosphere. He feels it around and inside him. He exhales it and he inhales it. For him, a Cuban atmosphere is both landscape and inscape, environment and *in*-vironment. Those he meets often think that *he* is the atmosphere, a Cuban caballero or a whispering palm tree. But he knows better: the atmosphere others see in him is not the atmosphere in which he dwells, perceptible only to him. A locale without a location, with contours rather than coordinates, this rarefied air he breathes is his portable island.

* * *

Atmosphere is feeling, affect—or rather, a particular affect. If exoticism, according to Victor Segalen's classic definition, is the feeling that diversity stirs in us, the chronic exile's atmosphere is the feeling stirred in him by something as familiar as his own first name, but also something that has been lost, like his own first name. We move through the familiar as through a vacuum. Only when the familiar becomes estranged from the everyday does it precipitate into atmosphere.

* * *

Since tourism is touring, turning, some may think of atmospheric Cubanness as virtual tourism, a mental and sentimental *retour au pays natal* accomplished by traveling in place, without ever moving from the house from which the chronic exile gazes at his homeland. But whereas the tourist seeks the unknown, the unfamiliar, the chronic exile worships sameness: Cuba, Cuba, Cuba. The tourist comes and goes, while the chronic exile, having left once, has decided not to leave again.

* * *

Nonetheless, he knows that he has become some sort of tourist, an occasional Cuban, sporadic rather than diasporic. In the almost fifty years that he has spent in exile, there have been many days when he has not heard a word of Spanish, but none when he has not heard a word of English. This is one reason, among others, why the chronic exile talks to himself—in Spanish.

* * *

Cuban graffiti: Havana, during the *balsero* exodus of the 1990s: *Yo me quedo*; Miami, at about the same time: *Yo no voy*. The chronic exile dissents from both sentiments. He cannot leave because he already left. He cannot stay because he never left. Were he to indulge in graffiti, he would scrawl on the walls of his house: *Yo aquí, allá ellos.*

* * *

In the 1950s, Cuban children used to learn geography from a textbook by Leví Marrero, *Geografía de Cuba*, whose first illustration showed a map of the world with Cuba at its center. Its caption: *El mundo alrededor de Cuba.* Anyone familiar with Cubans will recognize that the belief that the world revolves around Cuba is more than a cartographic projection. It's one of countless examples of the *ombliguismo* that scholars and pundits have discussed (and of which these pages may be another instance). A line from a song by the Cuban-American singer Willie Chirino sums up Cuban exceptionalism in four words: *Como Cuba, ni Cuba.* Like Cuba, not even Cuba. If islands are exceptions to the rule of continents, Cuba is an exception to an exception, an incontinent rule unto itself.

The second illustration in *Geografía de Cuba* offers another map of Cuba, but this time the perspective is different. The caption reads: *Cuba vista desde el norte.* In Cuban slang *el norte* is the United States. For the last half-century, "Cuba seen from the North" has encompassed the gaze of hundreds of thousands of Cubans. Looking at this map, the chronic exile sees himself looking at his homeland, that is, navel-gazing.

* * *

The poet Orlando González Esteva, another of the chronic exile's heroes, likes to say, *El futuro ya pasó,* by which he means both "the future already happened" and "the future passed us by." The reason, González Esteva adds, is not that we are no longer who we were, but that we have already been who we were going to be.

* * *

The chronic exile knows that, whatever happens in Cuba, it will have happened too late. Change may come to Cuba—it may have already—but no change will come to him. In this he resembles those hundreds of thousands of other exiles, on both sides of the Florida Straits and also within them, who did not live to see the day of their country's liberation. Exile ends, chronic exile goes on.

* * *

But. *Sin embargo.*

* * *

But perhaps he is needlessly betting against himself. But perhaps his bitterness has misled him, making him believe that there are no third acts in an exile's life. Eduardo Galeano, not one of the chronic exile's heroes, once wrote that nostalgia is good but hope is better. It may be that when our day finally does come—it may have happened already—the cocoon of exile will fall away from him like dead skin. It may be that he will discover that he has not lost the ability to connect and commune. Hope—*esperanza*—is a word that he has seldom used, an emotion that he has never embraced. When he was younger, he used to toast to a next year in Cuba without really believing it. The toast was an obligatory formality, one of the rituals of exile. More given to regret than to expectation, he always enjoyed living in the land of what-might-have-been, his only *país*. Will he allow himself to give up what might have been for what could be?

* * *

He tells himself that it would be a relief not to have to explain what kind of Cuban he is, which side he is on: for or against, *gusano* or *revolucionario*. He fantasizes about the day when he can identify himself as Cuban without his interlocutors wondering, usually silently, what he means. (His worm's eye views never have been a secret.) Like others before him, he visualizes *un puente, un gran puente* spanning the distance between the *aquí* and the *allá*. Not a bridge to Cuba, but a bridge between Cubans. Were that day to come, he would scrawl new graffiti on his wall, no longer a wall: *yo aquí, pero con ellos; allá ellos, pero conmigo.*

Notes

La conciencia de ser cubano y la voluntad de quererlo ser (The consciousness of being [a] Cuban and the willing desire to be one.)

Yo me quedo (I am staying.)

Yo no voy (I'm not going.)

Yo aquí, allá ellos (I'm here; they're over there [colloquially: To hell with them!].)

El mundo alrededor de Cuba (The world around Cuba.)

Ombliguismo (navel-gazing, self-centeredness.)

Un puente, un gran puente (A bridge, a great bridge [a line from a well-known poem by José Lezama Lima].)

Yo aquí, pero con ellos; allá ellos, pero conmigo (I'm here, but with them; they're over there, but with me.)

CHAPTER 22

A Cuban Dorothy

Eliana Rivero

(Translated by the author)

POETIC PREAMBLE

Mirror of the World, Garden of the Soul, Pearl of the East, Center of the Universe.... This fabled oasis on the edge of a desert has never lacked breathless admirers. Another name, City of Famous Shadows, reveals it as witness to the full sweep of its history.[1]

Across the street from my house lives a family of immigrants. They speak loudly in their own language, get together often on weekends and cook in their backyard, gather as children and elders and adults to remember stories and to share anecdotes in this place where they now have their home. They have prospered in the United States, they have their own business, and also own a great number of cars that they park all along the block. They are dark haired and dark skinned and speak little English, except for the young adults and the children. Women in the family look beautiful, well dressed, and very modern; the men have a very masculine manner, and greet neighbors by shaking their hand and asking "How are you?" with a ready smile.

Across the street from my house lives an example of the universal diaspora. They are individuals from a tribe, very close knit in their immigration and very happy to reside in prosperity. They left their country fleeing from political circumstances, and perhaps also due to religious motives. They come from a small republic in Central Asia. They are Jews from Uzbekistan, who migrated a few decades ago to Iran and then to the United States. One of the young women in the family owns a sports utility vehicle, new and silver in color, whose license plate spells—instead of numbers—a string of letters: SAMRKAND.

Evidently, the car has turned into a proud proclamation of ethnic nationality and place of origin, and even in the midst of the race for economic well-being, its owner exhibits the symbol of the eternal city of her childhood and its diasporic memory: Samarkand, second city in Uzbekistan, at a junction on the Silk Road where Turks and Persians and Mongols convened a millenary settlement as old as Rome or Babylon, and according to tourism guides, "Mirror of the World, Garden of the Soul, Pearl of the Orient, Center of the Universe." Its name alone, only the name of the city, becomes a cipher for dreams and an homage to the nation left behind, remembered, beloved.

At some point, I thought of having the word "HAVANA" inscribed on my license plate, but I opted for anonymity. I think that message wouldn't have left any doubt about my place of origin, but I believed it was a bit showy, and I decided to keep the cherished name in a more hidden place, in the memory of the heart. Other Cubans place flags with the lone star in their cars. However, after more than forty-five years dwelling in lands other than the one where I was born, I have been thinking that my diasporic Cubanness can be expressed also by the name of another mythical city, remembered in our fantasy, present in dreams and in the imagination of readers of children's literature and spectators of classic films.

No, I am not going to have "Havana" written on my license plate. I would simply like to have two letters on my Toyota Camry that would spell "OZ."

Cuba as Metaphor

The process of turning Cuba into a metaphor goes through the heart of its capital: the tropical image that persists in memory, what lasts and shines in the corners of my mind is that of the Morro Castle, the Paseo del Prado, or the Malecón. From that image one goes on to iconization, and from an icon, in turn, a trope is built that generalizes the concept: from the island nation to the capital of that world, to the city as representative of the original and "legitimate" culture. As *madrileños* say: "From Madrid to heaven, and a little hole to see it," meaning that only in paradise can one feel better than in the capital of Spain, and then only if you keep looking down at it through a peephole.

All that process of metaphorization, that winding journey like the meanders of a river, is an integral part of my search for identity as a *Cuban(a)-plus* (a term that I use to describe my multicultural performance of Cubanness, something that will be well understood by other "pluriCubans" who read these pages). The universal image of the city conflates with the immemorial representation of the Roman *urbis* (indeed, all roads lead to Rome), and with what we know about philosophical and imaginative religious readings; that is the way in which myths are constructed. *De Civitate Dei* was the title that Augustine of Hippo gave his book, speaking of the Christian community in opposition to the *civitas diaboli* of unbelievers, and though I don't equate (not even for a crazy instant) Havana with the divine and paradisiacal city in opposition, say, to a demoniacal New York—I can't do this because time and travels have immunized me against the madness of such myths, cultivated secretly by many insular as well as diasporic Cubans, and even recently by producers of films such as *The Lost City*—the temptation of the symbolic parallel is seductive. No wonder the neo-Romantic song collections of past decades referred to Havana as a siren lost in the waves of the sea. . . . But let's talk about other places before going back to the first one.

I went back to Niagara a few months ago. I say this not because I returned to a reading of the poem by Heredia, but because I have been able to gaze at the majestic falls, so dear to the memory of the exiled Matanzas poet, three times in my life. Although now I saw it from an airplane, I thought about the immortal lines, inscribed in my memory and also on a plaque placed on the Canadian side:

> What seeks my restless eye?
> Why are not here,
> About the jaws of this abyss, the palms—
> Ah—the delicious palms, that on the plains
> Of my own native Cuba, spring and spread
> Their thickly foliaged summits to the sun,
> And, in the breathings of the ocean air,
> Wave soft beneath the heaven's unspotted blue?
> This memory returns, to my chagrin . . . [2]

I was returning home from a seminar at the University of Buffalo where, with a group of "Cubanologists" and "Cubanophiles" residing in the United States, I had been discussing the intricate process of Cuban American cultural identity construction through several of its artistic expressions. There were not that many points on which we were in agreement, except in accepting that this is a complex situation and different for each of us. Of course, there were plenty of allusions to, and remembrances of, the text by Heredia in a place so close to where we were. Not everybody could remember the verses, but many recognized the importance of a basic cultural memory that can offer a background for discussion of what Cubanness is. Beyond the Cuban commonplace (no offense) of palm trees, present not only in the national emblem but also in many ashtrays and Cuban supermarket ads in New Jersey, there were other common denominators. We did not take into account nostalgia, that emotional discourse worn out by use and damaged by temporal distance, and we did away as well with classic essentialisms such as defining "what is Cuban." And yet we could detect something—that elusive something that is peculiarly affective—and which makes us feel an ethnonational solidarity in common. We were very clear that "that" which is peculiarly ours—La Cosa Nostra of the Cuban diaspora—is similar but different to whatever is also present in insular Cubanness; it has its origins in that original one, but it overflows its limits, transcends it physical and cultural borders, it metamorphoses, becomes more ample and diversified (and enriched, I think): it becomes transnational. And even then, "it" remains recognizable.

In that place close to Niagara I called our obsessive singularity by the name of *locura nacional* (national madness), which some partially refer to as "Cuban exceptionalism" and which borders on ethnocentrism, making us repeat ourselves on the same theme ad nauseam, to the boredom of others alien to our fixation on a persistent ontological search and confirmation. But since we are prone to build curious epistemologies based on that search, I want to construct right here a metaphor as long as it is culturally hybrid. I repeat: the process of metaphorizing Cuba is an integral part of my search for identity as a "Cubana-plus."[3] And in these lines I would like to begin living within my own self that identification, and configure a representation of Cuban culture in terms of the land of Oz, that mythical kingdom populated by the magic of his author's dream, the dream of L. Frank Baum, author of the book that serves as basis for the iconic film. The center of that utopia is a city of high shining towers, inhabited by people who serve and protect a mustachioed, mysterious wizard, axis and motor behind the urban miracle, whose name is a metonymic symbol for the place: Oz is the land because Oz is the wizard that created it, and both are one and the same.

In this manner, I want to construct a culturally hybrid allegory, and thus configure Cuban culture in a lyrical way, through the greenish veil of a reverie, as many other times the memory of that insular culture to which I once belonged is reconstituted. *Follow the yellow brick road, follow the yellow brick road....* Who has not seen Dorothy walking side by side with the cowardly lion, the brainless scarecrow, and the heartless tin man on the yellow brick road toward the shining city, where everyone is dressed in green, and where a mysterious wizard of legendary powers dwells and controls the destinies of that kingdom? What child has not trembled with fear when seeing the Wicked Witch of the West fly in her broom over the skies, intent on attacking the protagonist who travels in the company of the "good"? Have we not all laughed to see the Munchkins welcoming Dorothy, singing and dancing as the patriotic little people that they are, happy that Munchkinland, their country, has been saved from the spell of the Wicked Witch of the East? And who has not hummed—along with Judy Garland—the emblematic song of that place beyond the rainbow, the paradise that remains unreachable but that can be visited in our imagination? "Somewhere over the rainbow, way up high, there's a land that I heard of once in a lullaby...." (And beyond the rainbow, by the way, there is also the unreachable pot of gold filled with golden coins, according to the Celtic legends of Ireland, that other big island of green shamrocks and mysterious spirits, to carry the intriguing parallels further and to show that it is not only in Hollywood and Miami where webs of enchanted dreams are woven.)

The blue bird of happiness and the end of wicked spells await mortals in that mythical land, in the Emerald City: the perfect city-state, with marble columns and green tree fronds swaying in the breeze, populated with smiling, happy people who eat fruit jelly and promenade about in horse-drawn carriages, take pictures in front of artistic monuments, and live an unproblematic existence, telling jokes and composing music. Once its borders are crossed, sorcerers beautiful as fairies guide the traveler toward the Sanctum Sanctorum, the sacred and mysterious place where every wish is granted, where the heart is replenished with happiness, courage is recovered, and all pain ends; the center of centers, at the end of a shining corridor flanked with large colored-glass windows. That is Oz: mythic *locus, omphalos mundi*, nucleus of the universe where everyone experiences the plenitude of life's joys...in spite, or maybe because of, the wizard that gives it name and impulse. But Dorothy wants to go home, and wants her friends to be completed and satisfied, full of love, of brilliant ideas, and of courage to confront the dangers that lurk in any corner of life. The Wizard, a green-bearded personage, is all-powerful, and all granting. But woe! At the end, Toto, the little dog, reveals that everything is a mirage, after sliding a curtain open with his teeth. The Wizard ends up being just a figure invented by myth, hidden behind the smoke of machines, ultimately mortal, a reflection of our own limitations, and also of our own desires.

In my mind, the whole kingdom of Oz is represented on the same plane that the metaphorical Havana/Cuba that I describe here. They are one: the utopian place, the basic navel or center that we never had completely, that we sought to recover and thus (re)gain an original identity, as we approach the settling down of a diaspora whose citizens have much in common with the primeval island, as far as imagination goes. Cuba has ended up being, for her devotees inside and outside, the *umbilicus mundi*, and its capital city the center of that umbilical hole that carries one to the depths of one's being, in search of our original substance. Its/her charm lives on in our collective memory; in the words of a Cuban, recently immigrated to the southwestern deserts where I live, "Pompeiians would have celebrated it in a mosaic" (*la havana*, Osvaldo Cleger).

This is why I go through the world like a Cuban Dorothy, allegorically searching for the way home although afraid of the Wizard locked up in the green towers (who, for those who have not seen the film, ends up being a fraudulent and crazy man), or trying to find a *locus primus* where there are no supreme sorcerers, dangerous spells, or strange citizens. There are witches on the road, and flying monkeys enslaved by the Wicked Witch of the West, the general of those troops that maintain a reign of terror in the woods. I am afraid of those witches and those wizards, I fear witchdoctors and I don't even like mangoes (paradoxical detail in a person of Caribbean island birth).

Also contradictorily, I live in a country ruled by a character that, like a puppet, follows the design of the greater consumer society, sees imaginary witches where there are none, and uses them as a pretext to send armies of flying monkeys to conquer republics full of crude oil. At the end of the movie, nevertheless, innocence and kindness apparently triumph, à la Hollywood...taa-daah! All recognize that they have been deceived, but there is hope if one follows the road to self-knowledge (myth lives eternal in the heart of believers).

Parallel to that suggestive fable, my pages try to describe in symbolic, subjective terms what—in a poetic consciousness—is the imaginary kingdom of that transnational Cuba, a shining imaginary land of wizards and mangoes, of witches and witchdoctors, of bearded lackeys and of innocent or perverse creatures that populate the corners of the world, always sharing their *duende* and their grace, their angel and their *jiribilla*, constituting the polyvalent metaphor of a nation in search of itself.

CUBA AS FICTION

After all, through the fogs of memory, that place that is vaguely remembered with the adolescent awe of diluted remembrance, is a mythical kingdom. From the beginning, the great admiral of the Ocean Sea who arrived on its eastern shores described it as "the most beautiful island that human eyes have ever seen," a phrase repeated ad infinitum in our school classrooms, where visual and cartographic images were reproduced of that territory surrounded by water on all sides, with the contour of an alligator.[4] In that paradisiacal island space, sung by the poet Cucalambé as "Cuba delicious Eden / perfumed by your flowers / he who has not seen your beauties / has not seen the light nor enjoyed goodness" (translation mine), dreams were anchored that survive in the memory of many in later generations, light years after.

That Cuba with which poets dreamed, and for which sighs are heard among the old men in Miami who play dominoes on Calle Ocho, is a fiction maintained alive by means of the desire that it never end. But historical realities change, permutate, metamorphose; what always remains, immortal for posterity, are the fictions. Just ask Borges. And the Cuba that is expressed as a metaphor is also the filtering of a fiction. It is the original place, and thus idealized in memory and in hopes; but globally, in the diaspora, it is the common point of reference for those who live in the deterritorialized and open, plurisituated territory of a nation that overflowed its physical borders and spread throughout the world.

In the beginning of the twenty-first century, that transnationalized Cuba has already gone beyond many of the limitations that once circumscribed it: the weight of nostalgia, the murmurs of an eternal desire for return (today relegated more and more to generations that have left the island later, or to people in the last years of their life), the double life standard, bicultural and transculturated, in the present and in the past. All that overcoming, all that "leaving behind," is certainly more predominant outside of the duplicating environment of Florida, where many want to keep on living in the reverie of the Munchkins, the singing and dancing little people who welcomed Dorothy in the film about Oz, and are grateful that she landed in their middle. There, to a greater or lesser degree, the fiction called "Cuba" is kept alive by emotional and intellectual design. But in the final analysis, all its global citizens keep documents of spiritual identity in their hearts, although more and more the great majority of them—including of course their descendants, ethnic and cultural Cubans by heritage and by will—open themselves to the world, and only return to the fiction in leisure hours by means of music, gastronomy, or conversation, tied at times to the fresh memories of those who left the original beaches not too long ago to join the construction of a transnational nation.

Those who continue migrating today from the original paradise come to narrate the reverse of a fairy tale, but nevertheless contribute to the connection by means of their memories, and by the cultivation of ties with that place without realistic boundaries. The fiction called "Cuba," in spite of contact with the recently arrived, gets more and more diluted in the memory of the first migrants, it dissipates, turns into a foreign entity not so missed anymore, one that sometimes is (re)claimed and sometimes is just (barely) understood.

In my role as Dorothy, the amazed girl who declares she is not a witch but rather the inhabitant of a rural state—"Are you a good witch or a bad witch?" "I'm not a witch at all! I'm Dorothy Gayle, from Kansas!" (movie dialogue between Dorothy and Glinda, the beautiful and kind Witch of the North)—that home I yearn for in the depths of my soul is not precisely the real nation-state, the political and economic Cuba, the land of flesh and blood. A preferred place of one's own, representing the loft where one keeps childhood memories: that is the basis of my metaphoric Cuba... "I am not a witch, I am not treacherous or wicked because I am transnational; I am the Cuban Dorothy, formerly from Pinar del Río, now from the world!" In my personal meditations on identity, I identify with and reencounter the characters of Oz time and time again: sometimes the cowardly lion, some other times the bird-brained straw figure that can't think or decide, and even the patriotic midgets who dance and sing in gleeful noise upon discovering that the wicked Witch of the East has died, or is dying, she who terrorized the kingdom. My Florida family is made up of many of them, Munchkins who dance and talk all at the same time. Their joy at being free to say what they want is understandable because they have lived year after year, almost five decades, under the malignantly present shadow of a being with a long nose and green face, supposedly immortal, who once changed their lives. But there are no real wizards in the Floridian kingdom of Munchkinland, even though they have heard of a great OZ as all powerful and beneficent, and they think they live in the Emerald City.

In that imaginary city prosperity reigns, and there are tall buildings, beauty salons, and gigantic flowers, carpets, servants, consumer products, multicolored horses, carriages, and soldiers with halberds, walls that impede the entrance of any old mortal. And their unreal wizard has the same face as the bearded Uncle Sam. How is that possible? Could it be that OZ is also US? (Or that US can be OZ?) Do Cuban Americans living in these continental lands also dwell in the reverie of another myth, present in a parallel universe? Or is the original vision of a shining city confused with all the other cities that we have visited or inhabited in our diaspora? Londres, Madrid, Barcelona, París, Los Angeles, Nueva York, San Juan, México, Caracas, Buenos Aires, Bombay now Mumbai, Hong Kong, even Samarkand: are they all possible and exalted images of what Alejo Carpentier called La Ciudad de las Columnas (The City of Columns), Havana? I see the cobblestones in Old San Juan and those in the Boulevard Saint Michel in Paris, the ones in the old colonial city of Santo Domingo, the ones in Madrid's Plaza Mayor, even the ones in Rome, near the Colosseum and the Spanish Steps, and I think of the *adoquines* near the Templete or the Alameda de Paula in Havana, and those images are like tourist postcards: souvenirs of spaces visited, previously inhabited, shadows of a mythical city that repeats itself, navel reproduced in all latitudes, La Habana that was the center and is not anymore but that keeps reproducing itself in global space, Cuba with its palm trees remembered in Canada, the city with its deteriorated streets, remembrances of a visited space once inhabited and evoked in other countries, the nation that is another planet and an intriguing fiction that casts a spell with the memory of what is possible and the present horror of what is real.

I remember the line of verse by Octavio Paz: *Voy por tu cuerpo como por el mundo*, (I travel your body, like the world),[5] and I think that the fictitious and metaphorical body of Cuba is a live being, reproduced in similar manners but different in each one of the diasporic imaginaries that are scattered throughout the planet. Reproduced and alive, but not constantly contemplated: memory is sudden at times, and at other times blurry.

I travel your body like the world, Havana/Cuba, because you are the world (even if microcosmic), but at the same time only part of the world. Other transnational Cubans travel the body of the planet (I have seen them at the Louvre, at the Fountain of Trevi, at the Escorial, speaking with an unmistakable accent that, I do not know why, insistently preserves the cadences, the vowels, and consonants of popular Havana speech). They travel the world with their body, those diasporic Cubans (diasporocubans?), speaking also in other tongues, saying yes to foreign airs and opening a small café in London where they sell *mojitos* and *picadillo*. And I travel the world with my body as a Cuban Dorothy, thinking of a shining realm where the witches and wizards finally die because everything comes to an end, even that which is deemed immortal. In life everything passes on, "even the... even the... even the prune passes," as note the lyrics in the song by Liliana Felipe. And what persists is myth, for all eternity.

CUBA AS (PRE)TEXT

In a sense, my personal meditation on what Cuba *is* takes me to what Cuba is *not*. And what takes me everywhere else, to other bodies and other latitudes, is a bridge by which I hurl myself into exploration. I remember the words by Gloria Anzaldúa, in the preface to her book *This Bridge We Call Home:*

> Bridges are thresholds to other realities, archetypal, primal symbols of shifting consciousness... [that] connote transitioning, crossing borders, and changing perspectives... change is inevitable.[6]

And so it is with other bridges that we visit, after those in Michigan and the meeting that Ruth Behar called in Ann Arbor, bridges that take us to another shore and under which a lot of water has run, even more than when we pronounced, in 1994, that the river of time kept on flowing and took with it so many things. As Gloria (*que en paz descanse*) says, we are dealing with archetypes, and our consciousness changes. In this metaphoric field of land and water, when we cross borders and take steps toward the future, change is irreversible and inevitable. Bridges do not last forever, but in the transition toward other openings, Cuba is constituted again as the text and the pretext. Wherever there is the presence of those unmistakable transnationals, there will be conversation for the pure pleasure of fruition. Words in the mouth of Cubans sound and taste like guava paste, although at times they also smell like gunpowder. And that explosive sweet is the text, the textile, of an undeniable ethnoidentity, that can be heard and touched. But at the same time it is an excuse, the pretext to speak about the known and the recognized.

According to the sociologists who study diasporic phenomena, the world is now experiencing the largest migratory flux in the history of humanity. There are more than 185 million transnational migrants and refugees around the planet. It is also said that immigration nowadays generates massive transformations not only in the countries that send but also in those that receive migrants. That means that however much those on the outside (us) think that we are (or not) exiled from paradise, those who remain behind are (whether those who preside and decide want it or not) profoundly influenced by our allegorical, diasporic thinking. They dream what we dream because they ask themselves what happened to those who left. *Ubi sunt* our Vedado neighbors? Where did the gentlemen and ladies of the past end up? For the most part, they went to the other Land of Oz, Wonder of the Western world, surprisingly ruled now by a puppet and not by a wizard, even if the national avuncular icon has a beard.

And from the happy land of the Munchkins they send postcards, remittances, glitzy butterflies, little monkeys with mechanical tails, Internet visual images, messages, bottles coming from the Emerald City that are green and transparent, and they talk (in a soft voice) about the magic kingdom where anyone can walk on the yellow brick road, ho-hoing where are you going, I'm going to the countryside to seek my fortune, I'm going to take a ride around the planet, to saunter around the world, around the YUMA, around the UNAM in Mexico, to see movies by UMA (Thurman) in Los Angeles, to protest in front the United Nations, to visit UNESCO in Paris, in sum, to join the diasporic dance troupe around the planet, to use letters in a clever way, to say whatever comes to mind.

Such immigrants (as we are) organize themselves in transnational networks of social and cultural relationships that make borders porous, and in some way, redundant. The island becomes redundant, the text becomes redundant, and so do the margins: Havana, Cuba, free territory of the imagination (and not free from sin, as Frank Domínguez said in his bolero). But the city and the country, metaphor and allegory both of a diasporic, borderless kingdom, dimensions without land but nevertheless inhabited, continue progressing in their metamorphosis. By means of those bridges of the past we crossed to other margins and other shores, and that transnational Cuba (whether wanted or not by those who do not want it, and many of them must be in the island, discussing the matter in premodern terms) constitutes the most promenaded extension of the world outside the island borders. There they are: salsa dancers in Las Vegas, painters and artists in the DF, book dealers in Barcelona, cameramen in Madrid and Budapest, *sonero* musicians in Nueva York, yes, engineers in Venezuela, topographers in Ecuador, journalists in Coral Gables and Argentina, professors on the university campuses at Río Piedras and Mayagüez and Riverside, California, and writers everywhere, spilling out of car windows and planes, talking with one another on mobile phones and chatting on the Internet, the blessed addiction of planetary communication that makes talkers of all of us, that allows us to see Pinochet's funeral, the Catholic conversion of Daniel Ortega, the fashion runways in Milano, the secret illnesses of Caribbean caudillos, and that lets us return to Vegas to catch the show *Havana Nights*, whose insular performers liked the Nevada desert so much that most of them established their residence there in 2005.

Yes, it's a small world and the Cubans who walk the planet's roads get together to say *Oye, chico* and drink strong coffee on any street corner, which might not be *L y 23* but is more up-to-date, in any city on earth. The metaphor is globalized; the boundaries and borders of the city and the country become even more porous, there is no one who does not know what is happening in each corner, the world gets populated with travelers and mobilized people, even though the poor are left behind for lack of computers and passports and visas and freely exchangeable or acceptable currency. A cousin of mine who lives in Miami—not precisely known for her liberal ideas—on hearing the question "Are you thinking of returning to Cuba to live there some day?" answered with another question and offered a categorical answer: "Me? Move from the First World back to the Third? *Ni loca!* (I would have to be crazy!)." In the allegorical terms that I propose here, her reply could be stated like this: "Leave the actual kingdom of Oz to go back to that other imaginary, nostalgic kingdom? Please don't be foolish!" (Well, I would like to be the Queen of England, of course. At least I have the same initials, ER, as Elizabeth Regina in her monograms.)

CUBA AS TRANSNATION

If in the volume compiled by Damián Fernández, *Cuba Transnational*,[7] there is an attempt to define and situate in socially scientific terms the concept of a diasporic nation that some of us have creatively called "The Complete Cuba,"[8] in reality this phenomenon of the century has already been widely accepted by humanities theoreticians and students of global migration. At the October 2003 conference of Cuban and Cuban American Studies of the Cuban Research Institute (Florida International University), in a session titled "Cuba (Tras)Pasada, Cuba (Tras)tornada [Cuba (Trans)Fixed, Cuba (Dis)ordered]: Views on the Global Nation and Its Multiplicity of Being," there was a discussion on this topic that I now take the liberty of quoting extensively (I follow the pattern of what some critics term autocannibalism):

> I believe that there exists a transnational Cuba that has been spilling over the material boundaries of the island for decades, and that slowly (and painfully) is trying to transcend its past and look realistically at its present and future. At the same time that it experiences disorder and confusion, trying to imagine itself as a nation that evolves while it grows beyond its geographical borders, that transnational Cuba wishes to return to "being complete" after the disorder: the disturbing and emotionally troubling process of transference and translocalization of many of its original inhabitants. In that evolving process, the nation as a global community has become a "transnation," and many of its previous citizens are, in fact, transnational Cubans, diasporic subjects. There will always be, however, someone who will question these notions as dangerous to the integrity of a homogeneous "national essence" that has long been thought to define Cubanness. Although that essentialistic concept is extremely dubious in this postmodern age, nevertheless there are those who foresee that presenting national identity "as a cultural artifact open to handling and contestation is enough to provoke the worst passions on all the multiple sides of the Cuban divide." (Buscaglia-Salgado, 287, translation mine)[9]

I understand that some scholars in the island refuse to accept the concept of a transnational Cuba as we define it in the diaspora. I have heard comments about a meeting of Cuban studies at the University of Nottingham, England, in September 2006, where in a panel formed by participants from outside and inside the island the topic was intensely discussed, and some rejected the concept of Cuba transnational from the start (this is understandable, if what one attempts is to ideologically defend the integrity of the insular nation-state as complete in itself; global studies suggest the opposite, nevertheless).

On the other hand, as the Dorothy that I am, I believe in the power of imagination, in a postmodern vision that considers the profound influx and reflux of ideas with respect to *"Cubanidad"* and diaspora, and that can accept that today borders can be electronically erased because most of us have access to the dissemination, and even more importantly, the formation of ideas. Transnationalism is an exchange across those borders, carried out by nongovernmental individuals, by similar organizations, by information networks. As Damián Fernández asserts, the predominant image of Cuba as an geographically and politically isolated nation, "a sort of social Galápagos" (xiii), has been recognized as a myth, and the discourse about that Cuba "disconnected from the world" serves primarily to promote interests that arise from opposite, contending angles, as those of tourist agencies that encourage possible travelers with images of exotic destinations. A transnational Cuba, as the one known by those who live from the outside the nationality paradigm that includes us (whether we want it or not), is the image by which the insular *and* the diasporic society of the largest Caribbean island is presented to the world.

Given that perspective, I am of the opinion that notions such as citizenship and nationality change and metamorphose to the extent that they are reexamined by the light of these times in which we live. Some theoreticians even affirm that transnationalism refers to global cooperation among peoples, independently of the nation-states in which they inhabit. In that way, to be transnational is to be cosmopolitan. And a transnational lifestyle would be the dream of this Cuban Dorothy (to tell the truth, who wouldn't like to commute among several places in the European Union and North America—let us say, Nice, Vancouver, or Venice—with the change of seasons?) The cafés on Calle Florida in Buenos Aires and those in Brussels are not bad, and today even clubs in Shanghai are fine. In the People's Republic of China, the economic middle class that exists already lives a strange life: they cannot have access to all sites on the World Wide Web at home, but one finds tourists from Beijing in the casinos of Montecarlo and Lake Tahoe, at Lima shopping malls, and at the discos in Santiago de Chile...the world is a little ball, as Peruvians are wont to say. And we Cubans from the outside (though truly from *inside* the world), *los cubanos de fuera*, live to that beat, waiting perhaps to see our compatriots drinking coffee on La Gran Vía and talking to diasporic Cubans in Berkeley.

From that viewpoint, the diaspora is a precursor of postmodern transnationalism. That does not mean that all Cubans must leave their beloved birthplace, but the idea is that they might be able to face the world with open arms in the twenty-first century by stepping (voluntarily) on a foreign soil that they already know through the Internet and the World Wide Web. There are still so many of them that don't know what they are missing. In this way, the whole world is my kingdom of Oz, with wizards or without them. In the elaboration of my metaphors and my fictions lies the dream of an international/transnational humanist union in which witches have no place, and where the yellow golden road represents not only the bricks of a happy construction of life, but also the building of a homeland-nation that was what it was, is what it is, and will be what it will be in a not so distant future: worthy of being memorialized, visited, remembered in its hopes and its personal imaginaries, capable of belonging to all who love her, because she allows all her citizens to be global, to communicate widely, by electronic live transmission or in the (live) flesh.

I remember anew the verses of *Piedra de sol/Sunstone*, and I think of Havana/Cuba as the nucleus of that fiction, illusory but real at the same time—Mirror of the World and Garden of the Soul, Pearl of the East (Antilles) and Center of the Universe—that Samarkand of which one can dream in any place on the planet:

> you are a city that the sea assaults,
> a stretch of ramparts split by the light
> ....
> a domain of salt, rocks, and birds.[10]

And I go on as a Cuban Dorothy, singing over the rainbow and laughing with the little people, or at them. It is fine if anyone accuses me of being a romantic; that is why I believe in fairy tales, in allegorical metaphors, in the future, and in poetry.

NOTES

This essay is my own English version/translation of the original Spanish "Una Dorotea cubana." I am solely responsible for any changes, additions, and/or errors present herein.

1. As one of the ancient poets said, "You can travel through the whole world, have a look at the pyramids and admire the smile of the Sphinx; you can listen to the soft singing of the wind at the Adriatic Sea and kneel down reverently at the ruins of the Acropolis, be dazzled by Rome with its Forum and Coliseum, be charmed by Notre Dame in Paris or by old domes of Milan; but if you have seen the buildings of Samarkanda, you will be enchanted by its magic forever." From "Samarkand—the Gem of the East," http://www.tashkent.org/uzland/samarkand.html.

2. This translation, online at http://www.niagarapoetry.ca/heredia1827.htm, is attributed to William Cullen Bryant, American poet who also sang the glories of Niagara. The translation of the last line by Heredia, not present in Bryant's version, is mine.

3. In my article "In Two or More (Dis)Places: Articulating a Marginal Experience of the Cuban Diaspora," in Andrea O´Reilly Herrera, ed., *Cuba: Idea of a Nation Displaced* (Albany, NY: State University of New York Press, 2007), pp. 194–214, I discuss the notion of multiple positionality for a diasporic "Cuban-and-other" subject, characterized as possessing cultural markers that do not correspond to our paradigmatic and hegemonic discourse of exile. This is a model of identity construction that represents Cuban Americans (especially those who are not part of the southern Florida enclaves) as multi-cultural agents who demonstrate their adaptation by tolerating hybridity and even celebrating it, and who ponder—at many levels of interpretation—their dislocation from the cultural epicenters of Havana and Miami (*dislocated* is meant here as separated, taken out, dispersed, dismembered).

4. By the way, some irreverent Cubans in Miami have also seen in the island the profile of a vacuum cleaner, a contemporary version of the plow that characterized it before, and which places the wheels and the motor in the old Oriente province, the bag in Camagüey, and the handle in my native Pinar del Río.

5. Octavio Paz, with translation by Eliot Weinberger, *Piedra de sol / Sunstone* (New York: New Directions, 1987), pp. 12–13.

6. Gloria Anzaldúa and Ana Louise Keating, eds., *This Bridge We Call Home: Radical Visions for Transformation* (New York: Routledge, 2002), p. 1.

7. Damián J. Fernández, ed., *Cuba Transnational* (Gainesville, FL: University Press of Florida, 2005). The volume is a compilation of some of the papers presented at the Fifth Annual Conference of Cuban and Cuban American Studies, Cuban Research Institute, Florida International University, Miami.

8. See my "Cuba (In)Completa: Del sueño a la realidad" [(In)Complete Cuba: From Dream to Reality], in *Discursos desde la diáspora* (Cádiz: Aduana Vieja,

2005), pp. 47–57. In that essay, I give credit to the novelist Mayra Montero for the first use of such a phrase.

9. José F. Buscaglia-Salgado, "Leaving Us for Nowhere: the Cuban Pursuit of the American Dream" [review of Louis A. Pérez, Jr., *On Becoming Cuban: Identity, Nationality, and Culture*], *The New Centennial Review*, v. 2, n. 2 ("Origins of Postmodern Cuba," Summer 2002), p. 287. The quoted paper, which I read at that CRI conference in 2003, was titled "Cuba (Tras)Pasada: los imaginarios personales de una generación," or "(Trans)Fixed Cuba: The Personal Imaginaries of a Generation."

10. Octavio Paz, translated by Eliot Weinberger, *Piedra de sol/Sunstone* (New York: New Directions, 1987), p. 13. The verses quoted correspond, in order of appearance, to: José María Heredia, "Al Niágara"; Juan Cristóbal Nápoles Fajardo (*El Cucalambé*), "Décimas"; Octavio Paz, "Piedra de sol" (excerpts). They are all classic texts that can be found in Spanish on the Internet. The poem "la havana" by Osvaldo Cleger is included in his unpublished collection "Desertares" (included here by permission of the author).

CHAPTER 23

Becoming Cuba-Rican

Jorge Duany

Writing this essay has proven more difficult than other essays.[1] As someone trained primarily in the social sciences, I was taught to use the third person and erase most personal references from the text in order to sound more "objective" in my analyses. Moreover, the first person is problematic for me when referring to Cubans and Puerto Ricans, because I often feel caught between the two groups, as I'll elaborate below. Composing an autobiographic narrative on my subjective positioning as a "diasporic Cuban" therefore forced me to find a different voice from most of my previous publications on the intertwined topics of identity, migration, and transnationalism. I've been asked to reflect upon how my own experiences as a Cuban-born immigrant in Puerto Rico have affected my scholarly work, and to assume a personal rather than a "sociological" tone, a daunting task for someone not used to writing from this perspective.[2]

I was born in Havana in January 1957, but left Cuba with my mother and older brother on December 26, 1960. My parents' momentous decision to leave the island has always intrigued me and I still don't understand it fully. When the Cuban Revolution triumphed on January 1, 1959, my father was temporarily working as a television director in Costa Rica.[3] Meanwhile, I remained in Cuba with my mother and brother. My father went back to Havana sometime thereafter but couldn't find a job, so he had to move again, this time to Panama. Among other reasons, he felt displaced by the swift nationalization of the main Cuban television station, CMQ, where he'd worked before. My mother, who then strongly identified with Fidel Castro's Revolution like most of her family, stayed on, until she followed my father, together with my grandmother, who returned to Cuba after three months. My young mother must have been torn by the dilemma of keeping her marriage together or staying in her home country with her relatives.

Initially, we settled in Panama but moved on to Puerto Rico in 1966. I remember looking at a map of the Caribbean and wondering why on earth we were going there; I felt completely Panamanian by then. My growing family (I had two more siblings now) relocated in San Juan because my father was offered a job producing and directing television programs, including *telenovelas* (soap operas) and game shows. Also, my *padrinos* (godparents) were living there, as well as two of my parents' cousins on both sides of the family. I spent the rest of my childhood and adolescence in the San Juan metropolitan area. After graduating from high school in 1975, I studied in the United States. I earned my bachelor's degree at Columbia University in New York, my master's at the University of Chicago, and my Ph.D. at the University of California at Berkeley. I married in 1985, the same year I finished my doctoral studies, returned to Puerto Rico, and started a full-time teaching career. I later worked for a year at the University of Florida in Gainesville. Since 1988, I've lived in Puerto Rico, with short absences abroad related to my academic career. I finished writing this chapter during my tenure in Gainesville as a visiting professor in the spring of 2007.

Since I was very young, I was troubled by the constant question, "where are you from?" I usually answered, "I was born in Cuba, but I grew up in Puerto Rico." But that answer never settled which country I felt most attached to, a question that became periodically urgent, as when Puerto Rico's national team faced Cuba's in basketball or baseball competitions. I must confess that I have to think twice when I see the flags of the two countries, with their identical layout and inverted colors, before deciding which is which. One way in which I tried to solve the puzzle of my divided loyalties was by visiting Cuba since the early 1980s, first as part of organized groups,[4] then as a participant in academic conferences, and lately as an ordinary member of the "Cuban community abroad," as I took my wife, daughter, and son to meet my extended family in Cuba. Over the past three decades, I've returned about ten times to Havana and once to Santiago, the city of my father's birth, largely to reconnect with my uncles and cousins, as well as to better understand contemporary Cuban society and its ongoing exodus, including my paternal aunt and four of my cousins who left in the 1990s. Every time I've been back to Cuba I've felt differently. At first I was very much at home, almost like a prodigal son, easily reconciled with my relatives on the island, especially on my mother's side. More recently, I've grown more distant from Cuba and increasingly convinced that I couldn't live anywhere but in Puerto Rico, where I've spent most of my life and where I've nurtured my own family. I now prefer to say that "I live in Puerto Rico, but my parents came from Cuba." Sometimes I'll declare that I'm Cuba-Rican, rather than Cuban-American, since I've never lived continuously for long periods of time in the United States, even though I'm a U.S. citizen since 1985.[5]

My personal diasporic condition has undoubtedly shaped my research agenda, especially on transnational migration from the Hispanic Caribbean. In the early 1980s, I began to study Cuban exiles in San Juan for my doctoral dissertation. Afterward, my first postdoctoral research project focused on Dominican migration (much of it undocumented) to Puerto Rico. In the early 1990s, I conducted a field study of Dominican transnationalism in

New York City. Over the past decade, most of my intellectual efforts have dwelt on the Puerto Rican diaspora in the United States. Despite the shifting terminology and objects of study, I've been largely concerned with how massive population displacements impact personal and collective identities. I hope this autobiographical disclosure will show more clearly the connections between my life history and those of many others who have left their countries of origin in the Caribbean over the past six decades. As C. Wright Mills put it so well, capturing the intersections between biography and history is one of the hallmarks of the sociological imagination.[6] As an anthropologist, I'm primarily interested in exploring whether my self-revelations might resonate with the experiences of other people like myself.

STUDYING CUBAN EXILES, KNOWING MYSELF

I completed my doctoral dissertation in 1985, after a year and a half of fieldwork with Cubans in Puerto Rico. At the time, I thought of my work as an "autoethnography," in the sense that I went back "home" to study "my people," not an exotic Other. It was clearly an autobiographical intellectual project, as I struggled to understand the community in which I had grown up but no longer belonged to. I felt estranged from older Cuban immigrants who seemed fixed on recuperating *la Cuba del ayer* (the Cuba of yesterday, as they often referred to prerevolutionary society). Because I was too young to remember anything about my childhood in Cuba, I had no emotional investments in that period of time, except through my parents' memories. Still, I retained strong family and friendship connections with Cubans in Puerto Rico. As I approached this sensitive issue, I sought to abandon the popular myth of the "Golden Exile"[7]—the almost instantaneous economic success of Cubans in San Juan as well as in Miami—and to explain their mode of incorporation, cultural adaptation, and ambivalent relationship with Puerto Rican society. Writing my dissertation, it was difficult to assume a "neutral" tone in describing the Cuban community in Puerto Rico, a tone that was neither celebratory nor condemnatory. It was even more difficult to place myself within a narrative dominated by a social scientific perspective in the third person.

To interpret the situation of Cubans in Puerto Rico, I've frequently resorted to the theoretical framework of "middleman minorities" (or trading minorities, to use a less male-centered expression).[8] I elaborated this model in my dissertation as well as several articles and a book coauthored with the Cuban-American sociologist José Cobas.[9] Basically, a trading minority is a culturally distinctive group that specializes in the distribution of goods and services within the host economy. Examples of this type of socioeconomic adaptation include Jews in Western Europe, Chinese in Malaysia, Asian Indians in East Africa, Pakistanis in London, and Koreans in Los Angeles. Unlike most immigrants, who cluster in the lower rungs of the receiving society, trading minorities occupy an intermediate position between the local elite and working classes. Such a position largely derives from the group's socioeconomic traits, such as their previous class background, educational resources, and transnational business connections. One of the attractions of the "middleman minority" model was that it illuminated significant angles of my family's and my own experiences.

Overall, Cubans in Puerto Rico fit the occupational profile of trading minorities. To begin, most are employed in commerce and services, especially retail trade and professional and business services. In San Juan, many exiles have excelled in "the art of buying and selling," particularly as managers, administrators, sales, and office workers. My own mother worked as a cosmetics sales clerk in a large department store, as an itinerant clothing seller, as a beautician, and as an insurance agent (although she had studied to be a schoolteacher in Cuba, she never practiced her profession in Puerto Rico). My father became programming director at one of Puerto Rico's leading television stations, until he lost his job as a result of a corporate takeover and had to start again in Ecuador, where he died years later. My parents' occupations mirrored the strong concentration of Cuban exiles in the middle and upper levels of trade, communications, and other tertiary sectors of the Puerto Rican economy, such as finance, insurance, and real estate.

Second, trading minorities everywhere tend to arouse hostility and suspicion from ample segments of the host society. Such groups are usually stereotyped as stingy, unscrupulous, clannish, and materialistic in their ruthless pursuit and accumulation of wealth. In addition, Cubans everywhere have been attributed a proverbial arrogance and have often been dubbed "the Jews of the Caribbean" because of their business acumen. Puerto Rican folk humor typically portrays Cuban exiles as pushy, ambitious, and sly entrepreneurs.[10] For instance, a Puerto Rican once told me the following riddle: "What do humble Cubans and Superman have in common? That they don't exist." Many Puerto Ricans associate the exiles with the *blanquitos* (literally, little whites) and *riquitos* (the little rich people), the white elite of San Juan. Although I'm often called a *blanquito* in Puerto Rico, I resent the implication that I feel superior to members of the lower class.

Moreover, trading minorities often generate antagonism as well as sympathy from different sectors of the native population. In Puerto Rico, the proindependence movement and some nationalistic elements of the middle classes have tended to reject Cuban exiles, while the prostatehood movement has welcomed them as ideological allies. Most Puerto Ricans still perceive the exiles as unwanted outsiders who should not meddle in the island's internal affairs.[11] In turn, many exiles continue to harbor deep-seated racial and ethnic prejudice against Puerto Ricans. A slur commonly used by Cubans to refer to Puerto Ricans is *boniato* (literally, sweet potato), a folk term for country bumpkin. To recycle Lola Rodríguez de Tió's famous metaphor, Cuba and Puerto Rico may well be like "the two wings of the same bird," but they're still far apart from each other.[12]

Personally, I didn't suffer direct discrimination as a Cuban growing up in Puerto Rico. Perhaps my middle-class status and light skin color shielded me from outright exclusion based on national origin. Nonetheless, I did experience more covert forms of prejudice. For me, being Cuban in San Juan—especially a *cubanazo*, a "full-fledged" Cuban—was the object of friendly humor more than scorn. For instance, if you drew too much attention to yourself, appeared conceited, or spoke Spanish with a strong Cuban accent, some Puerto Ricans would disapprovingly exclaim, *tenía que ser cubano!* (you had to be Cuban!). Cubanness remains a stigma for many immigrants in Puerto Rico.

Finally, trading minorities are distinguished by a high degree of ethnic solidarity that Cubans in Puerto Rico have displayed over the years, as well as by a persistent cultural identity that has weakened in the second generation, due among other reasons to a high outmarriage rate. On this last point, Cubans in Puerto Rico deviate from the typical experience of trading minorities, such as Jews or Chinese in other countries, who often remained endogamous for long periods of time. Linguistic, cultural, and religious affinities have encouraged intermarriage between Cubans and Puerto Ricans, at least among persons of similar class and racial background. In my study of marriage licenses in San Juan, nearly 56 percent of Cubans had Puerto Rican spouses by 1983.[13] (I myself represent a minority trend, because I married a Cuban-born resident of Puerto Rico.)

Nonetheless, Cubans in San Juan maintained more than thirty-five voluntary associations in the mid-1980s, which helped them to maintain strong symbolic bonds with their homeland. The most active among these organizations were Casa Cuba, a private club where I spent much of my teenage social life, and the Unión de Cubanos en el Exilio, a Catholic charity that I've studied in more detail elsewhere.[14] Both institutions exemplified a strong trend toward ethnic encapsulation among first-generation immigrants. But most members of the second and third generations didn't follow that trend. As an adult, I haven't joined any Cuban associations in Puerto Rico, as a result of my growing ideological detachment from the dominant institutions of the exile community. In this regard, I feel closer to the experience of the second generation than the first generation of Cubans in San Juan. Most of my social life currently revolves around Puerto Rican rather than Cuban friends.

In my experience, Cuban and Puerto Rican cultures do not differ markedly. Regarding language, music, food, or religion, the two countries are indeed as closely linked as two wings of the same bird. That's one of the reasons why many Cubans resettled in San Juan in the first place and Cubans' integration into Puerto Rican society has generally been swifter than in south Florida's enclave, where many Cuban practices and values remain virtually intact and relatively isolated from other cultures. Altogether, Cuban Americans and Cuba-Ricans like me have developed distinctive identities, depending on where we grew up and how we blended into the receiving countries. Other scholars have argued that the meaning of the Cuban diaspora is strongly conditioned by when, how, why, and where one settled outside of Cuba.[15] I believe it's been easier for Cubans to "assimilate" into Puerto Rican culture than into mainstream American culture. Still, you must lose your Cuban "accent" in order to "pass" as Puerto Rican, as I often do, unless I'm asked about my birthplace. In some quarters, I know I'll never be fully accepted as part of the Puerto Rican nation because of my foreign birth. At best, I can aspire to become *un cubano buena gente* (loosely translated, a Cuban who's OK). Passing has its limits.

A continuing source of friction with many Puerto Ricans is the exiles' political ideology. Although many, perhaps most, Cubans in Puerto Rico favor the island's complete annexation to the United States, not all do. Nor can most exiles be caricatured as reactionary *batistianos* (supporters of Fulgencio Batista's dictatorship) who long to recreate "the Cuba of yesterday" once Fidel Castro dies. I certainly wouldn't describe my parents' ideological preferences that way, although my father was more conservative than my mother, partly as a result of their different class and generational backgrounds. Many exiles in Puerto Rico belong to the moderate sectors of the Cuban population abroad, who felt betrayed by the Revolution when it turned more radical in the early 1960s. My analysis of various Cuban organizations and publications in Puerto Rico revealed an ample spectrum of opinion, ranging from the far right to the far left.[16] Nonetheless, most Cubans in Puerto Rico are staunch advocates of the island's permanent association with the United States.

An apparent paradox is the exiles' combination of a strong diasporic nationalism (vis-à-vis Cuba) and pragmatic annexationism (vis-à-vis Puerto Rico). My mother often pointed out that contradiction to her friends and acquaintances, who didn't find it worthy of further discussion. I tend to identify with my mother's critical perspective, which has won me few allies among exiles. Over time, I've come to support either independence or free association to resolve Puerto Rico's colonial dependence on the United States. Needless to say, this political position has put me at odds with some Cubans in Puerto Rico. In the 1980s, many exiles also considered traveling to Cuba blasphemous, a concession to peaceful coexistence with Castro's revolutionary government. According to recent polls, however, most Cuban Americans now support unrestricted travel and sending money to their relatives in Cuba.[17]

Unless a new migrant wave from Cuba to Puerto Rico arises in the near future—an unlikely event, given the sluggish performance of the Puerto Rican economy since the mid-1970s—Puerto Rican society will completely absorb its Cuban community within the next generation, that of my children born on the island. If you ask them what they are, most will quickly respond "Puerto Rican," even though their parents were born in Cuba. Unlike me, my children have no qualms about their national identity. As a member of the 1.5 (or perhaps 1.75, to quote the Cuban-American sociologist Rubén G. Rumbaut) generation of immigrants, my position is much more precarious.[18] If Cuba plays baseball against Puerto Rico, I'll root for the Puerto Rican team. But when Cuba faces the United States in international sports, I'll usually side with the Cuban team.

PLACING MYSELF IN THE NARRATIVE

Writing about Puerto Rican national identity, I'm often painfully aware that I'm not one of the island's native sons. My Cuban birth, coupled with longtime residence in Puerto Rico, gives me an odd status somewhere in between stranger and near-native. I've often felt uneasy straddling this outsider/insider dichotomy, as when I'm called a "Puerto Rican sociologist" (who is neither Puerto Rican nor a sociologist, but rather an anthropologist). But being called a "Cuban-born anthropologist" doesn't entirely resolve the problem either. This issue emerged sharply in a February 2004 interview with a Puerto Rican graduate student, Verónica Toro Ortiz, who translated several chapters of my book *The Puerto Rican Nation on the Move* into Spanish. Toward the end of our long and intense conversation, Verónica asked me about the use of the first person in my writing. I can only quote a passage from my response:

> I've realized, in the course of writing this book, among other things, that although I generally use the third person, when I'm going to introduce myself as part of the text, as part of the environment I'm observing, then I use the first person and I make the distinction, and that has to do partly with my own biography. To give you an example, a Political Science Professor, Angel Israel Rivera, told me one day in the hallway: "I'm glad that you're now saying, 'we Puerto Ricans.'" And it's difficult for me to say that, because I don't feel totally Puerto Rican, since I was born in Cuba, although I grew up here. Nor do I feel very comfortable saying "we Cubans." Therefore, given that duality, that ambiguity, I normally don't say one thing or another. I resort to the third person: Cubans do this and say that, as well as Puerto Ricans. Every now and then, I use "we" when I feel part of what I'm writing. Perhaps that appears more explicitly when you're translating, the way in which sometimes I'd rather remain on the margins and don't place myself there.

Let me add a personal note on language and identity. I was recently asked when I first "became" bilingual. I responded that my parents had sent me to an all-English missionary school in the Panama Canal Zone during my third grade. Initially, I couldn't understand most of what was taught, except for Spanish class. But that year forced me to learn English quickly to survive academically. Moreover, I was often confused with an American because of my pale skin, blue eyes, and formerly light hair color, and many of my classmates were children of U.S. military personnel stationed in Panama. I'd try to darken my hair by dampening it with water, combing it constantly, and repeating in front of the mirror, "I don't want to be a *gringo*." Anti-Americanism was firmly entrenched in Panama City during my childhood years.

After moving to Puerto Rico, I was again placed in an all-English seventh-grade group called "Continental"—referring to the children of American business people on the island—because I did well in the English entrance exam. I didn't like that experience, as I felt isolated from Spanish-speaking students in other classrooms. Again, many thought that I was American because of my physical appearance and I was commonly associated with the *gringos*. Even today, people routinely mistake me for an American, especially in public places with many U.S. tourists, such as airports, restaurants, and hotels. "But you don't look Puerto Rican," I'm frequently told, and when I respond that I'm actually Cuban-born, I may hear the rebuttal, "You don't look Cuban either." To which I may reply rhetorically, "What does a Puerto Rican (or a Cuban) look like?" I've often reflected on the irony of "looking American" while living in three of the countries where that attribution is most problematic (Cuba, Panama, and Puerto Rico), because of the long history of U.S. interventionism in the Caribbean region.

Lastly, a decade of study in U.S. universities gave me the opportunity to develop fluency in the English language, to the point that I feel almost (though not quite) as comfortable writing in English as in Spanish. But language is a minefield for Puerto Rican cultural politics because of the island's colonial relation with the United States, and the unequal status of Spanish and English. As I noted in my interview with Verónica (cited above):

> This is the first question I'm always asked... "Why did you write this book in English?" One always feels under attack and I always think, noting the differences, of the case of [the noted Puerto Rican writer] Rosario Ferré, who decided to write a book in Spanish and rewrite it in English, and she's still criticized for it. When my book is published in Spanish, I think the audience will be similar [to the original one]; we'll see how the translation affects the socioeconomic and educational composition of the audience. I think that it'll be more self-reflexive; for example, some things in the English version are explained thoroughly, which won't be necessary in Spanish [because most of my readers will be Puerto Rican].

CONCLUSION

Exiles, undocumented migrants, transnationals, and diasporas: these have been focal points of my research and writing for more than two decades. The terms are all various ways, each with its own particular inflection, of naming the massive population displacements that have reshaped Caribbean societies since the 1940s. Whether they migrate primarily for political reasons (as exiles) or economic reasons (as undocumented migrants), Caribbean people are constantly moving, circulating, and thereby creating transnational communities. The diaspora has become a defining feature of daily life, for those who live abroad (mainly in the United States), those who remain back home (in the Caribbean), and those who circulate between the two places. But the challenge of locating and identifying with the "homeland" is ever more difficult for many migrants, including myself. I was born in Cuba, live in Puerto Rico, and don't plan to return to Cuba, except for short stays. To use the terms I've often applied to others, I'm a member of a trading minority that migrated to a semiperipheral country, itself engaged in a massive diaspora and increasingly a transnational nation. In short, I've become a Cuba-Rican.

Where are you from? Where do you belong? What's your nationality? Where's home? Which is your mother tongue? To ponder such questions, for myself and for others, I've relentlessly pursued the dilemmas of cultural identity among Cubans, Dominicans, and Puerto Ricans, both in Puerto Rico and the United States. Thus, my academic work has become as transnational as its primary object of study. Reviewing my curriculum vitae for such practical matters as applying for promotion, tenure, and sabbatical leaves, I realize that I've devoted much time and energy to understanding transnational migration. A Puerto Rican colleague, Aarón Gamaliel Ramos, once quipped that it takes about ten years to specialize in a research topic and another ten years to "despecialize" from it. In my case, it's difficult to avoid being typecast as a "migratologist." At the same time, studying contemporary migrations has allowed me to gain insights into broader social processes, such as the transnationalization of cultural practices and identities that are increasingly common as a result of globalization. It's also helped me to better understand myself.

The editors of this volume, Ruth Behar and Lucía M. Suárez, have raised poignant issues for the contributors. What kind of relation do I still have to Cuba? How has linguistic and geographic displacement affected me? How has migration shaped my life and intellectual production? What are the multiple bridges, whether familial, generational, geographic, political, or linguistic, that I experience in my daily life? Without pretending to exhaust all the possible responses to such queries, being born in Cuba, raised in Panama and Puerto Rico, and living on and off in the United States have left an indelible imprint. One result of these experiences has been the constant shift between Spanish and English throughout my life. Spanish has always been the "native" language I speak at home, but now I read and write in English every day. Spanish is the primary medium for my most intimate thoughts and feelings, while English is a more academic and professional mode of expression for me. I suppose this linguistic split is part of many migrants' lives, as well as a sign of increasing cultural hybridity. In an interview for the newspaper *El Nuevo Día*, I once told the Puerto Rican literary critic Carmen Dolores Hernández that being an immigrant had led me inexorably to probe my own identity and that of others, especially when the sources of identity are increasingly fragmented. Returning to Cuba, if only infrequently and for short visits, has helped me regain my sense of wholeness and connectedness to my childhood past, distant homeland, and family dispersed throughout Cuba, the United States, Puerto Rico, Panama, Ecuador, Chile, Switzerland, France, and Russia.

My ailing mother's last letter to her older brother in Cuba is dated December 31, 1994, more than thirty-four years after we left Havana. I still keep a copy of that letter in my laptop computer. Because she couldn't write easily anymore, my mother dictated the following sentence to me: "Thank God, Jorge was able to travel to Cuba, which was a great dream of his, and that way we'll have the opportunity to see each other through him." When my mother passed away four months later, on April 11, 1995, I felt like I'd become the main liaison between my relatives in Cuba and abroad—that they somehow had to "see each other" through me, that it was now my turn to repair the family ties that were ruptured as a consequence of the Cuban Revolution nearly five decades ago. It's a great burden to have inherited my mother's role as a safe keeper of those fragile links that must continually be renewed across generations, long distances, and political differences. Like many transnational migrants I've met throughout my research, I too find it indispensable to maintain emotional, family, and cultural connections with my country of birth. Going back to Cuba every so often is a way of not burning the bridges back "home." Even though I might never go back to live there again, I'd like to claim, with the exiled poet Heberto Padilla, that I've always lived in Cuba, if only in my mind.[19]

NOTES

1. This chapter is loosely based on my earlier article, "Exiliados, indocumentados y diásporas: la migración contemporánea en Puerto Rico," published in the Cuban journal *Del Caribe* v. 31 (2000), pp. 13–20. I was especially proud of this publication, because it's sponsored by the Casa del Caribe in Santiago de Cuba, located in Vista Alegre, the neighborhood where my father was born and grew up. I appreciate the suggestions for revision by the editors, Ruth Behar and Lucía M. Suárez, as well as stimulating comments by Yolanda Martínez-San Miguel, Silvio Torres-Saillant, Eliana Rivero, and Yeidy Rivero.

2. Ruth Behar has eloquently argued for a more intimate narrative style that takes into account the anthropologist's vulnerable position vis-à-vis her ethnographic informants. See Behar, *The Vulnerable Observer: Anthropology That Breaks Your Heart* (Boston, MA: Beacon, 1997).

3. Based on her archival research in Havana, Yeidy Rivero (e-mail letter to the author, April 9, 2007) notes that Cuban television had entered a period of crisis since 1954, leading many TV directors, producers, and actors to leave the island, mostly to Venezuela, Colombia, and Puerto Rico. I don't know why my father ended up in Costa Rica. See Rivero, "The Cuban Connections: Havana as a 1940s–1950s Latin American Media Capital" (unpublished manuscript, Department of Communication and Culture, Indiana University, 2007).

4. Although I didn't belong to the Brigada Antonio Maceo and the Círculo de Cultura Cubana, I took the opportunity to travel to Cuba as part of two trips sponsored by these organizations. For a moving testimony of the first group of young radicalized Cubans who returned to the island, see Grupo Areíto, *Contra viento y marea: jóvenes cubanos hablan desde su exilio en Estados Unidos* (Havana: Casa de las Américas, 1978). For a broader set of personal narratives of traveling back home, see Ruth Behar, ed., *Bridges to Cuba/Puentes a Cuba* (Ann Arbor, MI: University of Michigan Press, 1996) and Andrea O'Reilly Herrera, ed., *ReMembering Cuba: Legacy of a Diaspora* (Austin, TX: University of Texas Press, 2001).

5. Here I use "Cuba-Rican" to designate someone born in Cuba and raised in Puerto Rico. Other scholars have employed the term to refer to the extensive exchanges between Cuban and Puerto Rican cultures since the nineteenth century, especially in popular music, creative literature, and the media. See César A. Salgado, "Cubarican: Efectos de la capilaridad colonial" (paper presented at the Second Conference on Cuban and Cuban American Studies, Cuban Research Institute, Florida International University, Miami, FL, March 18–20, 1999); and Yeidy M. Rivero, "Caribbean Negritos: Ramón Rivero, Blackface, and 'Black' Voice in Puerto Rico," *Television & New Media* v. 5 (2004), pp. 315–337. Yolanda Martínez-San Miguel has aptly analyzed "the constitution of a diasporic Cuban-Rican imaginary" in the scant literature produced by Cubans in Puerto Rico. See her essay, "Puerto Rican Cubanness: Reconfiguring Caribbean Imaginaries," in Andrea O'Reilly Herrera, ed., *Cuba: Idea of a Nation Displaced* (Albany, NY: State University of New York Press, 2007), pp. 47–76.
6. C. Wright Mills, *The Sociological Imagination*, 40th anniversary ed. (New York: Oxford University Press, 2000).
7. To my knowledge, Alejandro Portes first used the expression in a sociological article in "Dilemmas of a Golden Exile: Integration of Cuban Refugee Families in Milwaukee," *American Sociological Review* v. 34, n. 3 (1969), pp. 505–515. The term has become synonymous with the first wave of migration (1959–1962) after the Cuban Revolution, which drew mostly on the middle and upper classes. See also my essay, "Neither Golden Exile nor Dirty Worm: Ethnic Identity in Recent Cuban-American Novels," *Cuban Studies* v. 23 (1993), pp. 167–183.
8. The best statement of this perspective remains Edna Bonacich's classic essay, "A Theory of Middleman Minorities," *American Sociological Review* v. 38, n. 3 (1973), pp. 583–594.
9. See Jorge Luis Duany, *The Cubans of Puerto Rico: Socioeconomic Adaptation in a Caribbean City* (PhD dissertation, University of California, Berkeley, 1985); Duany, "The Cuban Community in Puerto Rico: A Comparative Caribbean Perspective," *Ethnic and Racial Studies* v. 12, n. 1 (1989), pp. 36–46; Duany, "Ethnic Identity and Socioeconomic Adaptation: The Case of Cubans in Puerto Rico," *The Journal of Ethnic Studies* v. 17, n. 1 (1989), pp. 109–127; and José A. Cobas and Jorge Duany, *Cubans in Puerto Rico: Ethnic Economy and Cultural Identity* (Gainesville, FL: University Press of Florida, 1997).
10. See Duany, "The Cuban Community in Puerto Rico" and "Ethnic Identity and Socioeconomic Adaptation."
11. See Duany, "Two Wings of the Same Bird? Contemporary Puerto Rican Attitudes Toward Cuban Immigrants," *Cuban Studies* v. 30 (1999), pp. 26–51.
12. Rodríguez de Tió (1843–1924) wrote the poem "A Cuba" while exiled in New York City in 1893, at the height of the nineteenth-century liberation struggle in Cuba and Puerto Rico against Spain. The poem's best known stanza is as follows: *Cuba y Puerto Rico son/de un pájaro las dos alas, / reciben flores o balas / sobre el mismo corazón.* (Cuba and Puerto Rico are/like two wings of the same bird, / they receive flowers or bullets / over the same heart.)
13. Duany, *The Cubans of Puerto Rico.*

14. Cobas and Duany, *Cubans in Puerto Rico.*
15. See, for instance, Silvia Pedraza, *Political Disaffection in Cuba's Revolution and Exodus* (New York: Cambridge University Press, 2007); and Mette Louise Berg, "Memory, Politics, and Diaspora: Cubans in Spain," in Andrea O'Reilly Herrera, ed., *Cuba: Idea of a Nation Displaced* (Albany, NY: State University of New York Press, 2007), pp. 15–34.
16. Cobas and Duany, *Cubans in Puerto Rico*, Chapters 6 to 8.
17. See Institute for Public Opinion Research, School of Journalism and Mass Communications, Florida International University, *2007 FIU Cuba Poll* (http://www.fiu.edu/~ipor/cuba8/pollresults.html, retrieved on April 20, 2007).
18. Rubén G. Rumbaut coined the term "1.5 generation" to refer to the children of Indochinese refugees in California and the literary critic Gustavo Pérez-Firmat later developed it in a Cuban-American setting. Basically, Pérez-Firmat argues that persons born in Cuba but raised in the United States are neither fully Cuban nor fully American. Thus, they straddle the linguistic and cultural boundaries between the first and second generations of Cuban immigrants. See Pérez-Firmat, *Life on the Hyphen: The Cuban-American Way* (Austin, TX: University of Texas Press, 1994). More recently, Rumbaut has written about the "1.75 generation" to describe immigrants who were born abroad but came to the United States before the age of five, and whose experiences are closer to the first than to the second generation. See Rumbaut, "Ages, Life Stages, and Generational Cohorts: Decomposing the Immigrant First and Second Generations in the United States," *International Migration Review* v. 38, n. 3 (2004), pp. 1160–1205.
19. Heberto Padilla included the poem "Siempre he vivido en Cuba" (I have always lived in Cuba) in his controversial collection, *Fuera del juego* (Havana: Unión de Escritores y Escritores de Cuba, 1968). Lourdes Casal later wrote a poem with the same title, included in her posthumous anthology, *Palabras juntan revolución* (Havana: Casa de las Américas, 1981). Thanks to Eliana Rivero for reminding me of Casal's poem. See also Román de la Campa's memoirs, *Cuba on My Mind: Journeys to a Severed Nation* (London: Verso, 2000).

CHAPTER 24

Crossing Borders: Notes on Forgetting

Mabel Cuesta

(Translated by David Frye, Achy Obejas)

ARRIVAL: MONTHS TWO THROUGH FOUR (SPRING)

Bergenline Avenue may be the busiest of the smaller avenues in Hudson County. It's the route I take when I travel back and forth to the International Institute of New Jersey, where I work with recent Cuban emigrés, and where I still get my own monthly stipend as a new arrival myself. It's where, for four endless hours each day, I hand out checks, make court appointments in Newark or welfare appointments in Jersey City, send out faxes and take requests for counseling about applying for U.S. residency, gaining citizenship, taking advantage of the Cuban Adjustment Act, or consulting with the lawyer who represents us before the immigration judge. Then the phone rings and it's someone who just crossed the border and his uncle or brother, in his Marianao or Ranchuelo-accented English, asks for an appointment and I explain, in Spanish—which makes him smile on the other side of the phone— that the case manager will see them, that they don't need an appointment, that they just need to come in. And then I write an e-mail asking my mother for my birth certificate, something to prove I'm Cuban, because the irony of my birthday, July 4, 1976, needs to be notarized, and I remember the Latin: *verba volant, scripta manent* (the words fly off, the writing remains). Then there's another knock on the office door and it seems somebody reached the coast of Miami on a raft but doesn't have the parole papers the immigration officer should have given him—and that's a big problem. Without them we can't process his work permit or his social security number, but please come in and we'll call Miami and see what we can do; in any case, you can come by Thursday afternoon when our lawyer is here; yes, he speaks Spanish, he was born in Cuba, he came over when he was little but he still remembers things; his last name is Saud—no, he isn't Jewish, he's Cuban-Lebanese, and he says *comemierda* as if he'd learned to curse downstairs from the Vedado apartment to which his parents will never return. And suddenly it's two in the afternoon, and even though I still have a few messages pending, I've got to cross Bergenline Avenue once more on my way to Manhattan, to teach Spanish at the Cervantes Institute.

I head over, happy to know that the group of students waiting for me are American citizens born in India, Canada, Turkey, Germany, Russia, Poland, and Trinidad and Tobago. I've been able to talk with the Polish student about the cartoons I watched as a kid, sharing my fondness for Bolek and Lolek, characters she loved, too. The German student and I talk about "Good Bye, Lenin!" Wolfgang Becker's obsessive film, barely seen in Havana.

I think about the fate of these students, about to reach the highest level at the Institute, and about the elderly couple I met at the office this morning, to whom we can't offer jobs or cash because they don't qualify for our program, because they're past working age and have to go straight to the Jersey City welfare office. They couldn't bring their grandson over with them, and the elderly woman cries while they wait for the lawyer so he can give them advice on how to claim their benefits. While they wait, the elderly man leads me by the elbow to the corner of my office and whispers in my ear: "She's very nervous, you know, it isn't easy to come here and leave your daughter and grandson behind, not knowing what's going to happen; but I'm strong, I can do any kind of work—if you hear about anything, you'll let me know, okay?"

And I tell him yes, I understand, and he asks me where I live, so I give him my address, and he asks if I came over with my parents, and I tell him I came alone, and he's surprised and continues with his indiscrete questioning: who do I live with, how did I get here, how long ago, do I know how to speak English, how much am I making, if I hear about any jobs, please, to not forget to let him know, and again I tell him yes, and I answer all his questions, though I'm careful not to scare him off, not to tell him that I'm a lesbian and that I live with my partner, that I crossed the Mexico and U.S. border at the exact point where the towns of Matamoros and Brownsville are simultaneously united and divided by the same bridge.

I'm careful not to tell the desperate elderly man how the Mexican authorities threw me off the bus and kicked the small suitcase that had accompanied me from Mexico City, where days earlier I had wondered what a borderland was, ensconced in my leather armchair, in my ivory tower. I'm careful not to tell him what I was before I crossed the border, about the possible me lurking down there, deep down, where other officers, this time American, give me orange soda and pat my head, welcome me to a country where I arrive torn between a love that was and a love that's just beginning: a woman's body; nights spent listening to the Salve Regina set to a contradanza that José María Vitier composed for his "Misa Cubana," his Mass for the Virgin of La Caridad del Cobre, all so I can get to sleep while Maya, by my side, meditates to stimulate the third strand of her DNA, or studies quantum physics, and we both burn Taj Mahal incense and light aromatic candles, the better to dream about that summer in St. Petersburg—the white nights, we repeat, watching an old documentary about the fall of the czars. I don't mention these things to the elderly man who has come precisely to the Guttenberg neighborhood, accompanied by his wife and her weeping, overcome with a desperation I don't know how to soothe. So here I am, sitting on the bus crossing Bergenline Avenue and thinking about these things, when my eyes come across a billboard: a well-lit ad placed by a food company called La Costeña. It's an ad for jalapeños, perfectly canned, and their slogan stops me cold, paralyzes me. It's printed in black letters, in a huge computerized font, and reads: You'll forget you're on this side. The promise is written precisely in the mother tongue of the jalapeños' most obvious customers, the ones whose palates haven't gone soft yet because they've just arrived on "this side," or the ones whose palates have never gone soft in spite of all the years, who get ticked just thinking about the milder tastes preferred by the children born "on this side," children who can't stand the fury of the best chilis from their parents' homeland and are addicted to Tex-Mex food and don't get past the bland chicken quesadillas and guacamole served at so many Midtown delis.

The promise to forget is showcased on the billboard that's a tin can, that's a row of cans at the supermarket, that later becomes one more can in any Mexican's shopping bag, that's finally an empty can in the recycling bin that's supposed to be set out only on Tuesdays on the curb by the house where the one who's eating forgets. The billboard that leaves me thinking is on the street I'll pass every day I live in this neighborhood and work at the office for Cuban immigrants; the billboard leaves me thinking about a ritual of oblivion, which I'd love to discuss on a theoretical level, Bailey's in hand, at my dear friend Madeline Cámara's super-Cuban home in Tampa, while we talk about the effectiveness of Buddhism, agnosia, or the Regla de Oshá in solving our troubles with love, and La Lupe falls to pieces so many times, proclaiming that "It's over, baby, over"; it ends with those two tongues in which she sings, the languages that will make me tell her, once more, ever so slowly: "I understand now, my dear.... I've left too, I'm also part of that distance, that impossibility of being one whole thing," and she smiles pleasantly and changes the music, in case we end up crying over nothing now, because we're better off thinking about our book project on rituals of return, all of them, so we can talk about the ways all those restaurants capriciously decorate with images of the cathedral, their *arroz con pollo a la chorrera* next to coffee cups that sport, with their best and most picturesque designs, the map or the flag of Cuba. Here I am, thinking about how much I'll enjoy discussing this billboard in December when she comes to visit and shows me photos from her trip to Morocco, where I know full well she went trying to forget her own grief for Cuba and her stubborn refusal to understand why she and her Algerian husband can't go back (a question that haunts her, that she toys with) and make couscous in La Víbora, while the four of us stroll down Boulevard East and gaze at Manhattan in the natural silence that winter brings, and Maya, feeling my arm around her back, again insists that no city celebrates Christmas as magically as New York, and I interrupt her with a touch of sarcasm to bring up her hometown, her faraway Cabaiguán, where she hasn't been in more than forty years, where Christmas is undoubtedly magical too, with its *lechón asado* and yuca that tastes like yuca, not like those balls of starch we wolf down once a week at the little place owned by that guy from Placetas that's so cheap it's a pity not to eat there more often; and, even though it doesn't have a slogan hanging outside, it does offer a thick slice of oblivion with *tasajo* and white boniato, about which it's best not to talk. I skip ahead to December and the conversations I make up beforehand and stage around the Swedish pine dining room set that we bought at the transnational store IKEA; we love to fantasize about the idea of a few futons covered with white quilts for when friends come over and we make room for them, and this sends me to a house that isn't the house we live in but a house made from wooden logs, with fire places to sit by and read the Persian manuscripts I've seen at the Morgan Library, where an original score by Mahler is still waiting for me. But there's the billboard, on the other side of the bus window, as it's rush hour and the bus is stuck...the billboard that makes my thoughts leap from one side to the other, totally addicted to psychoanalysis and free association; I consider over and over which side I'm on, which border is mine, which line I crossed blindly, unknowingly, on the verge of an abyss that may not exist, but which turns me into a shadow of the person I used to be, once more embedded in that vanished mirage that those who stay on the island talk about; the billboard makes my thoughts move from one side of my brain to the other and asks questions I'll have to learn to live with; people questions I've come to love.

LIVING IN THE LINCOLN TUNNEL: MONTHS EIGHT THROUGH TEN (AUTUMN)

The billboard is replaced months later by a new one that doesn't provoke the same restlessness in me. I've left the International Institute of New Jersey by this time, because I don't have the time to keep working there, because I've proved myself good enough to get a position as an adjunct lecturer at Baruch College, where I'm met in an agreeably large classroom twice a week by students born in socialist countries whose names I can't manage to rid myself of, obsolete names that I repeat, making them laugh and making me laugh, and where I return with my obsession for learning foreign languages through cultural immersion while trying to prepare for the TOEFL and the GRE—more exams for me, a professor who long ago passed all her exams; with these I know I'll have terrible problems enunciating the proper vowels into the microphone. I know I'll open my mouth so wide that everybody will be able to tell my absolute dominant language right away. I console myself by thinking that having an accent can be seductive and so I study grammar and immerse myself in the Cosby Show, so old-fashioned it makes my students laugh all over again.

I still struggle with the question of which side I belong on, but the billboard has been torn down; in its stead, I have a new Habana Abierta CD.

"Boomerang" is the name of the album sent by my ex-partner, who has stayed in Cuba, in the house where we once lived together, a house that I can't place precisely on either side of the blurry line that's still the border I've crossed; the CD arrives, and so does my birth certificate, along with new demands that are placed on me, my vaccination card, something to prove that I've been formally protected against measles, tuberculosis, and poliomyelitis. The card arrives with the songs I know I'll never stop playing throughout my overland journey to the point closest to the coast of Cuba, off shore, where I will offer my long seven-braided hair to the Virgin who watches over me, who turns into stone, coral, or foam on any seacoast. The same Virgin who's lent her name to so many botánicas in New Jersey, Miami, Madrid; songs that carry me through all my tunnels, including the tunnels of bitterness from all that rhetoric about special privileges and superiority that we got so sick of on those mornings with Pioneer kerchiefs, reveille, the national anthem, verses by Marti, lessons on how to conjugate vowels and consonants in which the final result was an outlandish and self-indulgent text on the privilege of being a Cuban child; superiority, inner exile appear like a boomerang just at the moment when we least need them, they make us yearn for a land whose telluric power, as imaginary as it is effective, tears us apart, doesn't let us recognize the image of a mixed culture, transnational, stateless, in which there's nothing to fear, in which almost all of us will take part, sooner rather than later.

Epilogue: Summer (a Year and a Day, Permanent Residency)

I don't cross Bergenline Avenue anymore. I've moved to a new neighborhood. The noise and the billboards have been replaced by small gardens, views of Manhattan, tiny ads selling big-name properties with Sunday-only open houses, and lots of silence. Every weekday I spend twelve hours in the city, running from one place to another, grading exams, showing film clips (almost always, and very suspiciously, scenes from Cuban films). I have my routines, my physical exhaustion, a few credit cards that I fear more than the devil fears the cross, and another card that proves I'm a resident of this country, yet something inside me continues to resist what everyone else calls my new status.

Something nameless keeps happening. All sorts of fears crowd my brain when I realize that from time to time I'm using English language constructions to speak Spanish, I'm losing words that come to me first in the new language and not my native one, and by the same token I'm going back more often than when I lived in Cuba to certain foods, certain kinds of music, a certain vocabulary, a certain love for Cuba, a certain tearfulness, not tears for what I've lost, but tears of rediscovery.

At least once a month I dream about the border crossing in Matamoros; I can't forget it. At least once a day I write letters to my Cuban friends scattered across the five continents, seeking their written gazes as they move from country to country. I imagine myself a radar, sending and receiving all sorts of signals that opt in favor of memory, and as I detach from one national identity, that in my case was always blurry, I take on a new one that's affected by the same fragility. Queer studies help me understand nonstagnation and the determination that sexual positioning implies, and I extrapolate these ideas to my condition as a naturally claustrophobic islander, as the amplification of the imaginary that I am, that we are, wherever I go, wherever I play music, put on an accent, take on doubts about being here, wherever I try to save us, to save me, from forgetting, no matter how many jalapeños, tamales, or yucas I consume. And in the end it turns out that I can't guess which side of this untamable border I'm on, nor on which side I ought to be.

CHAPTER 25

Cuba in my Heart: A Geo-Emotional Condition

Lucía M. Suárez

In finding the answers to my questions, like so many before me, I've become haunted by Cuba.

—*Elizabeth Hanly*

In 1964, the Cuban Revolution was five years old and the nation was sharply divided between those who fled, the derogatorily named *gusanos* (worms), waiting for Castro to leave sooner rather than later, and those who stayed to *sacrificarse por la patria* (sacrifice for their homeland), believing ardently, or at least hopefully, in the possibility of a country that offered citizenship, dignity, education, and equality to all of its residents. During this pivotal year of worldwide rearrangements, my parents, disappointed by speeches that did not improve their daily lives and terrified by overwhelming food shortages, suddenly closed businesses, and silently emptied apartments and houses, joined the hemorrhage of Cuban nationals fleeing their beloved country. Like many Cubans, they went to Spain to await their papers before finding exile in the United States. In Spain, the Franco government kept the streets clean, and large immaculate avenues welcomed dictators such as Trujillo to *la madre patria* (the mother country). For my parents, the year was marked by disillusionment. They did not see the Revolution as an answer to anything. But they were blessed by hope, for they imagined life in the United States would be full of opportunities. Still, they felt overwhelmed by anxiety; they were abandoning their home, traveling without money, and arriving into the cacophonous rhythms of large metropolitan cities—Madrid and, later, New York.

My mother was seven months pregnant and without insurance when she arrived in Spain to live with my father in an unheated *pensión*. They had no time or money to prepare for my arrival, but a kind Spanish neighbor, Filomena, handed them an exquisite layette of white essentials for a new infant girl, donated by the Catholic Church. Filomena became my god-mother when I was baptized in a beautiful medieval chapel. The only picture that exists of my parents during this period shows happy, grateful faces, full of youth, truly trusting in the wonders of beginnings. I do not remember the cold, but my mother remembers bittersweetly how I slept tucked into her arms. She smiles when she recalls that, at three months, I was wrapped tightly and put into a basket that hung in the airplane that took our new family to New York. Of course, I can't "remember" any of this, but I do know that today I feel a comforting familiarity when I travel, flying high in the sky on an airplane to an unknown destination, brimming with the promise of unimaginable possibility. The humming lull of a plane's engine or a bus's motor rhythmically sways me to a place of calm abandon; I always welcome the new experiences that await me at a new destination.

Conceived in Cuba, birthed in Spain, and quickly whisked away to the United States, I consider myself a transit baby. My identity, from the beginning, encompassed two continents and would forever be marked by liminal

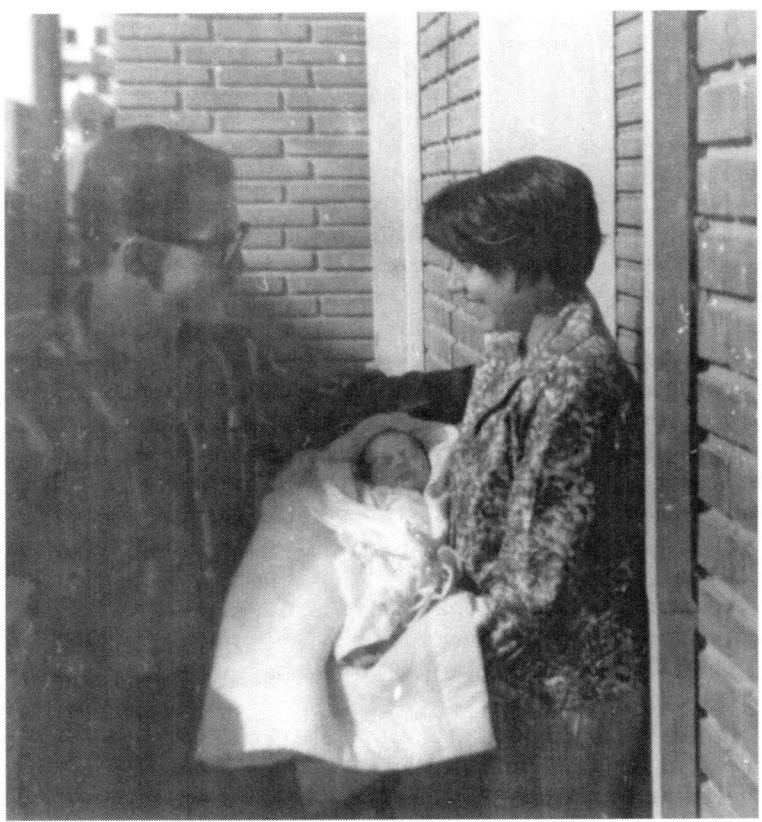

Anonymous, *Transit Baby* (photograph)

spaces of transition. The terms of endearment my family addressed me by, from very early on, defined me as a child of the world, traveling, discovering, and assimilating multiplicitously. I was *la españolita, la cubanita, la negrita linda* (I was born almost purple), and *la nueva americanita*. These loving epithets, which reflect the major historicopolitical events that led my parents and many other Cubans like them to displace themselves and reshape their lives, I believe, are at the core of my lifelong search for the meanings of plural identities and the intersections of diasporic realities.

I can't remember the 1960s. I was too young and too overprotected, especially in the early years before my sister was born. We lived in a building occupied by other young Cuban families with little children. Our doors were always opened to each other, and our stay-at-home *mamás* made memorable meals that included *arroz blanco con frijoles, plátanos fritos, tostones, picadillo, lechón asado*, and *fricasé de pollo*. In the morning we were greeted by the essential *café con leche* with *pan cubano*, and our afternoons were sweetened by Malta with *leche condensada*. I did not speak (and perhaps did not even hear) a word of English until I went to preschool at the age of four. It was not until that moment that I realized that my parents and our friends might be foreigners in the world we occupied. Until that moment, I imagined that everyone must have been Cuban of some sort.

But my family was changing. My parents learned of, and quickly put me in, a Head Start program. Available to economically disadvantaged children and families, with a special focus on helping young children develop early reading and math skills, the program promoted school readiness by enhancing the social and cognitive development of preschoolers by providing educational, health, nutritional, social, and other services to its participants. Particular emphasis was placed on the parents' involvement. My parents were thrilled; Head Start was a family affair in our house. Our concerted efforts to learn the English language initiated a series of transformations that included Velveeta cheese. My father thought it was the most American thing in the world and waved it proudly during snack time on weekends, when he announced that now we were becoming *americanos de verdad* (real Americans). I loved the stuff, but my mother was convinced that anything processed had to be made of plastic. She would announce skeptically, *Eso no tiene leche!* (There's no milk in that!) She missed the homemade cheese of her native Cuba.

As I got older, Mami and I traveled by bus and train everywhere. New York City was minutes away. But Coney Island was the hot spot to visit and when my father came along, he liked to take 16-millimeter films of me running in a red parka that made me look like a crimson balloon, bouncing up and down a very windy boardwalk.

In the 1960s and 1970s, a Cuban community, parallel in importance to the one in Miami, took shape in Union City and West New York, New Jersey. I was a *cubanita* raised along the Hudson River in West New York. There, I remember playing in a spacious park from which I admired the New York skyline and felt guarded by the distant and powerful presence of the Twin Towers. On weekends and for special occasions we explored the Macy's winter wonderland windows, saw the Christmas tree and skated at Rockefeller Center, and visited my grandparents in Washington Heights. During my childhood Fidel and the Cuban Revolution, as well as the stories of Cubans in Miami stoically waiting to return to a free Cuba, went unmentioned. However, on several evenings, when I was supposed to be asleep, I stole glimpses of packages of medicine to be sent to Cuba on our kitchen table. I could hear my mother complaining repeatedly to my father, *No puedo creer que con tanto socialismo para todos no tienen ni aspirina ni vitaminas* (I can't believe that with so much socialism for all, they have neither aspirin nor vitamins).

I tried my best to decipher nighttime conversations between my parents. And I learned that there was some communication between our distant families in Cuba and the United States. For example, I once caught them whispering about a letter from my grandfather, an ardent revolutionary who had stayed where he felt he belonged. *El viejo dice que está bien, que todo está mejorando* (The old man claims that everything is fine, that things are getting better). But overall the 1970s were the years of unspeakable separation. Cubans on this side were *gusanos*; Cubans on the island were learning Russian, figuring out lines and rations, still believing, and learning the art of silence. This, I now realize, was a deeply painful decade for all Cubans, and on the island the years 1971–1976 were called *el quinquenio gris* (the grey five-year period). As a child I could not understand any of this. In order to survive, my parents had no intentions of looking back, much less of returning. Their goal was to integrate, assimilate, and raise *Americanitas*. At the time, I felt that it was such an irony that our social conduct and moral codes were completely dictated by old-fashioned Cuban mores, while we were expected to become *Americanitas*. I had to figure it out on my own: how I would be 100 percent American while every night my mother lulled me to sleep with tender words that would not let me forget how strongly rooted to Cuba her life was. *Cuando salí de Cuba dejé mi vida, dejé mi amor.... Esta niña linda que nació de día quiere que la lleven a la dulcería....* (When I left Cuba, I left my life, I left my love.... This pretty little girl, born during the day, wants them to take her to the candy store....) Through these lullabies and the absent stories of a past that was too painful to mention, I was given a Cuba that was spectral.

In 1988–1989, I was studying in Paris, through a CUNY (City University of New York) exchange program. I had, by then, become a Francophile and found myself writing papers on Lacan in good schoolgirl French. I read Milan Kundera in French, thinking that somehow the contradictions I was discovering about the Cuban situation could be explained via his disturbing, yet astute, observations of the way dreams for utopia in Czechoslovakia were riddled with cynicism and crimes. For me, French was the language I explored identity with, Spanish the language I loved in, and English the language in which I thought critically. So I would sometimes buy books in English that I had read in French and reread them. I reread *The Book of Laughter and Forgetting*, a Penguin Books edition at the end of which there is a conversation with the author. Kundera pointedly notes: "People like to say: Revolution is beautiful, it is only the terror arising from it which is evil. But this is not true. The evil is already present in the beautiful, hell is already contained in the dream of paradise and if we wish to understand the essence of hell we must examine the essence of paradise from which it originated."[1] Revolution, paradise, dreams, hopes, terror, disillusion: these were words that I knew all too well from the "secret" conversations I sometimes got to overhear and from the tacit fear I felt my parents lived in. The contradictions exposed by family secrets, the public denunciations of Miami exiles, and revelations from Eastern bloc expatriates like Kundera led me to ask many questions. I was fascinated by the feelings and sensibilities experienced in the Soviet Union. What was the Eastern Bloc like? What had happened? How did dreams of equality turn into nightmares controlled by an intransigent state? How had Cuba, my parents' native island, joined the East from its golden spot in the Caribbean Sea?

In France, I discovered my Cuban self. While I was classified as *Américaine*, it became clear that my Cuban lineage made me different. Exiles from Argentina and Chile in Paris talked with light in their eyes about the Cuban Revolution and its free island in the Caribbean. I remember the look of awe in my dear friend Daniel de la Fuente's eyes. He had supported and fought for the socialist, egalitarian ideals introduced by the Allende government. Then he had survived torture in a Chilean prison cell under Pinochet's rigid rule of terror. Saved by Amnesty International and offered a new life in France, Daniel, a gifted and gentle artist, looked to the words of Che Guevara for comfort from his own dark experiences of censorship and erasure. Daniel believed that all humanity could have equal access to a life in dignity, and the goals of the Cuban Revolution, highlighting education and health, inspired him. After all, by 1962, the revolutionary government reported the adult literacy rate to be 96 percent. This was the highest in the world. Also, the Worker-Peasant programs in Cuba had helped large numbers of adults to get a sixth-grade education. In the 1960s, in contrast to the rest of Latin America, this was as groundbreaking as it was inspiring.[2] Daniel had witnessed the horrors of disenfranchisement in his own country and his dedication to a more humane world was immensely sincere. I remember that while drinking a glass of red wine at a busy Paris café, he somberly confessed that he needed to believe in order to not die. His small studio apartment in Paris was usually filled with songs of human possibility. His memories of torture and survival were accompanied by the voice and lyrics of his fellow Chilean singer, Victor Jara. Victor Jara sang about the people who worked the land. He valued their labor and belted out the changes to come. In his famous song "El arado," he sang:

> *Afirmo bien la esperanza,*
> *cuando pienso en la otra estrella.*
> *Nunca es tarde me dice ella,*
> *la paloma volará.*

[I uphold my hopes
when I think about the other star (Cuba, which, like Chile, has one star in its flag).

It's never too late, she tells me,
the dove is going to fly.]

But Victor Jara was a victim of the 1973 coup d'état led by Pinochet. On September 11, he was supposed to sing at Santiago University. Instead, he was arrested and taken to Santiago's boxing stadium, where he was tortured for four days before he was machine-gunned to death at the age of thirty-eight.[3] Jara's last words punctuate his tragic death: "Silence and screams are the end of my song." My friend Daniel listened to Jara's songs, and shared his own stories with me. Then he would sigh deeply, change his mood, and put on the music of Silvio Rodríguez, one of the famous singer-composers of the *Nueva Trova Cubana*. Through Silvio's music, Daniel saw Revolution embodied and alive. His need to believe in the world was nurtured by the romantic words cooed by Silvio. His memory of Silvio and Victor singing together in Chile in 1972 confirmed for him, and me, a particular unity between the peoples of Latin America, internationally. Interestingly, one year after these heartfelt conversations in Paris, Silvio returned to sing in Chile, where he sang "Venga la esperanza" (May Hope Arrive) and dedicated "El hombre extraño" (The Strange Man) to Victor Jara. Daniel's wife, also a Chilean exile, was by then suspicious of her ideals. She preferred the romantic, intimate lyrics of the Belgian singer-songwriter Jacques Brel to accompany her quiet hours in the evenings. "Quand on n'a que l'amour" (When All One Has Left Is Love) played in the background.

Cuba, Cuban history, and my own Cubanness, I learned in Paris, were important parts of global history and critical to Latin American reality. It was time for me to discover and value not only my parent's Cuba, but also my own experience of and with Cuba. Since my sense of its past (good and bad) was ridden with horrible, gaping lacuna, I embarked on a cultural and literary odyssey of all things Cuban. I read great authors—Cirilio Villaverde, Lydia Cabrera, Alejo Carpentier, Lezama Lima, Reinaldo Arenas—and listened to music old and new: Ernesto Lecuona, Pérez Prado, *la nueva trova*, and Los Van Van, among many others. In part, I wanted to have Cuba to myself; I also wanted to understand the ideological impact that the little country my parents had abandoned decades earlier had on the continent of the Americas, and the imagination of the world at large.

In effect, it is the rest of the world that has had a deep impact on the island. Although changes began in 1978–1979 when Cuban reconnections took place and *gusanos* (worms) were figuratively transformed into *mariposas* (butterflies), the real change came as a result of the Soviet Union's experiment with perestroika. The conclusive fall of the Berlin Wall in 1989 and the reunification of East and West Germany put an end to the dark grey, coal-polluted cities of the Eastern bloc. With the fall of the Socialist Bloc, the subsidies that Cuba had enjoyed came to a dramatic halt in 1990. Cuba had no choice but to welcome a *período especial en tiempos de paz* (the special period in times of peace). As the Cold War was morphing into globalization, the Cuban economy was forsaken.

It was at this critical point of global shifts that I felt an urgency about being in Cuba. New questions nagged me. What had I missed by not being a "real Cuban living in Cuba"? What would my life have been if my parents had never left? How could I possibly feel so Cuban when my life was cultivated in other geographies and languages?

In 1991, I figured out a way to get there, not on a brigade or through an official visit to relatives (our families were alienated, or so I thought), but rather as part of the CUNY Cuba Exchange Program. I arranged to go as a researcher with a grant from the United States and an exciting, intellectual home base at Casa de las Américas, where Luisa Campuzano, a literary critic, was my gracious hostess.

I was warmly welcomed: I received great support from my sponsors at Casa de las Américas, an open door at ICAIC (Instituto Cubano de Artes e Industrias Cinematográficas), and made an extremely emotional connection to my eighty-four-year-old grandfather and my impressively resilient step-grandmother. Yet despite all this I felt that I had landed on Mars. Despite the family stories and the myriad pictures, movies, and books that had informed my knowledge of Cuba, my senses were hit by uncanny unknowns when I arrived on the island. The humidity in the air wrapped my body like a warm blanket welcoming me to a home I had never known but knew so well. The language, its accents and missing consonants, belonged to me, and the sea was every bit as beautiful as I had imagined it. But there were no stores or food anywhere! There were no cash machines on corners. The public bus system was being decimated due to gas shortages. Bicycles were everywhere, and the romantic ruins I had seen in pictures, were, in effect, the squalid living conditions of Fidel's *pueblo*. Cuba, as it had come to develop during its Soviet years, was fast disappearing. Although I was thrilled to be in my inherited homeland, I was deeply distressed that it should be suffering so acutely. But I was not going to be critical; on the contrary, I wanted to be supportive of this country that had fought so hard to fulfill the dream of being the first utopia of the Americas. Supposedly, Cuba could lead the path for the rest of Latin America, encouraging a unification of *Nuestra América* and one day fulfilling the dreams so compellingly described in the writings of José Martí.

I planned to be there for three months and I was determined to experience life as a Cuban. As quickly as possible I exchanged dollars into pesos, expecting to get into lines to buy pizza or go to the Coppelia ice cream parlor. Although no one seemed to object—at least, they never made fun of me or put me down—I must have been the only one who believed that I could actually become a Cuban native. During the special period most Cubans were dreaming of getting out and moving into the daunting world of free markets; in contrast, I was enthralled, experimenting with the sacrifices the Revolution asked of its population. I gladly went to the field just outside of Havana to do volunteer work with a group from Central America to clear out weeds with a machete. Upon my return I showed off my painful blisters with pride to Luisa Campuzano and the secretaries at Casa de las Américas.

Everyone smiled respectfully and said nothing. In retrospect, I wonder how many Cuban-Americans they had seen go through the same steps of connecting to a life that had never been theirs. The mere fact that I was staying at a nice hotel in the *Vedado* (a modern neighborhood in Havana), and eating fresh fruit at the buffet breakfast every morning set me apart from the realities of my friends and family who were up at five in the morning to stand on line for eggs or powdered milk or bread.

But I was on a tight student budget, and since cheap meals on corners were impossible to find, I depended on that hotel breakfast for my nourishment. I lost 15 pounds during my first trip to Cuba. I could not afford three meals a day at hotels, which were almost the only places where food could be bought at all. At this point, I began to understand the power that hunger has on our bodies and minds. One night I went to one of the few public food places in Havana, by the Malecón. All they sold was pizza and soft drinks. I stood on line with a friend for about an hour. My stomach was growling and my head was spinning. Walking under the hot sun during the day, waiting for buses, and haggling to get a ride from a packed taxi with other tired folks, as well as the sea salt in the sea air, made me feel weak by nine in the evening. Then there was the wonderful smell of hot pizza. My mouth watered while I waited patiently, imagining that I was a *revolucionaria*. By the time we were almost up front, the last two pizzas were rationed to the couple in front of us. Suddenly the star-studded sky felt like an endless black hole. I was so hungry it hurt. The hunger made me feel very little and lost. My zeal, driven by the curiosity of knowing Cuba authentically and experiencing a life I believed I had missed out on, was quickly giving way to exhaustion and an animalistic mania for survival. Luckily for me, I was not a "real Cuban" and I used up my remaining energy to walk over to the hotel to get an *ajiaco* (a traditional Cuban stew with root vegetables and ham). The cheapest item on the menu was also the most nourishing source of warmth for my body. As I finished the last spoonful of stew I felt the deepest sadness. Now that my body was not empty, my spirit was. I thought about the other people who had waited behind me on line at the pizza place. Did they get something to eat elsewhere? If not, how did they placate that miserable hunger that cannot be cheated with any number of psychological exercises? I felt that I had not known how to stand in solidarity with them; even worse, I realized that I would never begin to even imagine what it might have been like if my parents had never left Cuba and if I had grown up there.

By the time that I had accepted my non-Cubanness, something almost comical occurred. I stood on another line to listen to Pablo Milanés. He would be performing live on stage, singing romantic boleros with his well-worn guitar for at least two hours. The queue I was so proud to be on was filled with people my age from the *Juventud Comunista* (Communist Youth). It was a beautiful early Saturday evening and there was flirtation everywhere. Love songs from a popular star's melodic voice were certain to nurture and inspire us all. It was clear that everyone waiting to experience this performance was thrilled to be there. We craved words and rhythms to soothe our physical hunger and our ethical misgivings. I was in awe that I would finally get to enter the famous Karl Marx Theater. In this state of simple happiness, the man standing in front of me introduced himself as Gustavo and asked where I lived. I started to explain that I lived in New York City but that after the summer, I was moving to Durham, North Carolina. I don't think I got past New York City, when this very handsome, doe-eyed man with hair that reminded me of Samson just laughed and said, *Ay, no seas comemierda. Aquí una cubanita no me va a engañar* (Oh, don't be a jerk—a Cuban girl can't fool me here). I couldn't believe it! My accent, by now hard-core Cuban, my looks, and my locally acquired skimpy dress did not even hint at my real residence in the diaspora. He was so sure that I was lying that I could not disappoint him. So I smiled and said, *Soy del Vedado* (I'm from El Vedado—where I really did spend most of my time). He was relieved that I wasn't going on with my "lies" about being an *extranjera* (foreigner). With a coquettish twinkle in my eye, I introduced myself as Rocío, the morning dew that sensually drapes on the leaves and flowers innocently awakening in the morning. It was magical, listening to Pablo Milanés and embodying my newfound Cubanness, even if for one brief evening under the Cuban moon.

At the same time that I was making emotional and spiritual re-connections to my ancestral homeland, a tourist economy was formally instated by the government. A new, two-tiered economic system abruptly ended the utopian ideal of equality once promised by the Revolution. Nonetheless, for me, it was an extraordinary summer that shifted my relationship to a place that had never been fully mine, to a place where I belonged, albeit as a *Cubana-Americana*. I interviewed twelve Cuban women writers, saw amazing Latin American movies, and got to see my favorite singer/song writer, Silvio Rodríguez, from a seat so close I could almost touch him. Most importantly, I met my grandfather for the first and only time, and connected to family I did not even know I had.

To date, I cannot recreate the conflicting emotional feelings that surged in my chest and remained lodged in my throat while I sought out my paternal grandfather. I only had a small piece of paper with the name of a neighborhood, *Reparto el Globo*, with which to find him. Nonetheless, I was determined, and convinced that I could. So, at the hotel where I was staying, I asked which bus would take me to the complex, close to the airport, with that name. Very early one morning I set out to find one elderly man who did not know I was in Havana. I descended from the bus at the central square of *Reparto el Globo* and had nothing else to go on. I was sweating from the hot bus ride and the fear of not finding my grandfather, a link I wanted more than anything in the world. There were some young children playing around the bushes, and two very elderly gentlemen sitting on a bench. I asked the men, "I am looking for my grandfather. I don't know if he is still alive. He should live here. Do you know where I might find Gil Suárez?" I held my breath. Maybe, one of these men would look into my eyes and respond, "I am Gil." But no such luck. They mumbled amongst themselves, and asked some questions about where I came from. I answered simply and honestly.

Then they waved with their hands and fingers. "We think he lives up there. Follow the dirt road, past the new block housing and ask up there." He existed! Or so I assumed by their answer.

I picked up the pace, sweated even more, and walked up the hill, admiring the 1950s Chevrolets parked along the way. Was I walking into the past? Would this encounter allow me to discover something I did not know I had always been looking for? As I was daydreaming and walking, I heard the shrieking voice of an elderly woman, "Stop! Stop! You have to be a Suárez!!!!" I stopped cold. I was being recognized. But how? This very tiny woman, four-foot nine (to be exact), wrinkled and bone thin, was walking back and forth between a charming wood house and a low gate. She wanted to make sure I did not leave; she wanted to awaken someone inside. I walked to the gate. She opened it and pulled me in with a grip so surprisingly strong for her body that I was sure she was either possessed or really an animal in disguise. She explained that I looked just like the daughter she had with Gil (my aunt, it turns out). We were like twins, she exclaimed, as she looked at me with the twinkle of discovery in her eyes. I walked into the house. And there I met my blue-eyed, five-foot tall grandfather. He was equally wrinkled but contrastingly calm and quiet. We looked at each other and could not speak. He reached out his hand; I reached out mine. We hugged for what seemed like a long time as escaped tears rolled down our cheeks.

The woman introduced herself as Farita and immediately brought me some coffee and asked many questions. She had all of the letters my parents had sent them over the years stored safely in a shoebox under their bed. She would run back and forth, getting proof of our connections: pictures of me as a young child, pictures of the family at Coney Island. Why had I not known about all of this correspondence? Why did we not have pictures in a shoebox at home? Or did we? I was so choked up I could not speak. My grandfather was clearly happy that she took charge of telling the stories, showing the pictures, and asking questions. Who was still alive? Who had died? How was so and so? Was so and so still so fat? Was so and so still courting too many women? I actually did not have the answers to many of her questions. Our family in exile had dispersed in such a way that I did not even recognize some of the names she mentioned. Farita, it seemed to me, had keys and memories I did not even know existed. My grandfather and I sat there. I could hear my heart pounding in my chest. I could hear my breath and see my grandfather taking in air, fast, slow, at last relaxed. I looked at his hands and a chill ran up and down my spine. His hands were exactly like my father's, exactly like my own hands.

What had started as a professional, educational trip ended up being the most personal voyage of my life. I journeyed to the epicenter of my family's memories and leftover links. There, I discovered the deep-felt love I had for them, the numerous ways in which we were disconnected, and the even deeper ways in which my Cubanness was anchored by family.

When I think of that time, bursting with emotions, a melancholic melody comes to mind. Silvio's words are: *Mi unicornio azul ayer se me perdió / pastando lo dejé...* / *no sé si se me fue, no sé si se me extravió...* / *se fue...* (I lost my blue unicorn yesterday... / I don't know whether it escaped or whether it got lost... / it's just gone...). It remains one of my favorite tracks because it highlights the ephemeral nature of beauty. Now, many years later, listening to it makes me think of the ideals of the Revolution. Before reading between the lines, etching restrictive codes for a new society, or turning to a different superpower for sustenance, the words that led revolutionary fervor almost fifty years ago were like a blue unicorn, exquisite and unattainable. Finally, the unicorn and the dreams are gone, and we don't know if we'll ever be able to find that ideal that had, for so long, sustained a nation in hope. My grandfather, the ardent revolutionary, had become quiet over the years. He spoke to me of family, of love, and a little bit of the advances in medicine that his revolution ushered. I could see pride and sadness in his eyes. I was beginning to understand the complexity of change and the challenges of utopia. Like my grandfather, I also wanted to grasp onto the dream of a better humanity.

Sadly, my grandfather died before I was able to make my brief second visit, when I went as part of an intellectual panel from the University of Michigan at a conference in the Casa de las Américas. The center was, as usual, fervent with creative, literary discussion and great energy. But I knew that I had to escape, if only briefly, to pay my grandfather's widow a surprise visit. This time there was no bus to take me to *Reparto el Globo*, so I took a taxi. My step-grandmother, who was going blind, was elated to see and hear me, and I was grateful for the opportunity to be with her and to listen to the details of the previous years and my grandfather's passing. Their little house had been torn asunder by hurricane Charley in August of 1994, and a somber shack was all that remained. Despite her losses, she was still energetic. She felt confident that the government would soon help her out. I listened and looked around. The darkness in the house underscored my grandfather's absence. I wished I could have seen more of him. I yearned for another opportunity to share histories that now no one else would remember. Before returning to my place in the literary scene at Casa de las Américas, I hugged Farita very tightly and cried because I knew that the distance between our lives could not be mended, and because I did not know if I would ever see her again.

During the course of the following ten years, I found myself on numerous flights searching the Caribbean. I hid behind the veil of academic discourses and intellectual investigation, but could not avoid the burning personal question based on, "How can I be so Cuban, so very *caribeña*, if my entire life has been molded by Cuba's very absence?" My research took me to Puerto Rico, Grenada, Antigua, la Guadeloupe, Martinique, the Dominican Republic, and Haiti. My curiosity led me to investigate the Caribbean condition of women writers before me who also defined themselves by a geography that was very far for them, and experiences that were shaped by memories, frozen reproductions of an island paradise, and travel. I researched and wrote a doctoral dissertation entitled *Caribbean*

Women Claiming Their Islands. With this work, I had hoped to connect my own experiences with the lives of others in a similar situation. I traveled to Cuba, Spain, and France researching two famous "Cuban" women authors of the nineteenth century, Gertrudis Gómez de Avellaneda and Madame La Comtesse de Merlin (María de las Mercedes Santa Cruz y Montalvo, also known as la Condesa de Merlín). Unlike myself, however, these two women had spent their childhoods in Cuba and never let go of the memories shaped in a paradise of turquoise seas and joyful playing in the lush tropics. For example, La Condesa experienced the first twelve years of her life on the island, and then lived the rest of her life in Spain and France. Unable to abandon the beautiful memories of childhood innocence, she returned to Cuba after her husband, the French Count Antoine Christophe Merlin's death in 1840, when she was fifty-one.[4] La Condesa published a major work, *La Havane*, based on that brief trip to Cuba. Despite her limited travel to Cuba, her writings allowed her to claim her Cubanness. Even though her place in French society (she wrote in French, had a famous literary salon in Paris, and generously sponsored writers like Balzac), it seems that her extensive writings in *La Havane* confirmed her much-idealized Cuban identity. Thus, La Condesa forever etched herself into Cuban history, not because she was an intrinsic part of that history, but because that history and the imagination of Cuba was an indelible part of her.

In contrast, I do not nurture an idealized Cuban identity. For better or for worse, my childhood "paradise" was urban and cold. Occupying both sides of the Hudson River, my memories of glistening waters do not recall the turquoise blue of the Caribbean, but rather the exciting contrasts between New York and New Jersey and the mercury vapor lights of the Lincoln Tunnel. When my mother and I took the bus into the Port Authority, my nose was at the height of the emissions from the buses. Then she bought me a donut before we took the train to Columbia Presbyterian Hospital for my checkups and shots. To date, the rare, and awful, mixture of exhaust and donuts at a bus station anywhere in the world takes me back to my own childhood paradise, when I had no questions and could not even imagine regrets.

In 2001, ten years after my first voyage to Cuba, I returned as a faculty leader for the University of Michigan Alumni Association. At first, I was just delighted with the prospect of going back as a teacher/guide. I had studied so much about Cuba, its histories, its writers, and its architecture, that I felt honored to be in such a position. By this time, I had accepted that my childhood and my identity were rooted in the United States, and that, much like the Condesa de Merlín, I had yearned for Cuba in a romantic and unrealistic way. Since I had accepted that my Cubanness was more imagined than actual, I was also going as a Cuban-American who understood (or so I thought) her place in the geo-emotional scheme of Cuban, Cuban exile, and Cuban diaspora identities. But, again, this trip proved all of my neat categorizations wrong. Once in Havana, I felt at home hugged by the familiar humidity that immediately draped itself around my body. But everything had changed quite dramatically. The economy was based on the dollar that flew about in tourist hands and was coveted by Cuban nationals, still holding on to their *libretas* (rationing cards). As I looked around and saw undernourished Cubans who did not have access to the luxuries of excess (extra chocolate, super-sized servings of yuca, or even regular servings of our traditional lechón asado) in contrast to robust libidinally charged tourists I felt a deep sadness.

The new, hyperluxurious buses were over air-conditioned and oversized. They accentuated the discrepancy between the tourists' gaze and the natives' condition. The members of the tour group were mostly retired, extraordinarily interesting people who had traveled the world over and experienced most of the things that I knew only through books. In fact, one of the couples on board had been the last owner of the Hotel Nacional before they fled the country. The hotel was forlorn during the Soviet years and reconstructed magnificently for the new tourist economy of the 1990s. For this couple, Cuba was not a curiosity or the latest bastion of communist failure; instead, Cuba held an intimate history of splendor and loss, memory and rediscovery. Despite the fact that the group that had signed on was wonderful in every way, my position as a sort of native, with real family and friends in Havana who could never mix with this group, made me uneasy. The smiles on the Cubans were always there, but as I thought of the dilapidated apartments and rooms most Cubans lived in, I understood that those smiles were part real and hugely performed. Indeed, these jobs at tourist spots are highly coveted and those who work in the tourist industry make a better living than others, including doctors and lawyers. But it can't be easy to serve cocktails when in real life one has an engineering degree.

What pained me the most was the begging that I had not seen previously in Cuba. On one occasion, when we were descending from the steep stairs of our tour bus in Camagüey, two emaciated women and their children greeted us with urgency. They asked for pencils, paper, shampoo, soap, and toothpaste. Fortunately, many of us had been properly informed to bring these kinds of items to distribute. And we did. Suddenly, I remembered a conversation I had once had with a Bulgarian friend who now lives in New York. She had told me of the hair color dilemma of the socialist days. When one color was available, everyone walked around with the same color. One year, it was a burgundy that became all the rage because it was all there was, if you were lucky enough to get it. I wondered if Cubans even had the fortune of having a hair color dilemma. I thought of all the CVS stores in the United States packed with products that promised beauty, youth, and ultimately simply made us dizzy with desire. It hurt to acknowledge that in Cuba soap was not a sign of excess but rather of desperate need.

I had a frightening experience during this trip. The only other woman my age, Tiara, and I decided to separate from the tour group and go to a nightclub in search of a local taste of the city's nightlife. It proved to be almost impossible. All of the nice places were exclusively for tourists and admitted Cubans only if they were escorted by foreigners with dollars. This meant that we got to observe many overweight, often drunk men in their seventies cavorting with beautiful Cuban girls in their teens. I tried not to stare. I understood, all too well, the human and economic needs that were being played out here. But I wanted to dance and I was not going to dance with any of these men attaining Cuban experiences while groping. Growing up in a Cuban family where dance and music were always at the center of our gatherings, dance has always been about communion with the soul. Dance for me is about joy. I did not want to soil that identification with some old man who could not dance heaving over me. Fortunately, Tiara had met some Cubans, more or less our age, who wanted to dance. They were great dancers and we were delighted to buy them their drinks and some appetizers. We had not planned to stay out late and were not drinking alcohol ourselves. We needed to get some rest for an early start the following day with the tour group. As we were getting ready to leave, calling an early night, the lightness of the dancing partners changed into a frantic appeal to hold onto us. "Ah, but the night is young," cooed Guillermo. Then Pablo interrupted, "I have to go to the bathroom." "Oh, it's right there," I innocently pointed to the door in the back. In a matter of seconds he was on his way, opened the door, and the nightclub bouncer attacked him. I watched as if it were an out-of-body experience. The hostility with which this young and very courteous man was being treated was completely uncalled for. I went back, told the manager (who had magically appeared out of nowhere) that Pablo was with me, he was my guest, and as such I felt that he had the right to use the bathroom. The manager looked me over with disdain. *Aquí es para los extranjeros, los hombres con sus niñas* (This place is for foreigners, men with their girls).

My stomach turned into a hard knot. Had I heard clearly? Did he tell me I couldn't negotiate the use of the bathroom because I was not a foreigner? Or was it because I was not "un hombre," but a woman? I stood my ground, even though I thought I was going to be violently hurled onto the street. Tiara, who was clearly not a *Cubana*, was standing at attention by my side. I could feel her arm sweating against my arm. They looked at her, allowed Pablo to use the restroom, and stared at us like cats about to pounce on a mouse while he was inside. I felt horrible. I couldn't dance anymore. Tiara and I went out to get a cab. We apologized to these dancers who had been so respectful during two hours of dancing. But they were angry. They took us by the arms and pressed us to go with them to some other party. I didn't like this. I panicked, hailed a cab, and grabbed Tiara. We moved quickly, determined to return to our hotels unharmed. We did not look back to see Guillermo and Pablo's reaction to our abrupt escape. Briskly, we were on our way. The cab driver did not say a word. We tried to catch our breaths as the last twenty minutes spun in our heads. Had we been hustled? Were we expected to take those dancers somewhere? Were they young students and professionals like us, deprived of an evening of dancing? Was it all about "business only"? Were we in the wrong because only men with *jineteras* were welcomed? I did not understand the codes that flew about me. I felt lost, and all I wanted to do was go straight to sleep and forget. Luckily, I'd be on the bus the next day, on route to yet another Cuban destination. I could forget. But could the two young men?

* * *

Recently, I went to a conference at the University of Connecticut, organized by Jacqueline Loss and José Manuel Prieto that addressed Cuba/USSR and the post-Soviet experience. One of the participants, a writer who had lived in Russia but now resides in Spain, looked at me and asked, "Where are you from?" I knew that he was trying to figure out, according to my accent and my looks whether I was Argentine, Puerto Rican, Cuban, or something else. I answered as honestly as I could, " My parents are Cuban." His face lit up with a huge, complicit smile, "I knew it. *Eres Cubana.*" He did not hyphenate me or qualify the place I lived in versus the nationality of my parents. Instead, he quite naturally added me to a growing list of Cubans at home in cities throughout the world. I responded with an accepting smile, "Yes, I guess I really am a *Cubanita* after all."

Lately, however, my trips "back" are rarely to Cuba but to what was once a Cuban community along the Hudson River. The area has since welcomed new immigrant groups from Central America and the Middle East. When my daughter runs against the wind with the New York City skyline as her backdrop, I look over to the right and see a huge absence. The World Trade Center is conspicuously missing. Those pillars of iron, glass, and concrete that looked over me throughout my childhood years were blown up and burned down by an unprecedented and, until that moment unimaginable, act of violence. I know that nothing, no matter how strong it may seem, can stand forever. And I understand the sadness of loss, the pain of bereavement, and the silence of impotency.

For me, an American with a Cuban soul, my parent's island nation will always be a place of inquiry, myth, illusion, disappointment, and hope. I have come to accept that their Cuba is long gone. Nonetheless, Cuba remains an integral part of my identity, even if in reality it has always evaded me, even if most of the time, I am in a country that is not Cuba.

NOTES

1. Milan Kundera, "Afterword," *The Book of Laughter and Forgetting* (New York: Knopf, 1981), p. 234.
2. See Louis Pérez, *Cuba: Between Reform and Revolution* (New York: Oxford University Press), p. 359.
3. "They Couldn't Kill His Songs," BBC News, Saturday, September 5, 1998. Viewed at http://news.bbc.co.uk/2/hi/americas/165363.stm.
4. See Adriana Méndez Rodenas *Gender and Nationalism in Colonial Cuba: The Travels of Santa Cruz y Montalvo, Condesa de Merlin* (Nashville and London: Vanderbilt University Press), p. 10; and Lucía de las Mercedes Suárez, "Caribbean Women Claiming Their Islands" (PhD dissertation, Duke University, 1999).

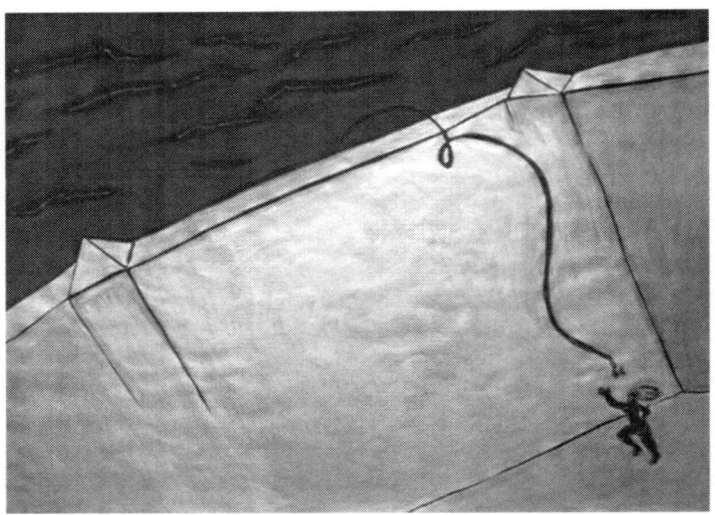

Rocío García de la Nuez, *Haiku: La noche* (Haiku: Night) (painting)

PART V

Esperando: To Wait Is a Cuban Condition

CHAPTER 26

Waiting

Ruth Behar

Our Caribbean island-nation tried to build a socialist paradise believing that a better tomorrow was just around the corner. Those who lost faith, left; those who stayed tried to keep the faith. But all of us Cubans have been waiting. Wherever we may be, on the island, struggling with the island, dreaming of the island, forgetting about the island, we wait. We each wait in our own way. None of us knows what will come of our waiting.

With wit and unflinching honesty, Rolando Estévez seeks to show us, through a set of visual metaphors, how waiting has come to obsess us as a people. In his remarkable series, *Gerundios para la espera*, or "Gerunds for waiting," he has produced twelve images in which a small naked male figure is shown in twelve different relationships to a huge boulder. This figure declares, "I wait thinking," or "I wait concealing," or "I wait dreaming," or "I wait trying," or "I wait triumphing," or "I wait believing." What this person is waiting for, we don't know exactly. But since this art was conceived and made in Cuba, we can give it a Cuban meaning. We know that Cubans live in a perpetual state of *espera*, of waiting, whether it's waiting in line or waiting for the bus, or waiting to see what will happen when the day finally comes that Fidel Castro has passed on. Cubans also live in a perpetual state of *esperanza*, of hope, to see when and how the promise of the Revolution that they longed for and fought for will truly be fulfilled.

Gerundios para la espera was completed in 1997 in Cuba. The work was exhibited publicly in the United States only once, while Estévez was at the University of Michigan as an artist-in-residence in 1998. Now, ten years later, these gerunds make their debut in print here in this book, adding their remarkable prophetic vision to our gathering of Cuban voices.

Estévez comes to his work as a visual artist from a long and continuing connection to the theater. He lives in Matanzas, Cuba, and his official position, for which he receives a state salary, is as set designer for the theater. The sense of high drama peppered with humorous masquerade that pervades his work comes from his years of dedication to the stage. Working in black and white tempera and ink on paper, he has produced several series of interconnected images on the themes of family, immigration, national identity, power, and sexuality. In these works he unites text and image into a brilliant fusion. "Gerunds for Waiting" is a truly magnificent example of the genre he has invented. It is part filmic storyboard, part comic strip, part mythic exploration.

In *Yo espero pensando* (I wait thinking), the boulder is balanced on the head of a man missing his forearms and lower legs, which suggests that thinking too much may be hazardous to one's health. In *Yo espero ocultando* (I wait concealing), the male figure deftly closes the curtain on the boulder as if it were a mere performance. The difficulty of escape is shown playfully in *Yo espero soñando* (I wait dreaming), showing a dreamer who dreams of a tiny boulder. *Yo espero intentando* (I wait trying) and *Yo espero triunfando* (I wait triumphing) depict the despair of trying to change the nature of things. But *Yo espero confiando* (I wait trusting) offers an endearing image of a man about to leap off the cliff of a boulder clasping a parasol. It is at once charming and terrifying, like all the images in the series.

Although these evocative images by Estévez arise from a thoroughly Cuban state of mind, they have a philosophical depth that makes them more than simply a commentary on our everlasting Cuban existential crisis. The "Gerunds for Waiting" are also about something much more elusive and universal. Let us say they are about *hegemony*, that difficult concept that Antonio Gramsci wrote about so profoundly while locked inside an Italian jail. Estévez's gerunds are about how reality becomes real. They are about how it is that we live in untenable worlds of our own making. Estévez assures us that we have agency, that we have free will, but whether we fight or accept our boulders, like Sisyphus, we are condemned to struggle with them, condemned to take little pieces of them into the long nights of our dreams.

CHAPTER 27

Gerundios para la Espera
(Verbs for Waiting): A Visual Coda

Rolando Estévez

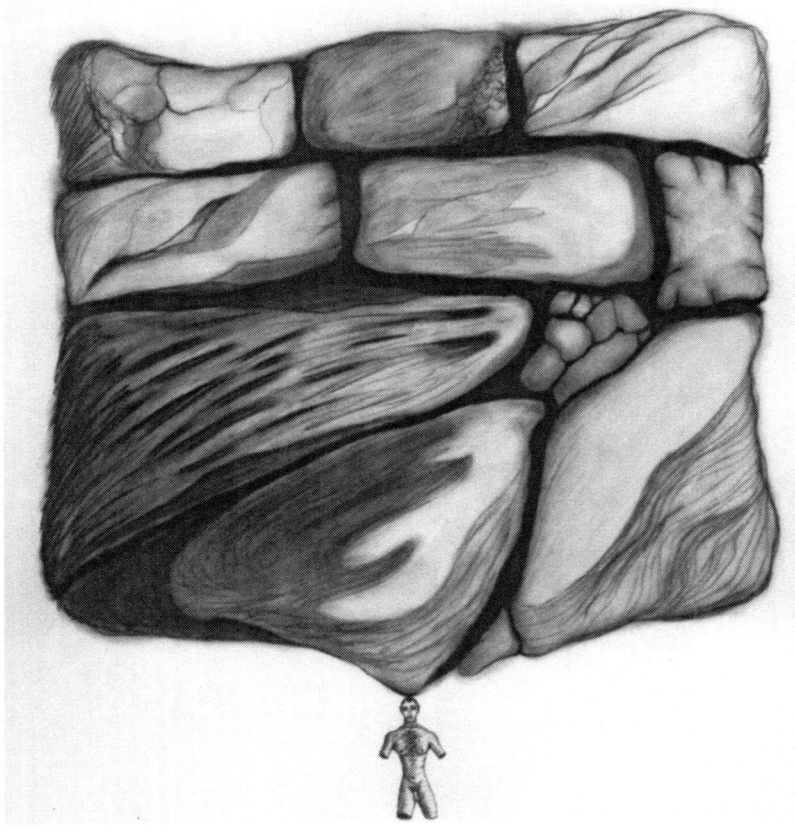

Yo espero pensando (I wait thinking)

Yo espero ocultando (I wait concealing)

Yo espero soñando (I wait dreaming)

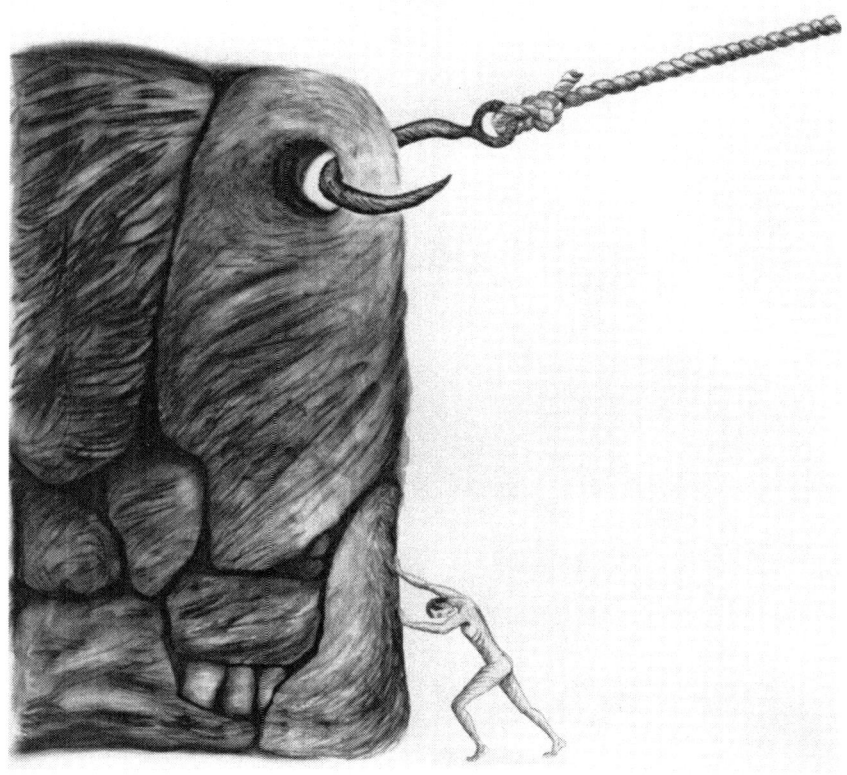

Yo espero intentando (I wait trying)

Yo espero triunfando (I wait triumphing)

Yo espero confiando (I wait trusting)

Yo espero pudiendo (I wait showing might)

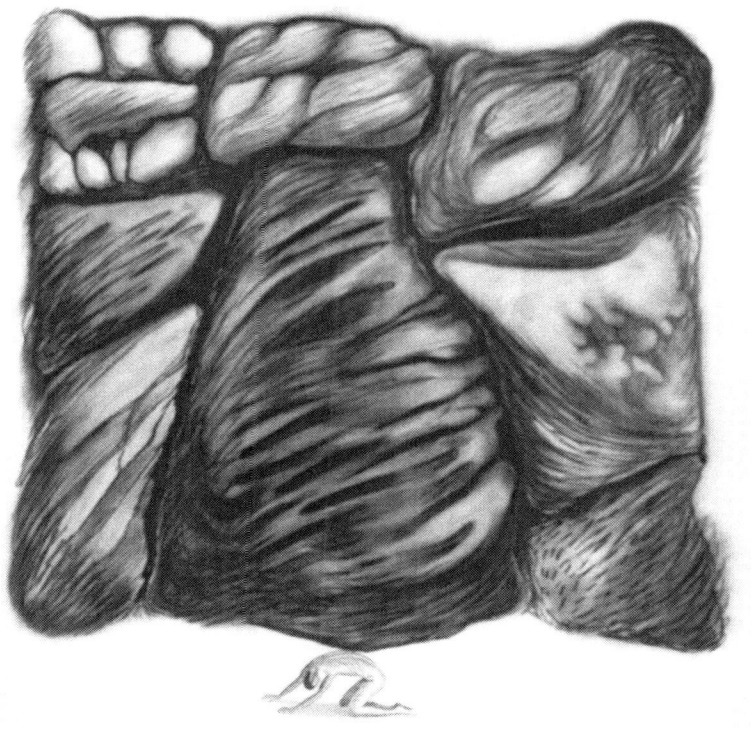

Yo espero alabando (I wait giving praise)

Yo espero buscando (I wait searching)

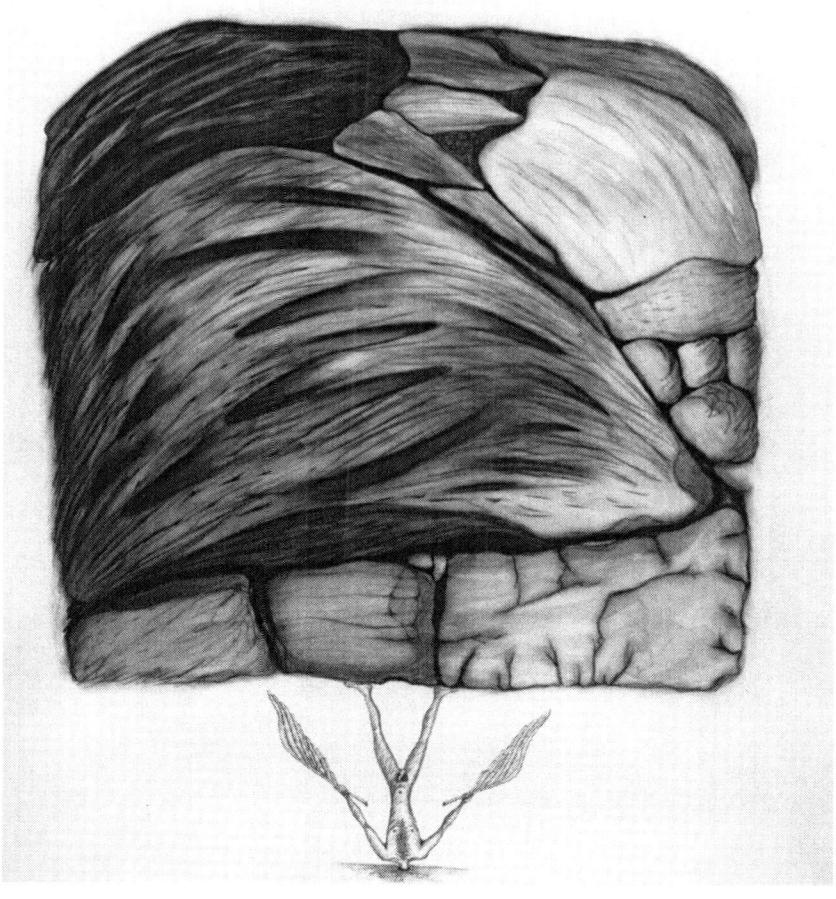

Yo espero escapando (I wait escaping)

Yo espero farseando (I wait joking around)

Yo espero gozando (I wait getting pleasure)

DISCUSSION TOPICS

GENERAL TOPICS

How do autobiographical works—whether presented as prose, poetry, or visual art—provide a nuanced understanding of Cuban identity?

In what ways do the contributors show that Cuban realities are currently in flux?

How do changes in the relationship between Cuba and its diaspora reflect changes that now exist globally between homelands and a wide range of immigrant communities?

What does the concept of a "bridge to Cuba" mean at this moment? Are bridges between Cubans ultimately possible? Or are they foreclosed by political impasses that are beyond the jurisdiction of individuals?

What are the many ways in which Cubans define and redefine, shape and reshape their Cubanness?

Has Cuba been commodified to the point that the diversity of Cuban experiences have been obscured?

EN LA MALETA: WITH A SUITCASE IN OUR HANDS

What is inside the suitcase of each of the contributors to this section?

In this section we have stories by a Cuban-American, a Cuban-Russian, a Cuban-Jew, a Cuban living in Germany, and a Cuban living in Chile. How do their narratives differ? Are there intersections of emotion and experience?

What are some of the pleasures of forgetting Cuba and developing a new hybrid identity?

Is the personal voice used in a distinctive way by each of the contributors?

What is the role of the Spanish language in maintaining a Cuban identity for Cubans who live outside of the island?

IDAS: AFTER EVERYONE HAS LEFT

Do you feel that hope or despair predominates in the poems included in this section?

Does the art work "look Cuban"? What expectations do we have as viewers about the meaning that Cuban art should convey about its cultural and national origins?

How does the witnessing of departures and the experience of saying goodbye become an integral part of Cuban identity for those who stay on the island?

What are the most commonly held stereotypes about Cubans? How do the contributors in this section challenge Cuban stereotyping?

How are those who stay in Cuba also part of the exile and/or immigrant experience?

REGRESOS: WHEN WE RETURN

What are the ways in which returning to Cuba is different than returning to other Caribbean islands from which many have immigrated?

How does the impasse set up by the governments of the United States and Cuba create a uniquely Cuban emotional condition of longing and loss?

In what ways are guilt feelings present in these autobiographical pieces? Why is guilt such an overwhelming emotion for Cubans who live abroad but choose to return to Cuba?

How do the authors revise their views over time as both they mature and Cuba changes?

What visual images come to mind when reading about the search for homecoming?

MAS ALLÁ DE CUBA: NOW AND THEN WE TRY TO FORGET ABOUT GEOGRAPHY

Can Cubans forget about geography?

How do Cubans remain connected to Cuba when they no longer live there and have built entirely new identities for themselves in other countries?

In what ways are new Cuban migrations similar to other migrations from Latin America and the Caribbean?

What are the differences between the migrations of Cubans over the past fifty years?

What roles do memory and nostalgia play in the Cuban imagination?

CONTRIBUTORS

Carlos Aguilera Chang (Berlin, Germany) was born in Havana in 1970. He is the author of *Das Kapital* (winner of the Premio Calendario Asociación Hermanos Sáiz, 1996). Aguilera Chang was the coeditor from 1997 to 2002 of the alternative magazine *Diáspora(s)* in Havana. He has published several volumes of poetry, fiction, and essays, including *Retrato de A. Hopper y su esposa* and *Teoría del alma china*, which have been translated into languages including German, French, English, and Croatian. He is also the editor of several anthologies of Cuban poetry and prose. In addition, his texts and articles have appeared in *Letras libres, Revista de Occidente, Diario de Poesía, Crítica, Manuskripte, Boundary 2, Tsé tsé, Mandorla, Encuentro de la Cultura Cubana, La Habana Elegante, Cubista, Babylon, Quorum*, and other journals, as well as newspapers such as Frankfurter Rundschau, El País, and Die Presse. He regularly writes reviews for The Miami Herald. He currently has a writing fellowship from Kulturstiftung and Dresdner Bank in Dresden.

Nara Araújo (Mexico City, Mexico and Havana, Cuba) was born in Havana in 1945. She is presently full professor at the Universidad de la Habana and at the Universidad Autónoma Metropolitana, Mexico. She received her PhD at the University of Moscow and has been an invited professor at the University of Paris 8, Saint Denis. Araujo has received several major awards including the Palme Académique de France and a Rockefeller grant. She is well known for her extensive presentations throughout the Caribbean, Europe, and the United States. Her publications include *Viajeras al Caribe*; *Visión romántica del otro*; and *Textos de teorías y críticas literarias*.

Jorge Luis Arcos (Madrid, Spain) was born in Havana in 1956 and has lived in Spain since 2004. A poet and essayist, he has published books on José Lezama Lima, Fina García Marruz, and the *Orígenes* group.His publications include the poetry collections *Conversación con un rostro nevado, De los ínferos, La avidez del halcón*, and *Del animal desconocido* (2002), and the essays collected in *La palabra perdida: Ensayos sobre poesía y pensamiento poético* and *Desde el légamo: Ensayos sobre pensamiento poético*. He also edited the anthology *Las palabras son islas: Panorama de la poesía cubana del siglo XX* and two collections of essays by María Zambrano, *La Cuba secreta y otros ensayos* and *Islas*. He is a member of the editorial board of the journal *Encuentro de la Cultura Cubana*.

Belkis Ayón Manso (Havana, Cuba, 1967–1999) studied art at the San Alejandro Academy of Art in Havana, specializing in printmaking, and graduated from the Instituto Superior de Arte in 1991. Her works, lithographs, calcographs, and collographs have been exhibited in Cuba, Japan, Germany, Switzerland, Puerto Rico, Mexico, and the United States.

Ruth Behar (Ann Arbor, Michigan) was born in Havana and grew up in New York City. She is the recipient of a MacArthur Award, a John Simon Guggenheim Fellowship, and the Distinguished Alumna Award from Wesleyan University. *Latina Magazine* named her, in 1999, one of the fifty Latinas who made history in the twentieth century. Behar has worked as an ethnographer in Spain, Mexico, and Cuba. Her books include *The Presence of the Past in a Spanish Village*, *Translated Woman: Crossing the Border with Esperanza's Story*, *The Vulnerable Observer: Anthropology That Breaks Your Heart*, and *An Island Called Home: Returning to Jewish Cuba*. Behar is coeditor of *Women Writing Culture* and editor of *Bridges to Cuba*, a pioneering forum of culture and art by Cubans on the island and in the diaspora. She wrote, directed, and produced the documentary, *Adio Kerida/Goodbye Dear Love: A Cuban Sephardic Journey*, which has been shown in film festivals around the world. She is Professor of Anthropology at the University of Michigan.

Richard Blanco (Miami, Florida), as a child of Cuban exiles, could claim citizenship in three countries only forty-five days after his birth. Naturally, questions about home and place have figured significantly in his life and poetry. But beyond nostalgia, the real consequence of the exiled condition is a perpetual sense of placelessness. In search of his proverbial home, which seems to be evermore distant, he has lived in Connecticut, Washington DC, Guatemala, Brazil, and in 2004 he returned to the city of his childhood, Miami. His *City of a Hundred Fires* received the prestigious Starrett Prize from the University of Pittsburgh Press. His second book, *Directions to the Beach of the Dead*, won the PEN/American Center 2006 Beyond Margins Award. Blanco's poems on the Cuban-American experience and the poetics of place have appeared in numerous literary journals and anthologies including, *Ploughshares*, *TriQuarterly*, *Michigan Quarterly*, *Best American Poetry 2000*, *Best American Prose Poems*, and National Public Radio. He is the recipient of a Bread Loaf Fellowship and a Florida Artist Fellowship. A former Assistant Professor, Blanco has taught at Georgetown, American University, and Connecticut State University.

Damaris Calderón (Santiago, Chile) was born in Havana, Cuba in 1967. She is a poet, narrator, and essayist. She completed her education at the Universidad de la Habana, and later received a master's degree at the Universidad Metropolitana de Ciencias de la Educación, Santiago de Chile. She has been living in Chile since 1995. She has published nine books of poems: *Con el terror del equilibrista*, *Duras aguas del trópico*, *Se adivina un país*, *Guijarros*, *Duro de roer*, *Babosas: Dejando mi propio rastro*, *Sílabas:*

Ecce Homo, Parloteo de Sombra, and *Los amores del mal.* Her work has been translated into English, Dutch, Portuguese, French, and Serbo-Croation.

Mabel Cuesta (New Jersey and New York) was born in Matanzas in 1976. She is the author of *Confesiones* and *Cuaderno de la fiancée.* She received her degree in literature from the Universidad de la Habana. She taught literature and theory in her native Matanzas for many years, and is presently teaching at the Instituto Cervantes in New York City. She resides in New Jersey.

Jorge Duany (San Juan, Puerto Rico) was born in Havana in 1957, but his family left Cuba for Panama in late 1960, finally settling in Puerto Rico in 1966. He later spent ten years studying at universities in the United States and one year working in Florida, but he has lived ever since in Puerto Rico, except for occasional absences because of his academic career. Duany is professor of Anthropology and Director of the Department of Sociology and Anthropology at the University of Puerto Rico in Rio Piedras. He has also been the director of the journal *Revista de Ciencias Sociales* and a visiting professor at the University of Michigan. He has published extensively on Caribbean and Latino/a migrations to the United States, as well as on issues of ethnic, national, and transnational identity. His most recent book is *The Puerto Rican Nation on the Move: Identities on the Island and in the United States.* He coauthored Los cubanos en Puerto Rico: Economía étnica e identidad cultural and *El Barrio Gandul: Economía subterránea y migración indocumentada en Puerto Rico.*

Abilio Estévez (Barcelona, Spain) was born in Havana in 1954 and now lives in Spain. He is the author of several plays, including the award-winning *La Noche (Night)*; a collection of poems, *Manual de tentaciones;* two collections of short stories; and two novels. His internationally acclaimed first novel, *Thine Is the Kingdom,* was translated into twelve languages and voted best foreign novel of the year in France. His second novel, *Distant Palaces,* was published to critical praise in 2002.

Rolando Estévez (Matanzas, Cuba) is a poet and visual artist. His set designs for the theater in Matanzas have won ten national prizes since 1990. As the cofounder and artistic editor of the artisanal press, Ediciones Vigía, he has designed more than 200 titles since 1985, some of which are now in the collection of the Museum of Modern Art (MOMA) in New York. His most recent exhibits of drawings and graphic art include *Postales pornográficas y filosóficas; Las vitrinas del Llanero Solitario; Dibujos para ponerse en la cabeza; Spotlights; Granos de miedo;* and *La vena rota.* His books of poetry include *El dios tardío, La cáscara profunda, Si perdonas al árbol, Cencerros de la noche, Suite para voz y corazón en traje negro,* and *Mar mediante.*

José A. Figueroa (Havana, Cuba) is one of the best-known photographers of modern Cuba. His works have been exhibited in galleries and museums from Guatemala to Milan, garnering numerous awards, and now reside in collections in Mexico, Milan, Parma, Paris, Los Angeles, and New York. His work is prominently featured in *Shifting Tides: Cuban Photography after the Revolution*, edited by Tim B. Wride.

Nely Galán (Los Angeles, California) is regarded as one of the entertainment industry's most dynamic creative executives. She has dedicated her career to bridging the gap between Latin culture and mainstream American media, and was dubbed the Tropical Tycoon by the New York Times Magazine. She was named one of the most powerful young executives in Hollywood by Entertainment Weekly. Galán, former president of Telemundo, currently heads Galán Entertainment, a multifaceted company that has produced over 600 episodes of television in all genres in both English and Spanish for clients such as Fox, HBO, Canal Fox, Sony, and MGM. Galán's first mainstream success, Fox's hit reality show "The Swan," aired in nearly sixty countries worldwide, evolving into an international brand. Galán penned the book *The Swan Curriculum*, created the *How to Swan Yourself* DVD, and has become a prominent speaker on the health, wellness, and beauty circuit. Recently, Galán created "The New You," a multi-platform brand built upon the "The Swan" experience and her years in the entertainment business.

Rocío García de la Nuez (Havana, Cuba) was born in Las Villas, Cuba in 1955. She graduated in 1975 from Cuba's San Alejandro Art Academy and later completed her MFA at the Repin Academy of Fine Arts in Saint Petersburg, Russia. Rocío is a renowned visual artist who focuses on the harrowing codes of gender and sexuality in the modern world. She generally structures her works in series that relate to a common topic or that aim at getting the viewer to reflect on the problematics of living in a world of dualities and appearances. She uses eroticism as a metaphor and a poetics to express the concept of liberty in the face of taboos and repression, given the need to defend the notion of diversity as a necessity in the sexual, social, and political realms. Her works have been exhibited in Spain, France, Russia, Switzerland, the United States, and Cuba, where she resides at present.

Nereyda García Ferraz (Miami, Florida) was born in Havana, Cuba. She graduated from the School of the Art Institute of Chicago, on a Ryerson Traveling Fellowship. She has received two National Endowment for the Arts Fellowships, in 1985 and 1989, and two Illinois Art Council Visual Arts Fellowships, in 1985 and 1989. García Ferraz coproduced the award-winning documentary "Ana Mendieta: Fuego de Tierra" (1987), about the life and works of Ana Mendieta. She was the 2001 recipient of the prestigious Richard Diebenkorn Fellowship from the San Francisco Art Institute. Her visual work has been included in numerous exhibitions throughout the United States, Latin America, and Europe. Her artworks are held in several major private and public collections.

José Kozer (Hallandale, Florida), who was born Havana in 1940, is the preeminent Cuban poet of his generation and one of Latin America's most influential writers. He left Cuba in 1960 and settled in New York, where he taught at Queens College until 1997. After a brief sojourn in Spain he and his wife, Guadalupe, settled in Hallandale, Florida. Kozer's first book was published in 1972; *Stet* is his thirty-eighth. He has written over 6400 poems. His recent books include *Mezcla para dos tiempos, Rupestres, No buscan reflejarse, Bajo este cien y otros poemas, Rosa cubica, La voracidad grafomana: José Kozer, Ánima, Madame Chu & outros poemas, Un caso llamado FK, Una huella destartalada: Diarios, Ogi no mato, Y del esparto la invariabilidad,* and *Íbis amarelo sobre fundo negro.*

Iraida H. López (New Jersey) has focused her research on Cuban American, Cuban, and Latino literature and culture. Her work has appeared in *Revista Iberoamericana, Cuban Studies, Anales del Caribe,* and *Temas,* among other journals. She is the author of *La autobiografía hispana contemporánea en los Estados Unidos: A través del caleidoscopio* and a contributor to *Bridges to Cuba/Puentes a Cuba.* Iraida directed the CUNY-Cuba/Caribbean Exchange Program from 1988 to 1995 and is currently an associate professor of Spanish and literature at Ramapo College of New Jersey.

Rosa Lowinger (Los Angeles, California) was born in Havana and emigrated to Miami with her parents in 1961. A writer and conservator of sculpture and contemporary art, she has worked on numerous historic preservation projects in Havana and Trinidad de Cuba. She has written about Cuban art and architecture for *Sculpture, Preservation, ArtNews,* and *Latina,* and is the author of *Tropicana Nights: The Life and Times of the Legendary Cuban Nightclub.*

Nancy Morejón (Havana, Cuba) was born in the Los Sitios district of Central Havana on August 7, 1944, the only child of tobacco worker and dressmaker Angélica Hernández and Felipe Morejón, who worked as a stevedore in the Havana docks. Her mother's Chinese and European ancestry and the African ancestry of her father created a blended duality in the poet, who eventually embraced the notion of transculturation. Morejón is a world-renowned poet whose writings have been translated into numerous languages. She has published more than twenty books of poetry, including her first book, *Mutismos*; three winners of the Cuban Critics Prize, *Piedra pulida, Elogio y paisaje,* and *La Quinta de los Molinos*; the bilingual anthologies *Where the Island Sleeps Like Wing* and *Looking Within/ Mirar adentro*; and her most recent book, *Carbones silvestres.* In 2001 she became the first Black woman to be honored with Cuba's National Prize for Literature.

Gustavo Pérez Firmat (New York) is the David Feinson Professor of Humanities at Columbia University. A writer and scholar, he is the author of *Idle Fictions, Literature and Liminality, Equivocaciones, The Cuban Condition, Life on the Hyphen, Next Year in Cuba, Bilingual Blues, My Own Private Cuba, Anything but Love, Cincuenta lecciones de exilio y desexilio, Tongue Ties,* and *Scar Tissue.*

Verónica Pérez Konina (Moscow, Russia) is the daughter of a Cuban psychologist and a Russian journalist. She is bicultural and bilingual in

Spanish and Russian. She studied journalism at the University of Habana, and then went on to study at the Gorki Institute in Russia. During her time in Cuba she was one of the founders of the literary group "El establo" along with Ricardo Arrieta, Sergio Asevedo, and Miguel Yozz. She received the coveted "David" prize from Casa de las Américas for her first novel, *Adolesciendo*. Her work appears in recent publications such as the Cuban anthology, *Escritos con guitarra*. She presently lives in Moscow and teaches Spanish and literature at the Cervantes Institute in Moscow.

Pedro Pérez Sarduy (London, UK), born in Havana in 1943, is an Afro-Cuban poet, writer, journalist, and broadcaster residing in London. He has worked in Cuba for national radio (1965–1979) and for the Latin American Section of the BBC World Service (1981–1994). He is the author of *Surrealidad* and *Cumbite and Other Poems*; coeditor of *AFRO-CUBA: An Anthology of Cuban Writing on Race, Politics and Culture*; and coauthor of the "Introduction" to *No Longer Invisible: Afro-Latin Americans Today* and of *AfroCuban Voices: On Race and Identity in Contemporary Cuba*, a book based on interviews with Afro-Cubans currently living and working in the island and discussing race issues. He has published a first novel, *Las Criadas de La Habana*, and is writing *Journal in Babylon*, a series of chronicles on Britain.

Ena Lucía Portela (Havana, Cuba), born in Havana in 1972, is a novelist, short story writer, and essayist. She received her degree in comparative languages and literatures from the Universidad de La Habana. She has published three novels, *El pájaro: pincel y tinta china*, *La sombra del caminante*, and the award-winning *Cien botellas en una pared*, which has been translated into French, Portuguese, Dutch, Polish, Italian, Greek, and Turkish. Her books of short stories include *Una extraña entre las piedras* y *Alguna enfermedad muy grave*. Her short story "El viejo, el asesino y yo" was awarded the 1999 Juan Rulfo Prize by Radio France Internationale. Her latest novel, *Djuna y Daniel,* will be published in Spanish by Random House Mondadori. She is an occasional contributor to the Spanish newspaper *El País* and the Mexican journal *Crítica*. In 2007 a panel of three prestigious Colombian novelists named her one of thirty-nine most important Latin American writers under the age of thirty-nine.

Sandra Ramos (Havana, Cuba) studied fine arts at the Higher Institute of Arts in Havana, graduating in 1993. Her works use such disparate techniques as installation, painting, engraving, and drawing to explore social and personal memories, the difficulties of daily life in Cuba, and such themes as solitude, emigration, and the political manipulation of history and memory. She has received numerous awards for her works and has been in residence at the Mattress Factory, Pittsburg; the Fine Arts Work Center, Provincetown; the Barbican Center, London; and the Civitella Ranieri Foundation, Italy. Her work is included in such important collections as the Boston Museum of Fine Arts, the Museum of Modern Art (MOMA) in New York, the National Museum of Fine Arts in Havana, the Fort Lauderdale Museum of Art, the Ludwig Forum für Internationale Kunst in Aachen, the Ontario Royal Art

Museum, the Fuchu Art Museum in Tokyo, and Thyssen-Bornemisza Art Contemporary (T-B A21) in Vienna.

Eliana Rivero (Tucson, Arizona), has been residing permanently in the United States since 1961. She is a poet, essayist, and critic of Latina American and Latino/a literatures; she focuses particularly on Cuban-American women writers. Her most recent book is *Discursos desde la diáspora*. Her article, "In Two or More (Dis)places: Articulating a Marginal Experience of the Cuban Diaspora," appears in Andrea O'Reilly Herrera, ed. *Cuba: The Idea of a Nation Displaced*. Rivero is Professor of Spanish literature at the University of Arizona.

Rafael Rojas (Mexico City, Mexico) was born in Santa Clara, Cuba, in 1965. He received his BA in philosophy from la Universidad de la Habana and his PhD in history from the Colegio de México. He has been living in Mexico since 1991, where he is professor and researcher at CIDE (Centro de Investigación y Docencia Ecónomicas, Center of Economic Research and Teaching). He is the author of numerous books on the intellectual history of Cuba, Mexico, and Latin America, including *Isla sin fin: Contribución a la crítica del nacionalismo cubano* (winner of the Anagrama Award for an Essay), *Cuba mexicana. Historia de una anexión imposible* (winner of the Matias Romero Award for Diplomatic History), and *La escritura de la independencia: El surgimiento de la opinión pública en México*.

Laura Ruiz Montes (Matanzas, Cuba), born in Matanzas in 1966, is a poet who has received many awards and is translated into English, German, Swedish, among other languages. Her poetry can be found in anthologies such as *El camino sobre las aguas*, *Las voces de un fin de siglo*, *Antología de poetas cubanos*, and *Poetas cubanos actuales*. She is the chief editor of Ediciones Vigía and the director of its journal, *Revista de Vigía*. Her works have won several prizes, including the José Jacinto Milanés Prize for Theater (2002) and the Hermanos Loynaz Prize for Children's Literature (2003).

Karla Suárez (Paris, France), born in Havana in 1969, has a degree in electronic engineering, a profession she continues to practice. She has published two books of short stories, *Carroza para actores* and *Espuma*, as well as the novels *La viajera* and *Silencios*, winner of the 1999 Premio Lengua de Trapo and a finalist for the 2004 Prix "Amedée Huyghues Despointes" des Amériques Insulaires et de la Guyane. Her novels have been translated into French, Portuguese, Italian, German, and Slovenian. Her short stories have appeared in anthologies and journals published in England, the United States, Finland, Iceland, Poland, France, Italy, Spain, and several Latin American countries. Two of her short stories were adapted for television in Cuba, and one was also presented as a play in Cuba. In France she has received several creative fellowships, including one from the National Book Center. After residing for several years in Rome, she now lives in Paris.

Lucía M. Suárez (Amherst, Massachusetts) is Associate Professor of Spanish at Amherst College. Born in Spain of Cuban parents and raised in the United

States, her creative and critical writings focus on the personal stories of international Caribbean diaspora writers and their impact on sociopolitical and human rights issues. She has received fellowships from Mellon-Mayes, the Rockefeller Foundation, and the Woodrow Wilson Foundation. Suárez has recently published *The Tears of Hispaniola: Haitian and Dominican Diaspora Memory,* and is currently working on her book of critical essays, *Looking for Cuba: Imagining a Nation.* Suárez, who was also trained as a dancer (National Foundation for the Advancement of the Arts Award in Dance, 1982), is merging her artistic experience and her critical training in her research, examining the role of dance in constructions of citizenship in Brazil. She is a Ford Foundation Fellow (2007–2008).

María de los Angeles Torres (Chicago, Illinois) is director and professor of Latin American and Latino Studies at the University of Illinois at Chicago. She is author of two books, *The Lost Apple: Operation Pedro Pan, Cuban Children in the US and the Promise of a Better Future* and *In the Land of Mirrors: The Politics of Cuban Exiles in the United States.* She edited *By Heart/De Memoria: Cuban Women's Journeys in and out of Exile* and coedited *Borderless Borders: Latinos, Latin Americans, and the Paradoxes of Interdependence.* Currently, she is a Co-Principal Investigator for a National Science Research Foundation Project, "Civic Engagement in Three Latino Neighborhoods," and is Principal Investigator for a project on "Youth Politics in the Age of Globalization," funded by Chapin Hall and the Kellogg Foundation.

Alan West-Durán (Boston, Massachusetts) was born in Cuba and grew up in Puerto Rico. He is the author of two books of poems, *Dar nombres a la lluvia/Finding Voices in the Rain* (winner of the 1996 Latino Literature Prize for Poetry) and *El tejido de Asterión o las máscaras del logos,* as well as a book of essays, *Tropics of History: Cuba Imagined.* He has translated Alejo Carpentier's *La música en Cuba,* Rosario Ferré's *Language Duel/Duelo de lenguaje* and Nelly Richard's *Cultural Residues.* West-Durán has edited *African Caribbeans: A Reference Guide* and *Latino and Latina Writers.* He teaches at Northeastern University (Boston).